Going Online @HOME

How To Make The Internet A Family Activity

KEN REAVES

BROADMAN
& HOLMAN
PUBLISHERS

Nashville, Tennessee

0-8054-2136-X

Dewey Decimal Classification: 004.67
Subject Heading: INTERNET (COMPUTER NETWORK)—HANDBOOKS /
FAMILY—INTERNET / ONLINE DATA PROCESSING—HANDBOOKS /
COMPUTERS—HANDBOOKS
Library of Congress Card Catalog Number: 00-030346

Unless otherwise stated all Scripture citation is from the NIV, the Holy Bible, New International Version, copyright © 1973, 1978, 1984, 1987 by International Bible Society.

Permissions for graphics of screen shots located on page 322.

Library of Congress Cataloging-in-Publication Data

Reaves, Ken, 1954–
 Going online at home : how to make the Internet a family activity / Ken Reaves.
  p. cm.
 Includes bibliographical references and index.
 ISBN 0-8054-2136-X (pb)
 1. Internet (Computer network)—Handbooks, manuals, etc. 2. Online data processing—Handbooks, manuals, etc. 3. Microcomputers—Handbooks, manuals, etc. I. Title.
TK5105.875.I57 R4168 2000
004.67'8—dc21

00-030346
CIP

1 2 3 4 5 04 03 02 01 00

DEDICATION

To my wife, Diane, and my kids, Travis and Katrina,
who, like so many families, have taken the plunge into cyberspace.

TABLE OF CONTENTS

Section Three: Browsing

Section Seven: Family and Friends

ACKNOWLEDGMENTS

I thank my God every time I remember you.
Philippians 1:3

What irony. Here I am writing this book about cyberspace while thinking about another writer who wrote almost two thousand years ago. I sit, typing in words on a laptop computer, while Paul wrote using pen and parchment. The glow of fluorescent lighting illuminates my work space; I have no need to squint. The dim flick of an oil lamp was Paul's only light. With the push of a button, I can print out copy after copy of my manuscript. Paul would have had to painstakingly copy his manuscript word by word. With the push of another button, I can send my notes in a matter of seconds to my editor a thousand miles away. It sometimes took months for Paul's manuscript to be carried a distance we easily travel in a day or two.

For all the contrasts, there is one common thread in our writing experiences—people. People were important to Paul. People, who added value to his life, made it possible for Paul to expand his ministry.

Though writers write alone, they are not alone in what they write. We cannot—more to the point, I could not—write without people. Like Paul, I need to stop and say thanks.

To Terry Willett, who "pushed" me into taking what I'd learned about the Internet and sharing it with families. Thanks for not taking no for an answer.

To my father, Johnnie Reaves, who taught me that dreams are always worth pursuing and hard work pays off. Thanks, Dad.

To my father-in-law, Travis Young, who taught me the importance of a positive attitude. With God, all things are possible.

To Andy Lee and Larry Antonacci—my Aaron and Hur. You kept me accountable and prayed for me throughout this project. Your faithfulness in prayer humbles me.

To my church family, the members of First Baptist Church of Clewiston, Florida. It's been my joy to serve as your pastor these past twelve years. I am honored that you've kept me around so long.

To Matt Perry, Fredia Rackley, and Ginnie Fountain—my church staff. Your words of encouragement came at just the right moments. Thanks for being so sensitive.

To my editors at Broadman & Holman, Vicki Crumpton and Janis Whipple, who believed in me and gave me the opportunity. Thanks for believing in me.

To my kids, Travis and Katrina, who bring a daily dose of joy and laughter into my life. Thank you for being my cheerleaders.

And most importantly, to my wife, Diane, who has stood beside me, loved me, prayed for me, encouraged me, and worked alongside me to reach my dreams. My name may be on the cover, but I couldn't have done this without you.

INTRODUCTION

Sunlight dances off the surface of the pool, flashing in your eyes. "Come on, jump!" a voice yells from behind you. You turn and look back. You stand alone at the end of ten feet of wood and fiberglass. The four feet to the water below might as well be forty. The ladder is at least a mile away. You wonder how in the world you let yourself get talked into jumping off the diving board.

"Are you going or what?" another voice shouts. You can't turn back; a gaggle of kids waiting their turn blocks your retreat. Besides, retreat would forever brand you with the "C word"—*chicken.* You look down again, searching inside for the courage to jump. That's all it would take. One small hop . . .

Once you've taken the plunge, you swim to the side, grab the handrail, and pull yourself up out of the water. Looking back at the board, you smile at your accomplishment, wonder why you didn't do it sooner, and rush to get back in line again.

Taking the leap into cyberspace can be as fearful as your first jump off a diving board. You know it won't kill you, but doing it—that's the problem. Such feelings are normal. There's always a certain amount of fear and anxiety when faced with something unlike anything you've experienced before. But don't let those feelings keep you from taking the plunge. When you finally hop online, you'll wonder why you waited so long.

There's a new world to explore on the Internet. There's so much to do, so many places to go, so much to learn. On the Internet, you can keep up with family, make new friends, and find long-lost ones. You can stay up-to-date on the news, sports, weather, and stock market. Your children can find homework help and the information they need for that research paper due in the morning. You can grow in your faith, start a new hobby, or rediscover an old one. As a family, you can take a virtual tour of the White House, a college campus, a museum, or a distant city. You can walk the streets of Jerusalem or play a game. You might turn your browser to the stars and see the universe through the lens of the Hubble telescope. You can find health tips and information, plan your vacation, find a new home, shop for a car, or gather information for making a purchase decision. That's just for starters.

Going Online @ Home is a hands-on, how-to guide to help your family reap the benefits—while avoiding the dangers—of the Internet. Some how-to material you read in this book is the same as you'll find in other introductory Internet books. What *Going Online @ Home* offers is a strong family-friendly perspective. You'll find a strong emphasis on making the Internet a family activity. You'll find detailed information on the dangers of the Internet and how to protect your family from them. Illustrations and recommended sites are made with your family in mind. Lastly, this book is family-tested. Real families, including mine, have tested the activities and step-by-step guides. Best of all, it's all in plain English. *Going Online @ Home* is the only book a family needs to start using the Internet.

Who Should Use This Book

If you are new to the Internet, this book is for you. It will introduce you to the Internet and the World Wide Web. It will walk you through the process of selecting an Internet Service Provider (ISP) and help you get online the first time. You will learn how to use E-mail, browse the Web, and search for what you need. Once you've mastered the basics, you can move on to learning the skills that will enrich your online experience.

If you are looking for a book to help get your whole family online, this book is for you. *Going Online @ Home* gives you the information needed to make your family's surfing an enjoyable and safe experience. You will learn how to set up E-mail for your whole family and connect with family and friends. School-age children will get tips for finding help with homework and research projects. The final section of the book provides hands-on projects that develop Internet skills and enrich your family's online experience.

If you have some knowledge of the Internet but would like to do more, this book will help. Move beyond simple E-mail. Learn how to host your own newsletter. Discover the full scope of multimedia online. Delve deep into the Internet with advanced searches. Build your own Web page, and more.

How to Use This Book

Use this book to get started on the Internet. Grab a cup of coffee or glass of tea, find a comfortable chair, and read through sections 1 and 2. When you get to section 3, "Browsing," move to the computer, log on, and start surfing.

Use this book to take you beyond the basics. Find the advanced techniques you're looking for by scanning the chapter headings.

Use this book as a reference book. Chapters are organized so you can quickly find what you need. In the back of the book, you'll find a glossary and an index to help you find answers to your questions.

Use this book as an idea source. Section 8, "Family Activities and Adventures," is devoted entirely to giving you a plethora of ideas. Appendix 2, "Web Sites to Visit," is a list of Web sites for a wide variety of interests.

How This Book Is Organized

The material in this book is arranged in a family-friendly, user-friendly order. From front to back, sections are logically organized.

- Section 1, "Welcome to the Internet," gives the basics you need to know before getting online. You'll learn how the Internet works and the three essentials for going online: the right hardware, the right software, and the right Internet Service Provider. You'll receive helpful advice on making right choices in each of these areas. Finally, you'll learn how to keep your system running like new.

- Section 2, "Family-Safe, Family-Friendly," opens your eyes to the dark side of the Internet. You'll learn how to protect yourself, your family, and your computer from the dangers of cyberspace.

- Section 3, "Browsing," walks you through the process of getting online for the first time. You'll become familiar with your browser, learn how to connect and disconnect from the Internet, and start to move around both the Internet and a Web site. You'll discover how to personalize your browser, change your home page, and speed up your connection.

- Section 4, "E-mail," teaches you how to send mail without a stamp. You'll learn how E-mail works and how to use your E-mail program. You'll also learn how to send and receive E-mail, send attachments, add signatures, organize your mail, and subscribe to an online newsletter.

- Section 5, "Finding What You Need Online," introduces you to search engines and how they work. You'll learn how to perform a basic search, select the right search engine, and use advanced search techniques. You'll find tips for helping your children with homework and school projects.

- Section 6, "Downloading and Updating," teaches you how to find pictures and files online. You'll learn how to download images, files, and programs and how to update software. You'll also learn the right and wrong ways to install and uninstall what you download from the Internet. Finally, you'll discover how to enrich your online experience by using multimedia plug-ins.

- Section 7, "Family and Friends," shows you how to use the Internet to connect with family and friends, find lost friends, and make new ones. You'll learn how to trace your family history, begin a family newsletter, and chat online. There's also a chapter designed to help introduce senior adults to the Internet.

- Section 8, "Family Activities and Adventures," provides dozens of ideas for activities to do online or with the aid of the Internet. Learn how to plan your vacation with the help of the Internet. Plan a day trip, find hobby sites, or play online games. You'll even learn how to build a simple Web page.

Window Terms	
Term	**Action**
Click	To press and release the left mouse button.
Double-click	To press and release a mouse button twice.
Right-click	To press and release the right mouse button.
Drag	To move the pointer or an object by sliding while holding a mouse button.
Open	To start an application, open a dialog box, or access a document, folder, or file. This is usually done by clicking the appropriate menu item or keyboard shortcut.
Press	To push and hold down a mouse button or key.
Select	To highlight all or part of a window

Also, here's a list of action terms used in Windows formats. Make sure you are familiar with these actions before going online.

Have you ever noticed how kids get in the swimming pool? Some toss their towels aside, race to the edge, and take a flying leap into the water. Others walk to the edge, test the water with their feet, then slip in from the side. Still others tentatively make their way into the pool using the steps in the shallow end. No matter what approach they take to getting in the water, in the end, they are all in the water—laughing, playing, and splashing. That's all that matters.

Whether you choose to leap into cyberspace or take a slow, cautious approach, in the end, you'll be on the Internet. Before long you'll be writing old friends and making new ones, doing research, planning a family outing, listening to a recorded broadcast, helping your child with homework, and that's just for starters.

So, what are you waiting for? Turn the page and let's get started.

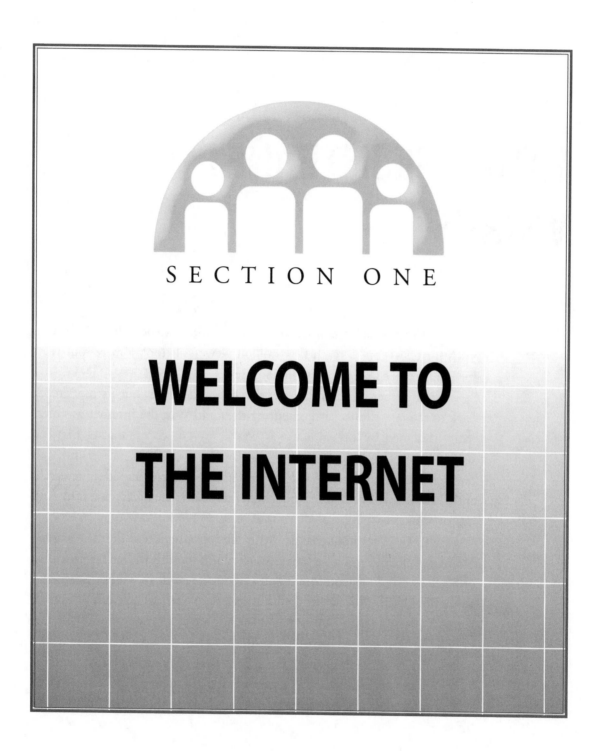

SECTION ONE

WELCOME TO

THE INTERNET

CHAPTER 1

HOW THE INTERNET WORKS

It took thirty years for radio to reach fifty million listeners. It took thirteen years for television to reach fifty million viewers. It took a mere four years for the Internet to reach fifty million users.

The Internet burst on the scene in the mid-1990s, but its roots reach back to the late 1960s. Birthed during the Cold War, the Internet was originally designed by the military. It was a way to communicate between scattered bases and command centers. By the mid-1980s, universities and research centers saw it as a way to communicate—exchanging ideas, research, and data. E-mail and electronic bulletin boards made it easier to find information.

In 1993, everything changed with the introduction of the first graphic browser, called Mosaic. No longer were you limited to white text on a blue or black screen. Now you could send and receive pictures, sound, video, and animation. With Mosaic (which later became Netscape), the rise of Online Services (like America Online), and the multiplication of Internet Service Providers, more people logged on to the Internet. To take advantage of the rush, businesses began posting Web sites. New companies, whose business was the Internet, were quick to seize real estate in cyberspace. News, sports, entertainment, and information of all kinds became the driving force of the Internet.

Still, it wasn't until late 1997 that the Internet really took off. Two things contributed to this growth. First, the price of computers dropped to the point where more families could afford them. Second, Internet service became available in most areas of the country.

As we ushered in the new century, an estimated 80 million Americans were online. Of that, 58 million were adults, roughly 30 percent of the adult population.[1] It is predicted that by the year 2005, 65 percent of Americans will be online. Worldwide, the Internet population is expected to quadruple, rising to 300 million by 2005.[2] For at least the next five years, the Internet will continue to grow. The amount and variety of information available online will grow at an even faster pace.

Learning the Lingo

Backdoor, cut, slam dunk, traveling. Fold, blend, puree, poach. Cash flow, debit, credit, liability. Every sport, every hobby, every job has its own lingo—a form of verbal shorthand telling us what we need to know without long explanations. The Internet, too, has its own verbal shorthand. Computer programmers and webmasters have taken verbal lingo to a new level, refining it to an art form.

Don't let the terms scare you. The more you use the Internet, the more familiar you will become with the lingo. As you begin your Internet adventure, here are eighteen of the most common terms. Don't worry about memorizing them; just familiarize yourself with them. Many other terms you'll encounter on the Internet will be self-explanatory within their context. If not, check appendix 1 at the back of this book.

1. Address

Every Web site and Web page on the Internet has an address. When you type in an address, it tells your Web browser what site you want to visit. Sometimes people will call a Web address a URL. This is short for Universal Resource Locator. Typically, addresses look like the following:

lifeway.com	LifeWay Christian Resources
nasa.gov	The National Aeronautics and Space Administration, NASA for short
family.org	Focus on the Family

2. Browser

This is the software used to access the Internet. Most people use either Microsoft Internet Explorer or Netscape Navigator. Casually moving around the Internet is called browsing, hence the name *browser*.

3. Download

When you connect to a Web site, you are downloading that page to your computer. The computer hosting the Web site, called a *server*, sends the information to your computer. Since the information moves from the Internet to your computer, it's called *downloading*. The term also refers to receiving a picture, program, or file from the Internet and saving it onto your machine.

4. E-mail

Sending and receiving E-mail is the most popular Internet activity. *E-mail* is short for *electronic mail*—messages sent from one person to another on the Internet. You can send pictures, files, and programs by attaching them to E-mail.

5. Favorite or Bookmark

Like an electronic Rolodex, favorites or bookmarks are set within your browser. To remember the address of a Web site that you plan to visit often, you can set a favorite or bookmark.

6. HTML—HyperText Markup Language

This is the language behind much of what you see on the Internet. All Web pages are written using HTML. You don't have to know it to use the Internet, but you will see the term.

7. http—HyperText Transfer Protocol

These are the first letters you see in the address bar of your browser. It is the "language" of the Internet. It is the standard by which information is exchanged between computers on the Internet. Hence it is the language your computer speaks on the Internet.

8. Hypertext

When you click on them, hypertext words will move you to a different Web page or Web site. Typically, hypertext appears as blue, underlined lettering. It can appear in different colors and without the underline, but it will always stand out.

9. Home

Home has two different meanings. First, *home* refers to the Web page your browser opens to every time you log on to the Internet. Second, *home* or *home page* refers to the "opening page" of any Web site. A Web site's home page is like the title and table of contents pages of a book rolled into one.

10. Internet Service Provider or ISP

Your ISP is the company through which you access the Internet.

11. Link

A link can be a picture, a word, a button, or a graphic image. Links "link you" to other parts of the same Web site or to a different Web site.

12. Load

As a Web page appears on your screen, it is said to be loading.

13. Modem

The modem is the part of your computer that dials your ISP's phone number and makes the connection to the Internet.

14. Online Service

America Online, MSN, and CompuServe are all Online Services. They differ from a standard ISP by providing custom content for their customers. This content consists of Web sites, magazines, entertainment, chat, etc. that may or may not be found on the Internet. All Online Services provide Internet access.

15. Search

Search engines and search sites are the "card catalog files" of the Internet. When you don't know where to find what you're looking for, start with a search engine. Search their catalog of sites by using keyword(s) or phrases.

16. Virus

You can't catch the flu on the Internet, but your computer can "catch a virus." Viruses are small, rogue programs. Once on your system, they replicate themselves and begin their "dirty work." Some are merely a nuisance; others can crash your system. Virus protection programs can protect your computer from them.

17. Web Site/Web Page

If the Internet were a library, then each book in the library would be a Web site, and each page in that book a Web page. Like the books in a library, some sites contain hundreds or thousands of pages, and others are small, containing just a few pages. Instead of pages made of paper, Web sites and Web pages are electronic files stored on computers scattered around the world.

18. World Wide Web

This is the most talked about segment of the Internet. It's also the largest. The World Wide Web, "www" for short, contains millions of Web sites and Web pages. When you enter "www" before a Web address, you're telling your browser to look for it on the World Wide Web.

Welcome to the World Wide Web

Ask questions of a research scientist in southern California. Play chess with someone in Tel Avi, Israel. Visit the Louvre in Paris, France. Watch the sun set over the Rocky Mountains. Listen to Dial-a-Deal on your hometown radio station—two thousand miles away from where you now live. Receive pictures of your grandchildren minutes after they are taken. Chat with your college student away at school or a missionary halfway around the world. Enter a bulletin board discussion of current events. Find spring gardening tips. Exchange hobby ideas with hundreds of others in a newsgroup. Plan your vacation. Preview a movie. Sample the latest music from your favorite group. Build your own family, hobby, or business Web site, and have others from around the world visit you.

It's not a stretch to say the world is as close as your computer's keyboard. In the time it takes for a Web page to load on your computer, you can be halfway around the world. So, hop on and let's take a quick spin around the Internet.

You may have heard the Internet called the information superhighway. Like a superhighway, you cannot get on the Internet from just any road. You have to find an on-ramp. Your ISP or Online Service functions as that on-ramp. When you call your ISP, the modem in your computer talks to the modem in their computer. Once connected, your call is directed onto the Internet.

As of July 1999 the Internet is a collection of an estimated 2.2 million public Web sites, containing more than 300 million Web pages.[3] All those Web pages reside on special computers, called *servers*, scattered across the nation and around the world. To get information from any of those servers to your computer, you must know the address of the Web site.

To move around the Internet, you enter an address in your browser. Your computer sends the request onto the Internet. That request travels to a special computer, called a *router*. Routers are electronic traffic cops. They read the address you've requested and send it on its way in the right direction. Often your request will travel through three to five routers, sometimes more, before it gets to the computer where the Web site you've requested is found.

When your request reaches the right Web site, the requested information is sent back to your computer in small pieces, called *packets*. Like an electronic jigsaw puzzle, these packets are "reassembled" by your computer on the screen. You will notice that some information, such as text, appears almost instantly, while graphics and pictures take more time to load. This is because graphics and pictures are larger files and require more packets of information to complete. The process is repeated each time you move to a new Web site or Web page.

Now that you're familiar with how the Internet works, let's turn our attention to what you need to have in order to get on the Internet and enjoy the experience.

CHAPTER 2

WHAT YOU NEED FOR GOING ONLINE

If you've purchased a computer in the last two to three years, then you probably have most of what you need to get online. Getting the most out of the Internet requires more than a good computer and a fast modem. You need the right software and the right Internet Service Provider. We'll look at selecting an ISP in the next chapter. For now, we'll focus on the hardware and software you need. Unless you're an experienced user, don't skip these chapters.

Computer

Shopping for a first computer can be as intimidating as shopping for a new car. On the outside, most computers appear the same—beige, plastic boxes with slots and buttons, keyboard, mouse, speakers, and a monitor. It's what's inside that makes the difference in power, speed, reliability, and price. Before buying a computer, you need to decide what kind of computer user you are. Most computer users fall into one of three broad categories: power user, mainstream user, or casual user.

Power User

The power user is looking for all the speed, power, memory, and hard-drive capacity he can pack into that beige box. If you plan to work with digital photographs, edit video, or play games requiring 3D graphics, video accelerator cards, and lots of memory, then you are a power user. Most people don't fall into this category. If you are a power user or you just want to have the biggest and fastest machine on the block, then plan to spend between $2,200 and $4,000 for a computer.

Mainstream User

The mainstream user is by far the most common computer user. Mainstream users use a computer for more than surfing the Internet and sending and receiving E-mail. If you plan to write letters; manage finances; create calendars, posters, or flyers for a church or civic club using a small desktop publishing program; trace your family tree; scan pictures; use a small database; or play games, then you will most likely be a mainstream user. Plan to spend between $1,400 and $2,100 for a computer.

Casual User

You are a casual user if you plan to use a computer to surf the Internet, send and receive E-mail, and perhaps write a letter or two. In 1999, the computer industry developed a new line of computers called *essential machines*, or *e-machines*. These computers lack the power, memory, hard-disk space, and monitor size of machines designed for mainstream or power users. Casual users are willing to make the trade for the sake of price. Essential computers range in price from $600 to $1,200.

WebTV is another option for the casual user. If all you want to do is surf the Internet and send and receive E-mail, check out WebTV. WebTV uses a small box, with a modem, to access the Internet. The box sits on top of your television, like an old cable converter box. Instead of a monitor, you view the Internet on your television. Add a printer, and you can print

E-mail and Web pages. WebTV is the cheapest way to get on the Internet. The WebTV box and keyboard cost less than $200.

Purchasing Tips

If you are purchasing your first computer, stick with a well-known computer manufacturer. Many computer magazines publish lists of the top computers on the market. Visit your library, or invest in two or three issues of the magazines. Compare the models listed. Notice which manufacturers appear on more than one list. Is the one you're considering on a list? If you're considering a computer that doesn't make it to anyone's list, that doesn't mean it's inferior to others; it does mean that you need to do some more checking.

When purchasing a computer, you might have a friend or a local computer store offer to build you a custom computer. It might be good, but keep in mind a few other considerations. What about tech support? Can you call your friend at midnight when your system crashes? How can you be sure that all the computer's hardware and software will work together, not just now, but two years from now? What recourse do you have if the computer you buy turns out to be a lemon (especially if you bought it from a friend)? If it does break down, how do you know they will fix it as fast as a national brand? How can you be sure you're comparing oranges to oranges, and not apples to oranges, when it comes to price? All things being equal, you'll spend the same amount or more for a locally built system as you would for a national brand.

Modem

Most computers today come standard with a modem. I can't think of a national brand that doesn't have a modem in it. At this writing, the standard modem is a 56K V90. If you have an older machine, you might have a 33.3K or even a 28.8K modem. The number represents the maximum speed at which data is transferred. Since many variables affect connection speeds, you won't always attain the highest rated speed for your modem. The federal government limits analog modem speeds to 53K. Even if you have a 56K modem, the maximum speed at which you can connect is 53K.

Several other types of modems are on the market today. Other than the 56K, the most common ones for home use are the DSL and the cable modem.

DSL stands for Digital Subscriber Line. Using existing phone lines, it sends data from four to a projected fifty times faster than 56K modems. The most attractive feature of DSL is that it doesn't interfere with your phone service. With DSL, you can surf the Internet while your teenager talks on the phone. Many computer companies now offer DSL modems as an option.

Cable modems allow you to receive data from the Internet by way of your television cable. Local cable companies provide Internet access using the same cable as your television. Like DSL, cable modems are much faster than 56K modems. They do suffer from slowdowns if a lot of your neighbors have cable Internet access.

With both DSL and cable, you'll need a special modem. You'll pay more for both services. Right now, DSL and cable Internet access are not available everywhere. As availability and competition grow, prices for both will drop. If you're interested in faster home connections and are willing to pay the extra price, cable or DSL is the way to go.

Software

Browser

When you bought your computer, it came with software. If you have Windows 95, 98, or 2000, you have Internet Explorer. You might also have Netscape Communicator. Though there are other browsers, these are the most popular. Both have built-in E-mail programs.

Many versions of both browsers are in use today. As of this writing, the latest versions are Internet Explorer 5.1 and Netscape 4.7. To find out which version you have, open your browser. Choose **Help** from the Menu bar, then

About. The version of your browser is listed in the About box (see figure 1). Compare the version to the one listed here or found on the maker of your browser's Web site. If it doesn't match the latest update, you might want to consider downloading an update from Microsoft's or Netscape's Web site. Updating to the latest version allows you to take advantage of the full range of multimedia and other Internet features.

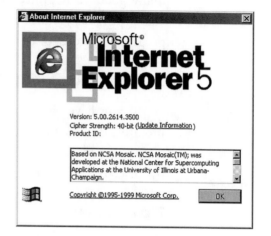

Figure 1. About dialog box

Your computer probably came with software for several Online Services or ISPs, such as America Online, Prodigy, Microsoft Network, MindSpring, and EarthLink. Many of these have their own browser. Don't install and sign up for these services unless you really want them. If you do try one (or more) of these services and then decide you don't want it, be sure to cancel the account. Use the program's uninstall feature to remove the program from your computer.

You're not stuck with the browser that came with your machine. You can install the one you'd like. You can even run Internet Explorer and Netscape Communicator on the same machine. If you choose to do so, just remember to specify which one will be your default browser. That way, the programs won't vie for top position.

Though you'll use your browser and E-mail program more than any other software, those are not all you'll need. You will definitely need virus protection and blocking/monitoring software. Additionally, you'll need to consider other software as you become more proficient with the Internet. We'll look at some of it in upcoming chapters.

Antivirus Software

When it comes to viruses, it's not a matter of if, but when, you encounter one. A virus is a small program that hides in a file or another program. When opened, the virus begins to replicate itself. Viruses range from being a mild nuisance to ones that will crash your system. There are many good virus protection programs available. If your computer didn't come with one, you will need to purchase and install one. You can find these programs in stores or download them from the Web.

Blocking/Monitoring Software

If you have children or grandchildren, you definitely need blocking/monitoring software. You might even want it as an adult to eliminate the temptation to view what you shouldn't or simply to avoid stumbling on it by mistake.

Zip Program

If you download programs, files, and images from the Internet, you need a zip program. To speed downloading, files are compressed, or "zipped." To use them, you must "unzip" them. You need a zip program to open them.

Uninstaller Program

If you install a program and then decide you don't like it, you can't simply delete the program's file folder. Every program you install makes changes to your computer and installs files in many different locations. The only way to safely remove a program is to use an uninstaller program. Most uninstaller programs now do more than just uninstall. They will monitor your system, clean the registry, remove bits of leftover programs, and move or archive programs. A good uninstaller program is well worth the money invested.

Software Checklist

Browser

- Microsoft Internet Explorer
- Netscape Communicator

Additional Software

- Antivirus
- Blocking/Monitoring
- Zip Program
- Uninstaller
- Adobe Acrobat Reader

Adobe Acrobat Reader

Today, many files on the Internet are offered for download in the PDF format. PDF stands for Portable Document Format. Designed by Adobe, this file format enables you to open, view, and print a file on any computer system. All you need is a free Adobe Acrobat reader.

You have a computer, modem, and software. All you need is a connection to the Internet. Which connection is right for your family? That is the subject of the next chapter.

CHAPTER 3

SELECTING YOUR CONNECTION

Rocky Road. Chocolate Chip. Vanilla Fudge Swirl. Pralines and Cream. Strawberry Delight. If you love ice cream, trying to pick one, and only one, flavor out of the dozens in an ice cream shop is a daunting task. Sometimes, selecting a connection to the Internet can seem just as daunting.

Your choices fall into two broad categories: Internet Service Providers (ISPs) and Online Services. Online Services include America Online, CompuServe, Microsoft Network, and Prodigy. Internet Service Providers range from small, local companies to larger, regional and national companies. Depending on where you live, you can have from one to dozens of options.

Online Services

Online Services provide a great way to learn how to use the Internet. The software is easy to install and set up. The simple interface (the browser window) is easy to use. The large, clearly-labeled buttons offer quick access to the rich and wide variety of what's called *proprietary content*. This original content is available only to subscribers. It doesn't reside on the Internet; it is only on computers belonging to the Online Service.

Most Online Services offer multiple E-mail addresses, so everyone in your family can have his or her own address. Many provide simple content filters to block unwanted access to certain sites and information. Services like America Online offer special communication tools for chat, such as AOL Instant Messenger, forums, and chat rooms.

There are trade-offs. With an Online Service, you have to use their customized browser and E-mail program. Often you'll pay more for an Online Service. You may have to contend with more frequent busy signals, lots of junk mail, and slower Web access, as all those customers compete for access. The content filters might not be effective enough for you. If you live in a small community, Online Services may not even be available.

After awhile, logging on to the Internet using an Online Service might begin to feel as if you're driving through the mall to get to the turnpike on-ramp. If you don't use it, all that custom content can become distracting. Besides, much of what you find in the proprietary content can be found on the Internet. You don't have to subscribe to AOL to use Instant Messenger. If surfing the net is your main reason for going online, you might want to consider an Internet Service Provider instead of an Online Service.

Internet Service Providers

Internet Service Providers don't offer the rich custom content of an Online Service. What they do offer are fast connections, personal customer service, special services such as Web hosting, and a variety of connection options (56K, Cable, DSL, or ISDN). ISPs allow you to choose your Internet software. When you dial up using an ISP, you log directly on to the Internet.

The number of ISPs is daunting. National ISPs, such as AT&T WorldNet, MindSpring, MCI, Sprint, and Sprynet, offer access throughout much of the country. Regional ISPs range in size from those covering a large portion of one state, to those servicing two or more states. Small, local mom-and-pop operations round out the choices you have.

In the last few years, a new breed of Internet Service Providers has developed. The family-friendly ISP offers a new level of protection for your family. These new ISPs do the work of blocking offensive sites and screening search results for you. Some block chat rooms and filter E-mail. Most block more than "adult" or pornographic sites, screening for sites that include: graphic violence, drug use, criminal activities, profanity, homosexuality, hate, gambling, and other dangerous content. Choosing a family-friendly Internet Service Provider can be a first step in giving your family a family-friendly, family-safe Internet.

Selecting the Right Internet Connection

Depending on the size of your community, you can have from one to dozens of Internet Service Providers to choose from. Finding the right one may take a little work and perhaps some trial and error. Selecting the right Internet connection begins with asking the right questions.

What ISPs are available in your area?

Start with the phone book and look up Internet Service Providers. You will find local and many regional ISPs listed there. It may not list national ISPs, unless they have a local office. You'll have to look them up on the Internet. If you don't have Internet service already, go to the library or ask a friend to do a search for ISPs in your area. Remember, just because an Internet Service Provider or Online Service calls itself "national" doesn't mean it's everywhere. Make sure they offer a local access number. Long distance charges or charges for 800 service add up quickly.

Are you interested in the custom content of an Online Service?

Would you feel more comfortable with an easy-to-navigate interface? If so, then you might want to try an Online Service. Many of them offer trial subscriptions.

From where do you plan to access the Internet?

If you plan to access the Internet only from home, then the size of your ISP is not as important as the quality and reliability of the service. If you travel a lot and you plan to use the same connection on the road, then you'll need to consider a regional or national ISP.

How often do you get a busy signal?

Before signing up, dial the Internet Service Provider's local access number at different times during the day. See how often you get a busy signal. Try dialing at the time of day you anticipate your family logging on to the Internet.

What are their customer support hours? Is it a toll-free call?

If they offer customer service from 9:00 to 5:00, Monday through Friday, and you access the Internet after 8:00 P.M. and run into a problem, how will you get support? Make sure tech support is available when you are most likely to need it. Ideally, you'd like to have toll-free tech support twenty-four hours a day, seven days a week.

What are others in your area using?

Ask around. Find out what Internet Service Provider your friends and neighbors are using. Are they happy with the service? What problems seem to recur regularly? Was tech support able to handle any problems they had?

What features do they offer as a family-friendly ISP?

If you're looking at a family-friendly Internet Service Provider, can you customize the filter settings? Can you override the filters? How do you report offensive sites? Can you request reconsideration of a filtered site?

What other features does the ISP offer?

Some offer multiple E-mail addresses, the ability to override blocking filters, or limited free Web site hosting. If these features are important to

Five Questions to Ask Yourself

1. Am I interested in the custom content of an Online Service like AOL, or am I looking primarily for Internet access?
2. What connection speed am I looking for?
3. What time of day will my family use the Internet?
4. Do I plan to use this connection while traveling?
5. What other features are important to me? Web hosting? Multiple E-mail accounts? Filtered access?

Five Questions to Ask Your Friends

1. What ISP are you using?
2. Are you happy with it? If not, why?
3. How often do you get busy signals? What time of day?
4. How often does the connection slow to a crawl?
5. Have you had any problems? Was tech support able to resolve them?

Five Questions to Ask Potential Internet Service Providers

1. What connection speeds do you offer in my area?
2. What other features do you offer free and on a fee basis?
3. Do you provide filtered content or blocking/monitoring software for customers?
4. What are your tech support hours and is it a toll-free call?
5. What is the cost per month? Is there a discount for paying quarterly, biyearly, or annually? Is there a sign-up fee?

you, make sure you ask about them ahead of time.

What connection speeds are available in your area?

An Internet Service Provider may offer 56K and DSL, but not in all areas. Find out what's available where you live. If you plan to upgrade to a faster connection, ask what their upgrade plans are.

How much does it cost?

Prices vary, so compare features. Is there a sign-up fee? If so, it shouldn't exceed twenty-five dollars. Find out if the fee is refundable if you're not satisfied with the service. Family-friendly ISPs typically run a few dollars more than others.

What is the minimum contract length?

Don't commit to a long-term contract. You may find their filtering is too strict or not strict enough, they've oversubscribed their service, they have slow connection speeds, or they lack adequate tech support. You don't want to lock into a service that isn't right for you.

Once you've settled on an ISP, sign up. You'll either have to prepay for service or give them a credit card. Their tech support should help you configure your software and get you connected the first time.

Before going further, it is important that you know how to keep your computer and Internet connection humming. Let's turn our attention to maintaining your system.

CHAPTER 4

MAINTAINING YOUR SYSTEM

While in college, I worked one summer at a Volkswagen repair shop. One day a tow truck arrived pulling a Volkswagen. The car had broken down on the nearby expressway. One glance at the engine and oil stick told the story. The owner admitted that because the engine was in the rear, he'd never checked nor changed the oil. He didn't know how. Consequently, a car with less than 50,000 miles on it needed a new engine.

Many computer owners treat their computer the way this driver treated his car. Since they don't know how to maintain their system, they don't do anything. Then they are shocked when their computer fails unexpectedly.

Seven Reasons Why You Shouldn't Read This Chapter

Before you read further, you might want to consider if this chapter is worth your time. After all, you've got a new computer, everything is working well, and besides, you're anxious to get on the Internet. You might want to skip this chapter. I don't want you to feel guilty about skipping it. To ease your conscience, here are seven reasons why you should not read this chapter.

1. You like living on the edge.
2. Your computer runs too fast and you'd like to slow it down.
3. You like the *click, click, click, click* sound your hard drive makes as it labors to find all the pieces of a file.
4. You don't mind losing important files and information.
5. You enjoy sleepless nights, high blood pressure, and migraine headaches.
6. You're lonely and like talking on the phone for hours with tech support.
7. You've always wondered what it would be like to reformat your hard drive.

If you don't own stock in Advil, if you like your sleep, and if you are allergic to needless work, read on. We'll look at what you need to do to keep your computer and Internet connection working smoothly.

Maintaining Your Computer

It's not as messy as changing the oil in your car, nor is it as noisy as vacuuming the carpet, but it's just as necessary. Regular maintenance can help prevent a host of computer problems. Before looking at what you need to do, let's look at how your computer stores information.

Maintaining Your Hard Drive

When you file a thirty-page paper report, you take the entire document, put it in a folder, and insert that folder in the proper file drawer. To retrieve it, all you need to do is remember the name under which you filed it.

A computer files that same thirty-page document differently. It takes the document, opens the first file drawer it comes to, and sticks as much of it in as possible. When that drawer is full, it goes to the next drawer, and then the next. When finished, your thirty-page report could rest in twenty-two different folders, scattered in ten different file drawers. Now try to find it.

A computer files this way because your hard drive is divided into hundreds of thousands of segments, called *clusters*. Since these clusters are small, it takes anywhere from a few dozen to hundreds to file a document. When it begins to save a file, it looks for the first empty cluster and starts saving the document. As you can imagine, your computer can slice and store your file in many places on your hard drive. Fortunately, your computer keeps a record (called the File Allocation Table) of where it stores all the pieces to each file on your hard drive.

Over time, files become even more divided and scattered. It takes longer and longer for your computer to find all the pieces to a file. This slows the performance of your computer. As your files become more fragmented, you run the risk of losing all or part of a file.

Fortunately, Microsoft provides two programs to help. Both Windows 95 and 98 include ScanDisk and Disk Defragmenter. To find them, choose **Start** from the taskbar, then **Programs, Accessories, System Tools**.

ScanDisk checks your hard drive for errors. It looks for "lost" files, bad clusters, and other problems. If it finds any, it automatically fixes them.

Disk Defragmenter sorts all the files on your hard drive, putting them "back together." It does this by moving data from cluster to cluster until all the pieces of each file are placed in adjacent clusters. It also puts all the unused space together. This speeds up your computer, because all the pieces of each file are now next to each other. In Windows 98, Disk Defragmenter speeds up your computer even more by arranging your files and programs according to which ones you use the most.

Windows 98 also includes a Maintenance Scheduler. This program automatically schedules ScanDisk and Disk Defragmenter. The first time you start your computer, Windows 98 automatically sets up Maintenance Scheduler. To check or change the settings, open Maintenance Scheduler by choosing **Start, Programs, Accessories, System Tools, Maintenance Scheduler**. From the dialog box, you can change the settings or run it manually. It's best to use the recommended settings.

To run ScanDisk and Disk Defragmenter automatically using Windows 95, however, requires *Microsoft Plus.* This is an add-on program. You can run each manually on a regular basis. It's too much to try to remember to do it every day. Instead, select a day and time to do it each week. After you've done it for a month or two, it will become a habit.

Backing Up Your Data

Keeping your hard drive in top condition is the first step in protecting your data. Yet even with the best possible maintenance, problems will occur. Software conflicts, hard-drive failures, power surges, and lightning can crash your computer. Consequently, it's important that you back up your important files. You can always buy a new computer, replace a hard drive, or reinstall your software, but you can't reload your data unless you have it backed up.

You have many options for backing up your data. You can back up data to a high-density removable disk (like an Iomega Zip drive), a tape backup, or another hard drive. Because of the size of many files, it's no longer feasible to try to back them up on floppies. What's important is that you develop some system of regularly backing up your data. If you are buying a new computer, I strongly suggest you spend a little extra and purchase a Zip, or similar, drive. These drives store anywhere from 100 megabytes to over a gigabyte of data.

When you back up your files, you can choose to back up the entire hard drive or just your data files. Backing up your entire hard drive will require more disks.

How often you back up your data depends on how often you use your computer. Major corporations and many small businesses back up their data every day. At home you won't need to back up as frequently. If you use a backup program, you can set it to back up all your files once a month. Then back up only those files that have changed on a weekly or daily basis. This is called an incremental backup. If you back up your data manually, you might not back it up as frequently, but you still need to do it regularly. Be sure to back up your data before installing new software or major upgrades to your system.

Organizing Programs

In the early days of computers, if you decided you didn't want a program on your machine, you simply deleted the files and folders associated with the program. Not any longer. Today, when you install a software program, it scatters files all over your hard drive, and the installation makes changes to key system files. If you try to delete a program by deleting its files, you risk slowing your computer's performance or crashing your system.

Today, you must uninstall a program. Many programs come with their own uninstaller programs. You can uninstall others by using the Add/Remove Programs feature in Windows. Double-click the My Computer icon on the Windows desktop. Double-click the Control Panel icon and choose **Add/Remove Programs**. Scroll down the list and select the program you wish to uninstall. Click **Add/Remove** and follow the prompts. If you try out many programs, you'll want to purchase a special uninstaller program designed to thoroughly rid your system of a program.

Maintaining Your Internet Software

When you access a Web site, your browser software downloads the text, graphics, and pictures to your computer screen. It stores those files in a cache. Internet Explorer calls this file "Temporary Internet File Folder." In Netscape it's called "cache." When you return to a site, your browser compares the Web page with what's stored in your cache. It then retrieves the files that haven't changed from your hard drive and only downloads the new items. This speeds up the display of frequently visited Web sites.

You also visit many sites that you never return to, or return to only occasionally. They, too, are stored in your cache. As your cache gets larger, it takes longer for your browser to search through the cache to find the files it needs. This can slow your browsing.

To clear your cache, open your browser. Choose **Tools, Internet Options** in Internet Explorer, or **Edit, Preferences** in Netscape. In the dialog box, find the cache options and follow the instructions for clearing it.

Both Netscape and Microsoft release periodic updates to their browsers. To take advantage of the ever-evolving features of the Internet, you need to update your browser. To update your browser, go to their Web site and follow the update instructions. If you have an earlier version of Internet Explorer 5 or Netscape 4, you can use their auto-update feature.

Your browser is not the only software that needs updating. The data files in your virus protection software and blocking/monitoring software need regular updating. Each of these programs can be set to update automatically. Consult the software's manual, help file, or Web site for how to automatically update.

SECTION TWO

FAMILY-SAFE, FAMILY-FRIENDLY

CHAPTER 5

THE FOUR-HEADED DRAGON

It's 3:00 P.M. School dismissed for the day thirty minutes ago. Mom's at the grocery store. Dad's at work. Big brother is in-line skating with friends. But do you know where little sister is? No, she's not playing alone in the park or exploring some dark alley. She's surfing the Internet. Is she safe? Can you trust where she goes, whom she meets, and what she "brings home" from the Web?

The world can be a dangerous place. In many ways the Internet is an electronic extension of the world. It contains all the good and all the bad you find in the world. Don't blame the Internet for the evil it contains. Blame the people behind the Internet. The dangers posed by the Internet mirror what you find in life. Those dangers fall into four categories: Moral Land Mines, Online Predators, Invasion of Privacy, and Computer Viruses.

Moral Land Mines

Mom sits down at the computer with her daughter. She's going to help her find the Web site for American Girl dolls. When she enters "American Girls" into the search engine and presses Enter, she gets more than she bargained for.

Another mother of two boys stumbles on an adult site while looking for the Toys-R-Us Web site. A teenage girl ends up on an adult site when she accidentally misspells "girl" in the Web address. A ten-year-old boy's assignment on the White House takes a wrong turn when he fails to enter "gov" on the Web address.

A teenage boy, looking for sports sites, types "sports" into a search engine. It returns the normal sites, CBS Sportsline and ESPN, among others. Yet the top site listed is an internal link on the search engine to a list of sixty-eight gambling sites.

You don't have to go looking for pornography, homosexuality, drugs, violence, cults, hate, and gambling to find them on the Internet. If you are not careful, they will find you. Those who build Web sites use every trick they can to "fool" search engines into listing their offensive sites as legitimate. That is why a search for American Girl dolls turns up far more than the Pleasant Company's Web site.

Like everything else on the Internet, if you want to find morally offensive material, you can. There are Web sites devoted to criminal activity, such as drug use and manufacturing, bomb making, software piracy, and computer hacking. Other Web sites, newsgroups, and chat rooms are set up for those interested in pornography, homosexuality, and worse. You can peep into college dorms, and watch babies being born in a high-tech form of voyeurism. Add hate groups, cults, and gambling, and you have a lot to avoid.

It's hard to put an accurate figure on the number of morally offensive sites on the Internet. The Internet is forever changing. A statistical snapshot taken today will be different tomorrow. Estimates range between forty-five thousand to a few hundred thousand morally offensive sites. Such sites present a danger to be aware of and avoided.

Online Predators

Cynthia thought her daughter was safe. Sixteen-year-old Jamie was raised in a Christian home. She was a home-schooled honor student. The family attended Covenant Christian Fellowship in Manteca, California. Then they got a computer and Internet service.

With no filtering software installed, Jamie began surfing the net. She found a local chat room—and a thirty-year-old pedophile found her. The man "groomed" Jamie, appealing to her emotions, convincing her to sneak out of the house at night for meetings. She got sexually involved.

In an effort to break the relationship, Jamie's parents sent her to live with relatives. She responded with slit wrists and a stay in a psychiatric hospital. Jamie plans to run off and get married when she turns seventeen. "I don't know if my child will ever be normal again," Jamie's mother says. "Our children are being stolen from our homes."[1]

Some have described the Internet as the playground of the twenty-first century. The Internet is actually more like a city, with playgrounds and dark alleys. There may or may not be someone lurking in the shadows.

Online predators cruise the Internet, visiting Web sites and chat rooms, reading wayward E-mail, looking for ways to take advantage of you and your family. The most common offenders making the news are the sexual predators, but they are not alone. Others want your money. They set up elaborate scams, often in the form of "can't miss" and "get all the money you want" E-mail scams.

Others set up false Web sites. This practice is called *spoofing*. They want you to buy software, books, or services from them. What they are actually selling are pirated goods or no goods at all. In either case, you may or may not get what you want; but they always get what they want—your credit card number and other personal information.

Invasion of Privacy

"Come check out our site," read the seemingly innocent subject line. Others were not so innocent: "College Coeds on the Web," "Girls, Girls, Girls," "Hot Pics." Suddenly, my fourteen-year-old son was receiving up to a half dozen such E-mails a day. Why? Where did they come from? How did they get his E-mail address? A friend had innocently signed him up to receive bonus points for surfing the Internet. The site was bogus.

A local franchise of a national company sent me an E-mail newsletter. Instead of hiding E-mail addresses using the blind carbon copy feature, they included the addresses in the "To" field. Everyone receiving the newsletter also received a list of all the E-mail addresses to whom it was sent. Later the same day, I and everyone else on the list were "spammed" by someone who received the same newsletter. Soon it was three to four unwanted E-mails a day, advertising various scams. In both cases, the spamming continued relentlessly until the E-mail address was changed. I'm not the only one. In April 1999, both Nissan and AT&T inadvertently sent a copy of thousands of E-mail addresses to customers who received their newsletter. Again, someone used the "To" field instead of the blind carbon copy.[2]

Spam (unwanted or junk E-mail messages) is a nuisance, even though there are ways to block much of it. But spam is only one way you can lose your privacy on the Internet. Sites you visit collect information from you. Every Web site you visit places a "cookie" on your machine. That cookie can only be read by the Web site that placed it there. Cookies can identify who you are, your UserID, E-mail address, Internet Service Provider, the site you came from, and the pages you visited on their site.

When you fill out a form on a Web site, that information is stored on someone's computer. You are up to the mercy of that Web site as to what they do with the information. They can keep it private, sell it to spammers, or post it in a database for anyone to find. A 1998 Federal Trade Commission study showed that 85 percent of 1,400 sites surveyed collected personal information. Less than 20 percent disclosed how that information was to be used. The same survey showed that 89 percent of children's sites were collecting information from children, and less than one in four of those sites told children to ask permission from their parents before giving the information.[3]

Others can use your personal information to hide their illegal activity. The damaging "Melissa" E-mail virus that made the news in early 1999 was sent using a stolen E-mail address. If someone gains your name, UserID, password, E-mail address, and other information (like Social Security and credit card numbers), they can become "you" in cyberspace. Your credit history and reputation can be ruined, not to mention the time it can take to straighten things out.

Viruses

You're typing along on your computer when suddenly a strange message flashes across the screen. Worse, the file you're working on disappears, or your screen goes black and your computer crashes. You've just been hit by a computer virus.

The virus software program I use lists over 41,000 viruses. Most simply make a nuisance of themselves, displaying messages or hogging memory. Others silently alter files, destroy data, and usually aren't discovered until it's too late. A computer virus is like the flu; it's not a matter of if, but rather when, you contract one. If you're not prepared, the virus could cost you more than a few headaches.

Are you ready to turn off the computer and yank the phone line out of the wall? Are you beginning to wonder if you did right in buying a computer? Are you ready to limit your kids to five minutes a week on the Internet? Yes, the Internet can be a dangerous place.

I grew up in Miami, Florida. There are areas of Miami I don't visit during the daytime, let alone at night. There are stores I drive by without a second glance. When I get in my car, I lock the doors. There are also areas I never worry about visiting. Miami has great restaurants, many wonderful places to visit, and lots of things to do. Every city is the same. It has both good and bad. You learn to enjoy the good and avoid the bad.

The Internet is like a large city. If you know where to go and where not to go, and if you know how to protect yourself, you and your family will be safe.

In the next three chapters we'll look at how to protect yourself, your family, and your computer. Hopefully, in the process, we will create a family-safe, family-friendly way for you to enjoy the Internet.

CHAPTER 6

PROTECTING YOURSELF

The number one concern of adults on the Internet is personal security and privacy. It's no wonder. Everything you do on the Internet leaves a trail. Every site you visit places a cookie on your machine, recording who you are, the site you came from, and what you did while visiting the Web site. Post a message to a newsgroup, and your name, E-mail address, and message is circulated to everyone on the list. Somewhere that message is archived on a computer. Electronic people finders (specialized search engines) distribute your name, address, phone number, E-mail address, and other information to anyone who asks. Use a chat program like ICQ or AOL Instant Messenger, and others can access your profile. Then there are marketers who are out to collect every bit of information they can about who you are, how you spend your money, your hobbies, interests, illnesses, and more.

If you want to get an idea of just how much personal information is already in circulation, look yourself up in a few people-finder search engines. (You'll find a list of them in appendix 2). Go to InfoSpace and do a "reverse lookup," using just your phone number. Some sites provide you with a street map and directions to your home. Others will search public records for you. Search professional associations, schools, and alumni group Web sites that might keep personal information. Is anybody in your family into genealogy research? You might want to check to see if they've posted their research on the Internet.

There is a good side to all this information. I once helped a niece find a sick uncle whom the family had lost track of. Others have found old college roommates, war buddies, or lost friends after thirty, forty, and sometimes fifty years. Some lost friends who were found didn't even own a computer. If you're doing research into your family tree, the Internet provides a wealth of information. The right newsgroups are a wonderful way to share ideas and information.

There are some simple steps you can take to safeguard your privacy. It won't insulate you completely, but it will make it much harder for snoops to pry into your personal life.

Ten Common Sense Rules for Protecting Your Privacy Online

Rule 1: Don't give out personal information

Web sites ask for information for various reasons. Some want it for marketing purposes or to compile a demographic profile of those who use their Web site. Others collect personal information to sell. Some want it in order to tailor their site to your interests. Before giving any information, make sure it's needed and know how it's going to be used.

You should always be careful in giving out any more information than your name and E-mail address. If asked to provide more information, make sure the site is secure. If it is, a closed lock will appear on the Status bar of your browser. This will keep prying eyes from viewing the information because it is encrypted. Always be wary of giving your Social Security number, date of birth, mother's maiden name, and credit or medical information. In the wrong hands, this information opens a lot of doors to your personal life, both on and off the Internet.

Rule 2: Read the privacy policy before giving information

This rule goes hand in hand with rule 1. The site's privacy policy should be easy to find. You should find a link to it on the home page or on the page(s) requesting personal information. Read it carefully. If a site doesn't have a privacy policy, then think twice before providing any information. Remember, privacy policies are voluntary. A site doesn't have to have one, nor does it have to abide by the one it's posted. In most cases, legitimate sites will have a privacy policy posted.

Rule 3: Protect your password

Don't tape your password to the front of your computer! Babysitters and children's friends have been known to memorize user names and passwords and use them later. Don't write passwords down. If you have more than three or four passwords, you may have to write them down. If you do, store them in a safe place.

Never give out your password. Sometime hackers, pretending to be tech support, call or E-mail people requesting your password. Don't give it out. Your Internet Service Provider will never need your password.

Change your password regularly. Don't use something as obvious as a name, anniversary, birthday, phone number, or zip code. Use a combination of numbers, letters, and symbols. Follow the example of those with vanity license plates (such as go2c4me), or use foreign words (chesed, lasagna).

Rule 4: Know the site

Be as familiar as possible with the site before giving any information. If they ask you to sign in, don't. Most sites allow you to explore the site as a guest. Make sure you feel comfortable giving them information. Some personal sites have guest books. They invite you to sign in so they know where their visitors are from. Be careful; unless you know the person behind the site, you don't know what they are going to do with the information. I've visited some sites where I could view all the entries in the guest book.

Rule 5: Clean out your cache and browser history regularly, and delete unwanted cookies

This prevents others from discovering where you've been online.

Rule 6: Handle E-mail carefully

Be careful in forwarding and responding to E-mail. If it looks suspicious, delete it. Never respond to junk E-mail. If the claim sounds too good to be true, it is. Read the subject header or first few lines in the preview pane of your E-mail program. This often provides all the clues you need to determine if it's junk mail. Don't read it. Delete it. Don't reply to junk E-mail, asking to be removed from their list. This only confirms that your E-mail is connected to a real person. A confirmed E-mail address can be sold to other spammers.

Question E-mail sent to you from someone you don't know. Don't respond to or forward any chain letter, no matter how good or appealing it sounds. Watch out for attachments. Attachments can carry viruses that could damage your data. Scan all E-mail attachments with your virus protection software before opening them.

Rule 7: Keep your E-mail and browser software up-to-date

Software isn't perfect; it's made by people. Sometimes "security holes" are found in the software after it's shipped. Both Microsoft and Netscape, as well as other browser and E-mail software manufacturers, post occasional "fixes" on the Internet. Use the auto-update of your software or check the manufacturer's Web site occasionally for updates. Check your software manual for specific information on how to update it.

Rule 8: Use a second E-mail address or post anonymously to newsgroups

Consider signing up for a free E-mail account to use for all newsgroups. Then if you get spammed (junk E-mail) or flamed (hate mail), you can cancel the account and open a different one. Consider using a handle (like in the CB radio days) or nickname, instead of your real name. Be careful about what you post to a newsgroup. You can infer a lot about a person by what they write.

Rule 9: Use caution when shopping online

Shopping online is becoming safer and safer. Many sites go to great lengths to protect the information you provide. It still pays to be careful. When purchasing online, buy from a company you trust. Make sure you are on their Web site, not a site pretending to be the real site. Read their sales and return policies carefully. Always place orders and give financial information on a secure site. Don't let a site store your credit card number or other account information. Reputable sites will give you the option of refusing to allow them to store your credit information. Always print out a copy of your order and keep it for your records.

Rule 10: Err on the side of caution

When in doubt, don't. Don't open that E-mail. Don't fill out that form. Don't visit that Web site. Don't post that message. It's not worth the headaches.

Reclaiming Your Privacy

OK, so you're following the above rules to protect your privacy, but what do you do about the information already on the Internet? There are some things you *can* do.

First, restrict or remove personal information on and off the Internet. People-finder search engines allow you to modify or remove personal information. If you use a chat program, go to where your profile is stored and remove all the information you can. Request that credit card information be removed from online stores where you've ordered items in the past. Request copies of your credit report and examine it carefully. See who has requested copies of your report in the last year. Check colleges, universities, professional associations, service organizations, and other Web sites that might store personal information. Check out the Federal Trade Commission site (www.ftc.gov) for other tips on how to protect your privacy.

Second, decide how you want to deal with the cookies that Web sites put on your computer. You can set your browser's preferences to "high," thus blocking all cookies. Some Web sites, however, will not work if you set your browser at this level.

There are a number of good reasons why you will want to accept cookies. For example, if you visit a weather site and request local weather, a cookie is stored on your computer. The next time you visit that site, it will automatically display the local weather. Cookies keep a record of where you've been on a site. When you return to a Web site days later, the pages you've visited before will be indicated by a change in the color of the hyper-text link.

A better way to deal with cookies is to either delete them manually or purchase a small utility program that manages them. These programs restrict the type of cookies you'll accept, delete all cookies at the close of your Internet session, or help you manage them offline.

Third, if you're worried about E-mail privacy, use an E-mail encryption program. Pretty Good Privacy (PGP) is one of the best. If you use an encryption program, whoever receives your E-mail must be able to decode it.

When you go to bed tonight, will you lock the front door? Of course you will. You don't want anyone walking in on you while you sleep. When you go to the ATM machine, will you guard your password and transaction? Yes, you will. The next time you log on to the Internet, will you be just as cautious about what you do online?

CHAPTER 7

PROTECTING YOUR FAMILY

Before you read further, I have a question for you. Are you going to do something *now* to protect your family online? Or are you going to wait until you have a problem before doing something?

If you're going to wait until you have a problem to do something, then skip this chapter. On the other hand, if you want to take a few simple steps to guard your family against the dangers the Internet poses, then read on.

For all our fear, when it comes to the Internet, most parents are reactive instead of proactive. We wait until problems arise before doing anything about them. It's as if we think, *It won't happen to my kids.* Why not? It can and does happen to kids like yours. Sometimes they stumble onto problems. Sometimes problems come looking for them. Sometimes others (their friends) lead them to problems.

You have locks on the doors, a fence around the yard, and rules concerning where your kids can and cannot go, what they can and cannot eat, watch on TV, or read. As good parents, you know who their friends are. You are involved in their lives. Protecting your family from the bad, and opening the door to the good, of the Internet is just an extension of what you are already doing as parents.

Seven Keys to Protecting Your Family

1. Learn to use the computer and the Internet

You'll never understand what your kids are doing online unless you learn how to use it yourself. Learning how to use the computer and Internet enables you to talk with your kids about what they are doing online. It gives you the confidence to take the steps necessary to protect your children's online adventures. By learning how to use the Internet, you gain firsthand knowledge of how the Internet works. You can know what your family is doing online. You can stay informed about issues affecting your family on the Internet.

2. Get involved

Arbitron NewMedia reported that more than half of all children turn to friends for information about the Internet. Only 5 percent turn to their parents.[1] Buck the trend. Make the Internet a family experience. Have your kids show you around the Internet. Let them show you their bookmarks. Ask them to tell you what sites they like and why. How do they find the sites that interest them? Do they follow links from other sites? Do they use a search engine? If they use a search engine, which one do they use, and why?

Talk about sites you like. When you find a site you approve of and one your children might enjoy, give them the address. Later, ask them what they thought of it. Find things to do together on the Internet. Play online games. Follow your favorite sports team. Plan your next family vacation using the Internet. Build a family Web site. Try some of the family activities in the final section of this book.

3. Subscribe to a family-friendly ISP

Many Internet Service Providers now offer some form of filtering. Check with your ISP to see what's available and then learn how to use it. If your ISP doesn't provide filtering, consider finding one that does. Check the sidebar for a list of national and regional family-friendly ISPs. If you use America Online, they provide a helpful set of blocking filters.

4. Use blocking/monitoring software

Subscribing to a family-friendly ISP is an important first step. Blocking/monitoring software provides a second level of protection against sites that might slip through your ISP's filters. With it, you can control when your children are online and the type of personal information they give out. Some of the better blocking/monitoring software keeps a record of where your family has been online. Even if your ISP has filters, it makes sense to invest in blocking/monitoring software.

5. Put the computer out in the open

Put it in the family room or another room where secrecy is minimal. Face the computer screen into the room. It's hard to hide what you're doing when others can walk by and see exactly what you're up to.

6. Don't allow children to use the computer when the rest of the family is in bed or not at home

You can't monitor what you don't see or know is going on. Resist the temptation to use the computer as a babysitting tool. Nor should you let a babysitter use the Internet when you're not home. The key here is parental involvement. If grandparents watch your kids, be sure they know the rules and the need to stay involved.

7. Create an "Online Family Agreement"

A clear, easy-to-read agreement will help protect your family and minimize conflict over the Internet. An "Online Family Agreement" helps children remember what is acceptable and unacceptable use of the Internet. By putting it in writing and posting it next to the computer, it eliminates future questions. It removes the fear factor by providing a way for children to talk with parents about problems they've encountered, without threat of punishment. It minimizes conflict because both acceptable behavior and consequences are spelled out in the agreement.

Know Where Your Kids Go Online

Both Internet Explorer and Netscape keep track of recently visited sites in a file called History. In Internet Explorer, click **History** on the button bar. In Netscape, click **Communicator, Tools, History**.

Scan the list of sites. To call up an unfamiliar site, double-click on it.

If the History folder is empty, make sure it's set to record sites. Choose **Tools, Internet Options** in Internet Explorer or **Edit, Preferences** in Netscape. Set the number of days to keep your history between fourteen and twenty days.

If after adjusting the settings the History list continues to be empty, someone is emptying it. You might have a problem. First, ask them not to empty the folder. If they continue to empty the list, then they are trying to hide where they are going on the Internet. It's time for you to act.

A better way to monitor and protect your kids online is by using blocking/monitoring software. Many of these programs keep a record of Web sites visited, search requests, and Web sites blocked.

Talking with Your Kids

Talking with your kids about the Internet should be an ongoing conversation. When you sit down with them the first time, make sure it's a conversation, not a lecture. Begin the conversation by talking about the things each person hopes to be able to do on the Internet. Parents want Internet service so their kids can get ahead in school. Kids want on the Internet so they can play games, keep up with their sports teams, follow their favorite musician, and chat with friends.

As you talk, discuss the importance of staying safe. You might use the analogy of a city, found in chapter 5. Introduce them to the idea of an Online Family Agreement as outlined later in this chapter. Begin working on it together. Discuss chat and E-mail. Decide what's best for your family, taking into consideration the ages of your children.

Read the *Internet Fable* with your kids. This story has been around the Internet for some time. No one knows who wrote it, but you can find it at the Parent Soup Web site (www.parentsoup.com/edcentral/alu/caution.html). This is a great story to help your kids understand some of the dangers on the Internet. Remember, though, don't spend all your time talking about the bad. Return to the fun, good, positive benefits of the Internet.

Never stop talking to your kids about the Internet. Show an interest in what interests them. If you permit your kids to chat online, direct them to monitored chat rooms. Occasionally, remind them of the dangers. Praise them if they come to you and report "making a mistake" or stumbling onto something offensive.

If they break the Online Family Agreement, don't panic. Discuss what happened and the agreed-upon consequences. Then enforce the rules. When the penalty is paid, discuss what they will do to avoid making the same mistake again. The goal is to be able to talk with your kids about the Internet. More important, the goal is for your kids to feel comfortable talking to you about the Internet.

Creating an Online Family Agreement

An Online Family Agreement can be a win for both you and your kids. It gives your children the freedom to operate within the rules, yet security in knowing the boundaries. It minimizes conflict by setting out the rules and penalties in advance. No one can ever say, "I didn't know" or "I forgot." It provides a nonthreatening way of communication when something uncomfortable or offensive is stumbled upon.

As a parent, an Online Family Agreement provides some security in knowing your kids will be safe online. It opens a channel of communication since the whole family is involved in establishing the agreement.

If your children are young, you might want to draft most of the agreement yourself; then sit down and discuss it with them. If your children are older, work out an agreement together. Part of what makes an Online Family Agreement work is the communication you develop in the process. If you hit a point you can't agree on, you might want to put that point off and come back to it later. If you still can't resolve the issue, you (as the parent) should have the last word.

Your Online Family Agreement should include the following points:

- When and how long they can be online. This should also include who has to be present for them to go online.

- What sites they can and cannot visit online. Establish clear boundaries of what is acceptable and not acceptable.

- How they will relate and respond online. Using bad language, getting into arguments, or responding to anything that makes them feel uncomfortable or that they know to be wrong is out. They will not respond to requests for personal information. Nor will they agree to call or meet anyone in person whom they meet online. They will inform you of all such requests for information.

- What information they can give online. Have them pick a nickname to use online. They must never give out their real name, address, phone number, family members' names, friends' names, school names, where parents work, theirs or other's E-mail addresses without permission. Make it clear if they are not to register for a free E-mail address, an E-mail newsletter or newsgroup, or fill out forms without your permission.

- The proper use of E-mail. Decide whom they can E-mail. Under what conditions must they seek permission before E-mailing someone? Decide if you will monitor your child's E-mail. You know what mail they receive through the Postal Service; shouldn't you know what they are receiving online? Let them know if you're going to monitor their

E-mail. If they have separate E-mail addresses, create a filter that sends a copy of their E-mail to you.

- How they are to report to you any Web sites or E-mail messages that make them uncomfortable or that they know are wrong.
- Will they be allowed to enter chat rooms or use a chat program, such as AOL Instant Messenger or ICQ? If so, set guidelines as to what chat rooms are acceptable, their conduct in the chat rooms, and under what conditions they are to leave the chat room.
- What online games and gaming zones are acceptable.
- What they can and cannot do on the Internet at a library, school, or friend's house. Decide if you will allow them to use the Internet any place other than at home. If you do, be clear on the conditions that are acceptable.
- Clear consequences for violating the agreement.
- A final statement that reads: "I will abide by my family's rules as to when, where, and what I can do online."
- Once the details of your Online Family Agreement have been finalized, have everyone in the family sign the agreement. Then, post it by the computer where all can see it and refer to it as necessary.

An Online Family Agreement is of little value if you don't also take steps to lock out the bad. Kids will be kids, and their curiosity and innocence can get them into trouble. As a parent, you must take steps to protect them from ever being exposed to the bad side of the Internet. Find out how to do just that in the next chapter.

CHAPTER 8

SLAMMING THE DOOR ON THE BAD

Kids will be kids. Their natural curiosity, their propensity to sin, can lead them into dangerous territory on the Internet. As important as the Online Family Agreement is, it's not enough. You need to take a few additional steps to protect your family. These steps will also help protect them from those online who will try to influence your children toward evil.

Family-Friendly ISP

If one is available in your area, consider using a family-friendly Internet Service Provider. Family-friendly ISPs do the work of blocking offensive sites and screening search results for you. When you log on to the Internet using a family-friendly ISP, your call is routed through their server. Their server then filters the content of your browsing. Most ISPs use software containing a list of offensive sites that is updated daily. If a site is on the list, your browser will indicate that you cannot access that site or that it cannot be found. Offensive links and search results are blocked. Many add a second level of filtering by screening for inappropriate words. This helps guard against new sites that haven't made it to the list, as well as offensive chat rooms.

Most family-friendly ISPs use the same list of offensive sites. Where they differ is in how they apply them. Some are stricter than others. For example, some filter gambling and others do not.

The number of family-friendly ISPs is growing. Though many call themselves national, that doesn't mean they are available everywhere. It means they offer access in many regions of the country. You'll have to do some checking to see if any national or local family-friendly ISPs offer services in your area.

Where to Find a Family-Friendly ISP

Here's a list of national family-friendly ISPs. This list is not exhaustive. There are many other national, as well as regional or local, family-friendly Internet Service Providers. Remember that national doesn't mean they are in your area. It simply means they have access in more than one region of the country.

• CleanWeb.net	877-253-2693	www.cleanweb.net
• CharacterLink	888-330-8678	www.characterlink.net
• FamilyConnect	800-800-6636	www.familyconnect.com
• Hedgebuilders	615-952-4200	www.hedge.org
• Integrity Online	800-585-6603	www.integrityonline.com
• LifeWay*online*	800-454-5965	www.lifewayonline.com
• Mayberry USA	888-734-3444	www.mayberryusa.net
• Rated-G	888-711-6381	www.rated-g.net
• Safeconnect	800-972-5800	www.safeconnect.com

For a list of other family-friendly ISPs, check out the following two sites:

- Focus on the Family CitizenLink
  www.family.org/cforum/research/papers/a0002551.html
- Kid Shield   www.kidshield.com

Family-friendly ISPs do have their limitations. Since more than two hundred new pornographic sites are posted every day, it is possible for a site to get through. Also these ISPs cannot monitor the time individuals spend online, nor do they track where someone has been on the Internet. Many filter only some chat and newsgroups. They don't guard against your children giving out personal information. Savvy teens can get around them by subscribing to a different ISP without your knowledge.[1]

Don't depend solely on a family-friendly ISP to protect your family. It should be a key part of an overall protection plan that also includes an Online Family Agreement (as outlined in the previous chapter) and blocking/monitoring software that you install on your family computer.

Blocking/Monitoring Software

Blocking/monitoring software adds a second level of protection for your family. Such software helps block chat, forms, FTP sites, and personal information. Many have a timer feature to limit when and how long each family member is online. All of them can automatically update their filter lists on a regular basis.

There are many different products to choose from. CYBERsitter (for PCs) and Surf Watch (for Macs) are two of the best. CYBERsitter is one of the easiest to set up and one of the most effective. It blocks sites by looking for key words and checking sites against an offensive site list. You can set the type of content filtered. The program automatically updates itself every seven days. It has an optional timer to limit online use. In my opinion, two of its best features are the violations log it creates and its ability to block ads. You can set the violations log to record only words and sites blocked or all online activity. You can review the log regularly, looking for problems and monitoring your family's online activity. If you discover any problems, you can save the log or print it out for reference. Sometimes the banner ads on legitimate sites can be offensive and tempting for your children. CYBERsitter's ability to block these ads is a welcomed added feature.

CYBERsitter is not the only blocking/monitoring software available, although it is the one we use and the one I recommend. Others include NetNanny, CyberPatrol, X-Stop, and Surf Monkey. Each of these programs works a little differently. They all have their strengths and weaknesses. All do some or all of the following: block access to offensive sites, chat rooms, and newsgroups; filter E-mail; establish time controls; and log Internet activity.

Another option is Crosswalk.com. This is a Christian Web site that provides free Internet filtering by way of a program called Crossing Guard. You can download their software free from their Web site. Crossing Guard blocks all chat rooms and chat programs other than their monitored chat rooms. In addition, Crosswalk's site offers a wealth of places to go online and a family-friendly search engine.

Using Your Browser's Built-in Protection Feature

If you choose not to purchase blocking/monitoring software, you can use your browser's built-in protection features. Both Internet Explorer and Netscape use voluntary rating systems by the Recreational Software Advisory Council (RSACi) and SafeSurf. RSACi divides its ratings into four categories: language, nudity, sex, and violence. SafeSurf has developed a far more extensive rating system based on eleven different categories. These include age, profanity, heterosexual themes, homosexual themes, nudity, violence, sex, intolerance, drug use, other adult themes, and gambling.

The problem with both systems is that they rely on voluntary site registration. You have to decide what to do with the millions of unrated sites. If you choose to block them, you will block millions of good sites. If you choose not to block unrated sites, then your child could access an unrated hate group or adult site.

If you choose to use your browser's built-in filter, you must set it up. Both Internet Explorer and Netscape allow you to use one or both rating systems. I recommend you use both. Some sites carry only one rating. I also recommend you choose to block all sites that don't carry a rating. This

means you'll have to manually exclude sites or override the filter when you
or your child need to access an unrated site.

Configuring Internet Explorer's Blocking/Monitoring Feature

1. From the Menu bar, choose **Tools, Internet Options, Content, Content
   Advisor.**
2. Click **Enable**.
3. In the Content Advisor box (see figure 1), use your mouse to select your
   filter settings using RSACi.
4. To add SafeSurf's rating system, click the **General** tab in the Content
   Advisor box. Click on **Find Rating Systems**. Follow the links to
   SafeSurf. Once on their Web site, follow the instructions for downloading and installing the SafeSurf rating system. (Click **More Info** at
   the bottom of the Rating tab to get
   a detailed explanation of the rating
   categories and levels.)
5. Once you've installed the
   SafeSurf rating system, return
   to the Content Advisor and set
   the rating levels.
6. When prompted, type in a
   password.

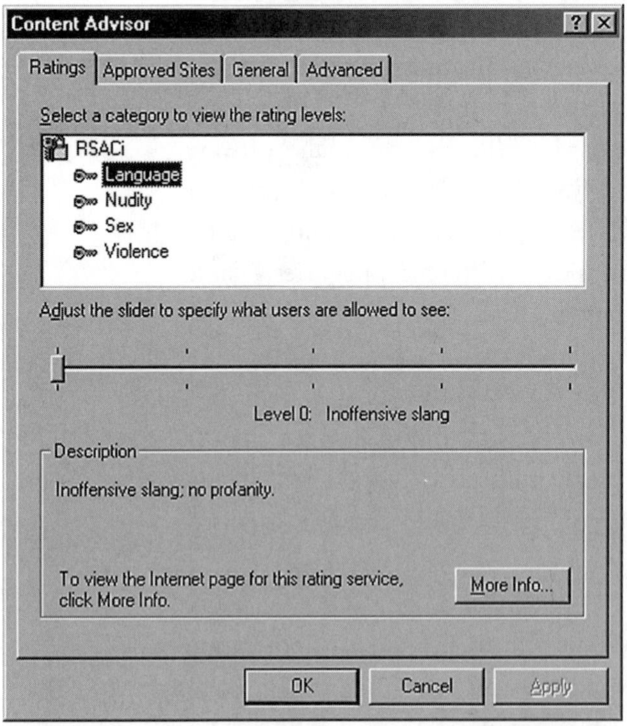

Configuring Netscape
NetWatch

1. From the Menu bar, choose
   Help, NetWatch. You must be
   online to set the NetWatch feature. If you are not online, you
   will be prompted to log on.

Figure 1. Internet Explorer Content Advisor dialog box

2. Once you log on, Netscape opens the NetWatch Web page. Read the opening page and click the appropriate link to set up NetWatch (see figure 2).

3. Setting up NetWatch is a three-step process. From the pull-down menus, select the acceptable viewing levels for both RSACi and SafeSurf. (NetWatch includes a hyperlink to a detailed explanation of each system's categories and filter levels.)

4. Choose and type in a NetWatch password.

5. Turn NetWatch on.

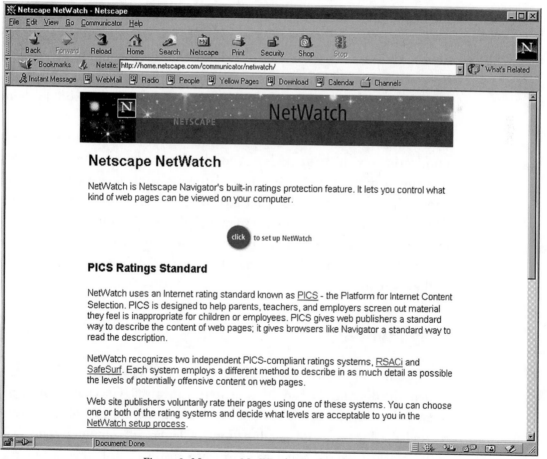

Figure 2. Netscape NetWatch Configuration page

You might choose to use your browser's protection system rather than blocking/monitoring software in two situations: (1) If you're a grandparent and your grandkids use your computer when visiting. (2) If you're on vacation and your kids will be using your notebook computer or a different computer. If they don't use the computer regularly, then it's not necessary to go through the added expense of blocking/monitoring software for it.

When You're Not Present

Studies show that students access the Internet away from home almost as often as they do at home. You need to decide how to handle those times when you're not there. What do you do when your kids are at school, the library, a friend's house, or a relative's home? This is the most difficult challenge you'll face. At home you can control their access with the use of software timers or by not giving them the password. But what do you do about other places?

The most important thing you can do is maintain open lines of communication with your kids. Second, discuss your Online Family Agreement with extended family and friends you know well. Let them know what is acceptable for your kids to do and not do on the Internet. Third, work with your school system and library to require parental permission and blocking/monitoring software. Fourth, make sure you specify in your Online Family Agreement what your children can and cannot do in these situations.

Stay Involved

I cannot stress this enough. Once you've done all you can with software to slam the door on the bad, it's time to stay involved. Check out your children's online activity. If you've installed blocking/monitoring software, learn to read the log. Ads and combinations of letters in computer codes will create blocked words. You'll have to learn to distinguish these from real violations. What you're looking for are sites accessed, sites denied, and words entered in search engines.

If you don't have blocking/monitoring software, use your browser's history feature to review the sites your family has visited. If you have a question about a site, visit it yourself.

The best insurance against the dangers of the Internet is awareness. Stay informed. Remain vigilant concerning what your kids are doing online.

CHAPTER 9

PROTECTING YOUR COMPUTER

It's not a matter of if, but when, you will encounter a virus. More than forty-one thousand viruses are floating around the Internet. A few, like Melissa in 1999 and I-Love-You in 2000, gain national attention. Most work anonymously, being sent from computer to computer by unsuspecting users. Once on your system, viruses do their dirty work.

In this chapter we'll answer the five most common questions concerning viruses: What are they? How do you get them? How can you tell if you have one? How do you avoid them? How do you get rid of them?

What Are Viruses?

Viruses are small programs. Some hide in other files and programs. Other attach themselves to E-mail messages. You "catch" a virus by opening the infected file or program in which it is hiding. It then moves into your computer's memory. Once there, it begins replicating, creating multiple copies of itself, much like an organic virus. Finally, the virus runs its built-in programming, called *code*. What the virus does depends on how the programmer designed it. Viruses can alter data, gobble up memory, crash programs, flash annoying screen messages, and even crash your computer.

Viruses don't damage computer hardware. Your monitor might begin to act strangely, or your keyboard may quit working properly when you have a virus. That simply means a virus has attacked the programs controlling the function of your monitor or keyboard. A virus on your hard drive or a diskette can only affect the data, not the actual drive. Remove the virus, restore your software, and your computer will function normally again.

Viruses are classified many different ways. The easiest way to classify them is by the files they attack. Microsoft Word and Excel viruses hide in macros attached to Microsoft documents. Macros are time-saving devices designed to automate tasks such as document formatting and calculations. When you open a document with an infected macro, you release the virus.

Boot sector viruses infect the start-up section of your hard drive. These viruses are potentially the most dangerous. They can prevent your computer from starting properly and damage the file structure of your hard drive, thereby crashing your machine.

File viruses target program files on your hard drive. These files are necessary to run your programs. Some attack key files in your operating system (such as Windows 95, 98, or 2000), disabling or corrupting them.

Other viruses infect JAVA and ActiveX files used by your browser when you surf the Internet. Some attack more than one area of your computer simultaneously.

There are other "viruses" that aren't viruses at all. They do their dirty work by getting people to waste countless hours sending useless warnings back and forth to each other. These are not real viruses. They are virus hoaxes. What's fascinating is that although they don't exist, some people insist on believing that they do. You can find a comprehensive list of virus hoaxes at all major antivirus software manufacturers' Web sites. Some more common ones are: WOBBLER, Blue Mountain Virus, BUDDYLST.ZIP, It Takes Guts to Say Jesus, Microsoft Virus, Returned or Unable to Deliver, and Win a Holiday.

It's easy to determine if a virus alert is a hoax or not. First, if it's a new virus and is spreading as fast as described, you'll hear about it in the media. Second, go to your antivirus program's Web site and look it up. If it's a real virus, they will know about it. If they know about it, they will probably already have a software update to protect you from it.

How Do You Get Them?

Viruses spread when people pass infected files from one computer to another. There are only three ways you can get a virus. One, you can get a virus from an infected diskette used to exchange data between computers. Two, you can get a virus by downloading an infected file from the Internet. Or three, you can get a virus by opening an infected E-mail message or attachment.

How Can You Tell If You Have One?

You have a virus if one of two symptoms show up on your computer. One, your computer (or a program) begins to act strangely. Or two, your antivirus program alerts you to the presence of a virus.

Just because a program quits functioning properly doesn't mean you have a virus. Nor does the loss of a file mean you have a virus. Programs quit functioning properly for many reasons. If you have a problem with a program, it probably wasn't caused by a virus if you have an up-to-date antivirus program running on your machine. To rule out a virus completely, open your antivirus program and have it scan all the files on your hard drive.

The best way to tell you have a virus is when your software alerts you to the fact. The type of virus often determines when it's found. For example, a macrovirus may not be found until you try to open an infected file. If it's a boot sector file, your antivirus program will alert you as the computer starts. Most of the time, viruses are found while the antivirus program works in the background. When it finds a virus, it alerts you to its presence and guides you through the process of removing it from your system.

How Do You Avoid Them?

Avoiding computer viruses is a lot like avoiding the flu. You limit your exposure and practice good hygiene (like washing your hands).

Limiting your exposure to computer viruses is a matter of being careful. Taking care in how you handle Internet downloads, E-mail attachments, and shared files on diskettes will prevent many problems with viruses. Don't download files from unfamiliar Web sites. Don't open E-mail attachments from people you don't know. If you weren't expecting an attachment from someone you know, don't open it. Make sure they sent it to you. Keep your E-mail program up-to-date.

Practice good hygiene by purchasing and using a good antivirus program. The program you select is not as important as the fact that you know how to use it. Set your antivirus software to scan automatically. Your program scans downloads and program files before they are opened from your hard drive. Set it to scan your entire hard drive monthly. Scan all E-mail attachments and downloaded files before opening them. These steps help you avoid infecting your computer with viruses.

How Do You Get Rid of Them?

When you discover a virus on your computer, you have two options in ridding your system of it. First, delete the infected file or program from your computer. Once you delete the file, replace it with a clean copy. One caution: Deleting an infected file or program doesn't always remove the virus from your system. Viruses can hide anywhere—on a diskette, in a macro, in a little-used program file, in a file meant to mimic another file, or in the memory. Even if you manually remove the virus from your system, you can reinfect your computer from an infected diskette, macro, or file the next time you use it. Therefore, it's important that you use an antivirus program.

Second, you can rid your computer of a virus by using an antivirus program to repair the infected file or boot sector. Sometimes totally removing a virus from your system requires both the repair of some files and the removal and replacement of others.

There are many antivirus programs from which to choose. If you purchased your computer in the last two years, you probably already have an antivirus program. To find out if there's one operating on your system already, slowly move your mouse pointer over the icons on the system tray. The system tray is in the bottom, right-hand corner of your computer screen. It usually contains the time. Hold the pointer over each icon long enough for a small pop-up window to appear, telling you what the icon represents. If you have antivirus software running, it will have an icon on this tray.

If one doesn't appear here, that doesn't mean you don't have a program. Check the list of software that came with your computer or scan the programs on the Start menu to see if it's listed. If one is installed, open it and follow the setup instructions.

You can find antivirus programs in any store that carries computer software. Three of the most popular programs today are Norton's AntiVirus, McAffee Anti-Virus, and Guard Dog. These are not the only ones. What's important is not which one you use but that you use one.

When you install it, be sure to make any emergency start-up disks it asks for. Label them clearly and put them with the other original computer program diskettes. If you have a virus, always follow your antivirus software's instructions on how to rid your system of it. Always back up your important data regularly.

Once you've suffered an infection, your risk for reinfection by that same virus increases. You can suffer reinfection from an infected diskette or from a file infected originally on your machine that now rests on another computer. To keep this from happening, scan all diskettes you've used to either transfer or back up files from your computer. Also scan for viruses on any other computer with which you have exchanged files.

Remember: It's not a matter of if, but when, you will encounter a virus. The best protection against a virus is a little prevention. Taking the necessary steps now will save you many headaches later.

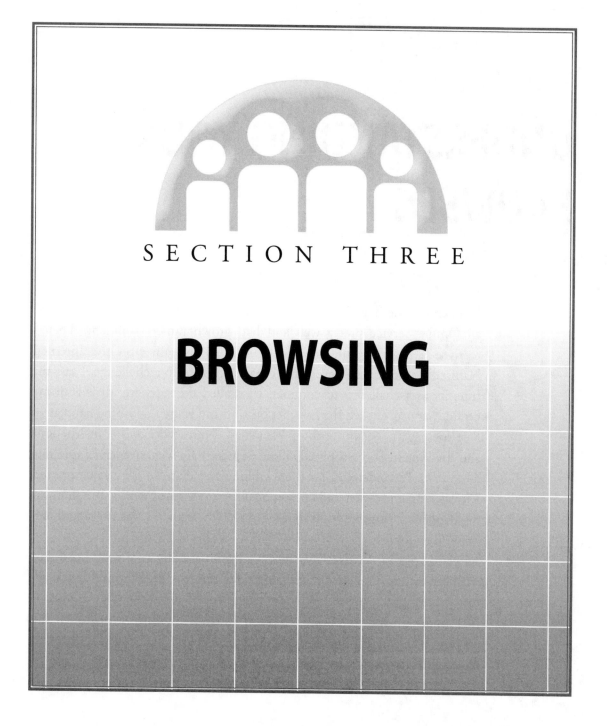

SECTION THREE

BROWSING

CHAPTER 10

UNDERSTANDING YOUR BROWSER

I remember the first time I logged on to the Internet. I had learned to use an Online Service pretty well and had grown rather confident. Then I received a program update, which included free time on the Internet. Naturally curious, and never one to back down from a challenge, I saw the Internet as a challenge to conquer. I installed the software, dialed up my Online Service, clicked the Internet button, and waited. Nothing happened. So I tried again. Again, nothing happened. I reread the online instructions and tried again. Success! I was online! At least that's what my screen told me. *Now what?* I wondered. I sat there looking at the screen for a few minutes. I scrolled up and down and clicked on a few underlined words. When nothing happened, I turned it off. I swore myself to secrecy. I wasn't going to tell a soul how foolish I felt. It was a month before I tried again.

I had no idea what I was doing. Eventually, by trial and error, and with more than a few tips from magazines and friends, I figured it out. So can you. Logging on and moving around the Internet isn't as hard as it first seems. This chapter, and the next three, will guide you through the process of getting online and beginning to discover all that the Internet has to offer.

Before You Connect

Now that you have a basic understanding of the Internet and have selected your Internet Service Provider or Online Service, it's time to connect. If you haven't done so already, pick up the phone and call them. You will need to set up an account. They will assign you a UserID and password. Without those two things, you cannot log on to the Internet. You can change your password whenever you like, but your UserID stays the same. Most ISPs ask you to select your UserID, so give it some thought. It can be anything you want, within the guidelines of your ISP. Select three or four possible UserIDs because your first choice might already be taken.

While on the phone with customer service, ask them to connect you to technical support. They will help you set up your software. Setting up your software is simpler with an Online Service, such as AOL or MSN. Because you use their software, it sets up automatically when you install it. Once you install the software, click on the icon for your browser. Provide some basic information, and you're ready to go.

A built-in Connection Wizard makes it easy for you to set up both Microsoft and Netscape. When you open your browser for the first time, this setup automatically runs. The Connection Wizard gathers the information your browser needs to connect you to the Internet. You can choose to sign up for a new account, transfer an existing account, or manually configure an account. If you use a local ISP, you will set up your connection manually. Don't be afraid of this. You need only three pieces of information: your local access number (the number you'll dial to log on to the Internet), your UserID, and your password. The Connection Wizard also has a built-in referral service. Clicking on this option in the Connection Wizard dialog box presents you with a list of ISPs in your area.

If you have any questions about setting up your software, call your ISP. They will help you set up your service, or troubleshoot it if you have any problems.

If you have "call waiting" on your phone, disable it. If you don't disable it, when someone calls while you are online, the click will disconnect you. To

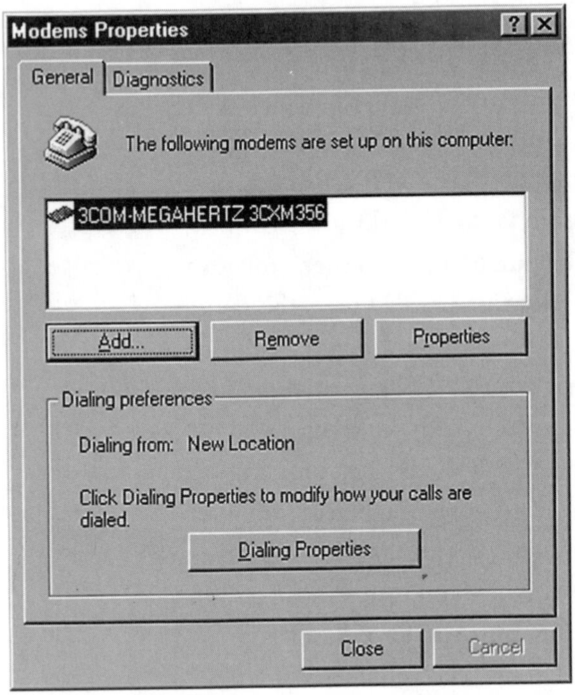

Figure 1. Modems Properties

disable call waiting, double-click on **My Computer**. Double-click again on **Control Panel**, and finally, double-click on **Modems**. This opens the Modems Properties dialog box (see figure 1). If it lists more than one modem, click on the one you use. Click **Dialing Properties**. Under **Dialing Properties**, click on **"This location has call waiting."** Enter your phone company's code to disable call waiting. (Check the front of your phone book or call your local phone company.) Click **OK** twice. Close the Control Panel and My Computer. Now when you log on to the Internet, your modem will automatically disable call waiting.

Understanding an Internet Address

An Internet address is called a *URL*, or *Universal Resource Locator*. A URL has a number of parts. The example below tells your browser to go to the November 1999 issue of the *Internet for Families* newsletter found on the *Internet for Families* Web site. Each part of this address is important.

http://www.internetforfamilies.org/iffezine/ezine1199.htm

Http:// tells your browser to use HyperText Transfer Protocol. This is the "language" your computer uses to "talk" with another computer. Typically, you'll see *http* at the beginning of most Internet addresses. At times, you will see *ftp, gopher, news,* or *telnet* instead of *http://*. These not only tell your computer how to communicate; they tell you the type of site you're on. *Ftp* is used to upload and download files. *News* is a newsgroup. *Telnet* allows you to log on to a distant computer as if you were sitting in front of the screen. *Gopher* is an older type of Internet file or site.

The *www* points your browser to the World Wide Web. As we saw in chapter 1, this is where you'll spend most of your time.

Internetforfamilies.org is the domain name of the Web site. Domain names have two parts. The prefix is often some form of the organization's name. The suffix tells you the type of site. There are five common address endings: *com* – commercial sites, *gov* – government sites, *edu* – educational sites, *net* – Internet providers or other networks, and *org* – nonprofit or other organizations. These are general classifications and don't always apply exactly. Other extensions designate different countries.

Up to five different sites can share the same prefix. What differentiates them is the suffix. Family.*org* is the address for Dr. James Dobson's Focus on the Family Web site, while family.*com* takes you to a site run by Disney.

The forward slash (/) is a separator. It is used to separate sections of the address. It is always a forward slash (/), never a back slash (\).

The *iffezine/ezine1199.htm* tells the Web site what section, Newsletter (iffezine); and what page, November 1999 Ezine (ezine1199.htm), you are looking for on the Web site. Depending on the size of the site and number of Web pages, this final section of the address can be quite long.

You'll often see Web addresses written without the http://www. This doesn't mean it isn't needed. It simply assumes that you know it's part of the address. With the newer versions of both Internet Explorer and Netscape, you can enter most addresses without using http://www. If it doesn't work then add www or http://www to the address.

Understanding Your Browser

Your browser software is like any other piece of equipment in your home. You can purchase a new VCR, bring it home, and plug it in. Without doing anything else, you can watch videos, tape a show (provided you're home), and watch it blink 12:00 unceasingly. However, if you take a few minutes to familiarize yourself with your new VCR, you can watch videos and do a whole lot more. You can record shows while you're away from home or even while watching a different channel. You can change recording speeds, copy from another tape, edit the sound or video, and even set the clock. In short, you'll enjoy your new VCR a lot more. The same goes for your browser. The better you know your browser, the more enjoyable and profitable your surfing will be.

Browsers have several common features. Figure 2 identifies six common elements of every browser. Beginning at the top and moving to the bottom, they are the Menu bar, Button bar, Address bar, Browser window, Scroll bar, and Status bar.

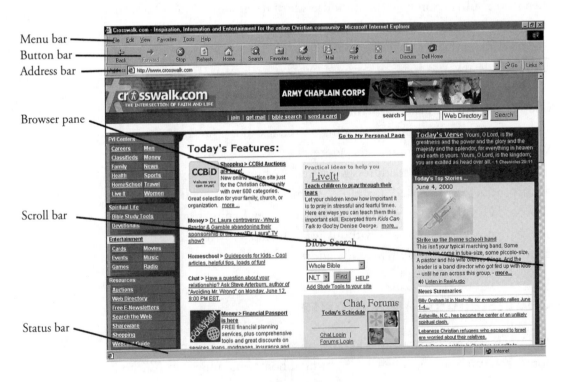

Figure 2. Browser features

The Menu bar lists functions of the browser in easy-to-access, pull-down menus. In Internet Explorer, these functions are under the following headings: File, Edit, View, Go, Favorites, and Help. Netscape groups them under: File, Edit, View, Go, Communicator, and Help. Both the Menu bar and toolbar function as in other programs.

The Button bar is a group of shortcuts for frequently used features found on the Menu bar. These buttons help you move around the Web and perform common features more easily than the Menu bar.

The Address bar contains the URL of the current Web site. This is where you enter an address to change pages or sites. The down arrow button on the far right allows you to view a list of recently visited sites. Clicking on any of them will bring up that address and connect you to the corresponding Web page.

The Browser pane displays the current Web page. Most Web pages are larger than your browser pane. That's when the Scroll bar helps.

The Scroll bar allows you to scroll down, viewing the entire Web page. Using the Scroll bar, you can move up and down the entire page.

The Status bar runs across the bottom of your browser window. Divided into three sections, it gives you an ongoing status of what's happening with your browser. Though Internet Explorer and Netscape Navigator displays are different, both include the same information. One section flashes bits of information telling you the site it's finding, logging on to, and finally, when it is done. A second section contains a moving bar that disappears when the page is downloaded. The third section gives you a series of icons, telling you the status of your Web connection. A lock indicates that you're on a secure site. Netscape adds an optional Component Bar for quickly opening Communicator features.

One final helpful browser feature is the logo in the top, right-hand corner. Depending on the version of your software, this logo may be different from that pictured in figure 3. When your browser is connecting to a site and loading a page, this logo animates. When the page finishes loading, it stops. This is another visual cue, letting you know the page is finished loading.

Navigating with Your Browser

The toolbar is your one-click stop for all the features you need in order to move around the Web. Clicking a button on the toolbar will execute an action, open a menu, open a dialog box, or change the size of the browser. Figure 3 shows both Internet Explorer and Netscape Navigator toolbars. You will notice they are quite similar, but they do have a few differences. The "Quick Reference: Toolbar Features" table summarizes these navigation aids.

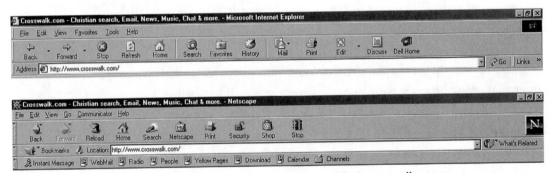

Figure 3. Internet Explorer and Netscape Navigator toolbars

Quick Reference: Toolbar Features

Button	Function	Internet Explorer	Netscape Navigator
Back/Forward	Moves you between pages visited during your current Internet session	Yes	Yes
Stop	Stops loading the current Web page	Yes	Yes
Refresh/Reload	Reloads the current Web page	Yes, called Refresh	Yes, called Reload
Home	Returns you to the Web page that opens every time you log on to the Internet	Yes	Yes
Search	Opens a directory of popular search engines	Yes	Yes
Favorites/Bookmarks	Calls up a list that you've created of frequently visited sites	Yes, called Favorites	Yes, called Bookmarks
History	Recalls a record of recently visited sites	Yes	On the Communicator menu
Mail	Opens your E-mail program	Yes	On the Communicator menu or the component bar
Print	Prints current Web page	Yes	Yes
Full Screen	Hides menu, address, and status bars, displaying more of the Web page	Yes	No
Guide	Opens site index called Netscape Guide	No	Yes
Security	Displays current security settings for site and browser	Called Internet Zone and is on the status bar	Yes

Enough talk. It's time to log on to the Internet and see what's out there in cyberspace. Turn the page, and let's get started.

CHAPTER 11

GOING ONLINE FOR THE FIRST TIME

Now that you understand Internet addresses and your browser, it's time to go online. But there's one more thing you need to do: decide where you want to go. Take a few minutes to collect a few addresses before you go online. You probably have a few sites in mind already. Find those scraps of paper you wrote them on. Find that old magazine that had a Web address at the bottom of an interesting ad. Make sure you have the full address.

Remember that Web addresses (domain names) are often the same as, or similar to, the name of the organization.

• Christianity Online	www.christianityonline.com
• Internet for Families	www.internetforfamilies.org
• LifeWay Christian Resources	www.lifeway.com
• MSNBC	www.msnbc.com
• Microsoft	www.microsoft.com
• USAToday	www.usatoday.com
• Netscape	www.netscape.com
• Moody Bible Institute	www.moody.edu
• Major League Baseball	www.majorleaguebaseball.com
• Promise Keepers	www.promisekeepers.org

Others are familiar abbreviations or company initials.

* Hewlett Packard   www.hp.com
* The National Football League   www.nfl.com
* The National Basketball Association www.nba.com

If none of these sites interest you, here are few more suggestions.

* Crosswalk   www.crosswalk.com
* Gospel Communications Network   www.gospelcom.net
* Insight for Living   www.insight.org
* National Geographic Online   www.nationalgeographic.com
* Focus on the Family   www.family.org
* Precious Moments   www.preciousmoments.com
* The New York Times   www.nytimes.com
* KidSurf Online   www.kidsurf.net

Making the Connection

It's time to log on to the Internet. Double-click on your browser's icon. Enter your user name and password in the Dial-up Connection dialog box (see figure 1). Make sure to enter them correctly. When you type your password, it will appear as asterisks. This protects your password from prying eyes. Do not check the "save password" box. By not checking it, you will prevent anyone from logging on to the Internet who doesn't have your password. When you have entered the information, click **Connect** to dial your ISP's access number.

The Dialing Progress dialog box appears, informing you of your computer's progress in logging on. At the same time, you'll hear your modem pick up the line, find a dial tone, dial the access number, and start "talking to your ISP's modem." After a few moments of what sounds like static, squeals, and whistles, your computer mutes the sound. You can watch the progress of your connection in the Dialing Progress box.

Once connected, an icon picturing two computers opens in the System Tray on the right side of the Windows taskbar. This icon flashes when your computer is sending or receiving information from another computer on the Internet.

Watch as your home page opens in the browser pane window. If this is the first time you've connected to the Internet, or you've never changed your home page, your browser will open to the default home page. Typically, this home page is set by the maker of your browser software. By default, Internet Explorer opens to MSN, or Microsoft Network start page, while Netscape opens to the Netscape Netcenter. You're not stuck with this page. I'll show you how to change it in the next chapter.

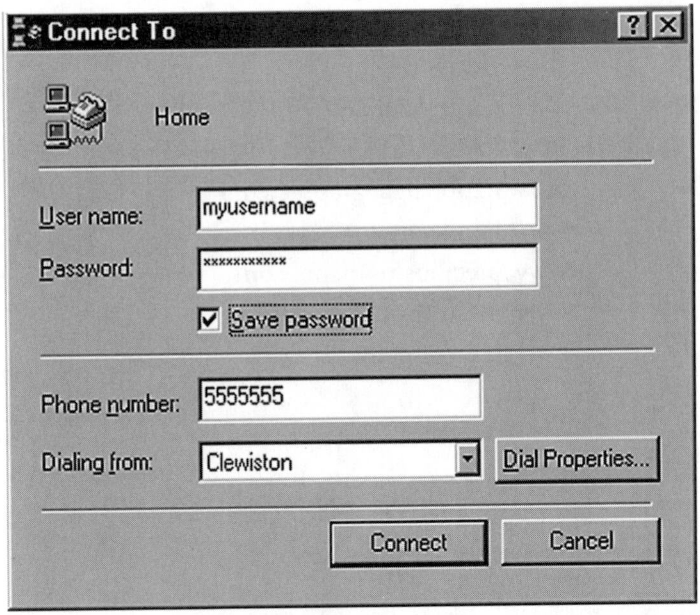

Before going any further, make sure the browser is full-size. (Click on the small Maximize button in the upper right-hand corner of the browser window. It is left of the Close button [X].) This enables you to view as much of the Web site as possible on your screen.

Figure 1. Dial-up Connection

Figure 2, on next page, is a picture of Crosswalk.com. This is the page my browser opens to when I log on to the Internet. Your home page will be different from the one pictured. Looking at the picture, you can see the Title bar, Button bar, site search box, hypertext, graphic images, banner ads, and, of course, the all-important text.

Now compare this figure to the page on your screen. Can you find the same features? Look for hypertext. It's the underlined text that's often a different color. The text contains a link to a different page or site. Look for other types of links. Move your mouse slowly across the page, stopping on pictures, graphic images, or buttons. If the arrow changes to a hand, then the image is a link to another page. (Notice how the address appears on the Status bar.) Clicking on the image will take you to that new address.

Now let's move around the site. If the Scroll bar is active, scroll down the page. If the page is wider than your screen, there will be a horizontal Scroll bar on the bottom of your browser's window. Never assume what you see on the screen is all there is. Most Web pages extend below the bottom of your monitor. Always use the Scroll bar to scroll down the page. Depending on your browser, the page up, page down, end, and home keys will move

Figure 2. Home page

you up and down the page. Some pages will have a *"Top of Page"* link at the bottom of, or spaced throughout, the page.

If you have Internet Explorer, press **F11** on the keyboard to change to the full screen view. Notice how you can view more of the Web page. The full screen view hides the window's taskbar (on the bottom of the screen), the browser's Status bar on the bottom, and all but the Button bar on the top. Press **F11** again to return it to the standard view.

Next click on a hypertext link and see where it takes you. Watch the Status bar at the bottom of the screen to see its progress in loading the requested Web page. When the animated bar disappears and the Status bar reads "done," the new page is loaded. Notice the URL has changed in the Address bar. Check out the new page. See if you can find a button or graphic link. Click on it and see where it takes you.

Now let's go to a site you've selected. Click on the text in the Address bar. It will highlight the address in blue. Type in the Web address of the site you want to visit. For now, be sure to include http://www. in your address. You don't have to enter this information in the latest browser versions. If you type in the domain name, it assumes http://www. If you are new to the Internet, it's good practice to type in this information. Sometimes, your browser won't recognize a URL without it. Once you've typed in the address, check to see if you typed it in correctly. Press **Enter** on your keyboard. Watch as your browser finds the site and connects to it.

You don't have to wait for a page to finish loading before you view it. Web pages usually load text first, then Button bars, frames, and graphics. This enables you to begin reading while the page finishes loading.

Move around the new site. See if you can find a feature that wasn't on any of the previous pages. Try it out. You can't break it.

Try another address. If you enter an address wrong, you will receive an error message. The most common error messages are: "server not responding," or "server cannot be found." Make sure you entered the address correctly. Make sure there are no spaces in the address. Check to see if you've missed a dot (.) or a forward slash (/). Perhaps you left out or transposed a letter. Slow down. The most common mistake is a typographical error. Proof the address before you press **Enter**.

If the address is correct, try again. If it still doesn't work, wait a few hours and try again. There may be too much traffic on the Internet, or your server may be busy. I've received error messages telling me: "microsoft.com cannot be found."

If you wait a few hours, or a whole day, and the address still doesn't work, there might be a mistake in the address. Try erasing the far, right-hand section of the address, back to the last forward slash. If that doesn't work, remove the next section. The Internet is always changing. Some pages are removed, or moved, and others added. If all else fails, go to the site by entering the domain name and search the site for the needed information.

After you've explored awhile, try backing up, using the Back button. Notice how you begin to retrace your Internet journey. Notice, too, how the color of hypertext has changed. This indicates what sites you've visited.

Before disconnecting, try a few more sites. Click on a few more links. Lastly, click on the **Home** button on the toolbar. This brings you back to your start page.

Disconnecting

When you've finished browsing, it's time to disconnect from the Internet. By default, your browser is set to disconnect after being idle for twenty minutes. If you get distracted and forget, it will disconnect automatically. When you're ready to disconnect, close your browser. Select **File**, then **Close** from the menu; use the Alt-F4 keyboard shortcut; or use the Close button ([X]) in the top right-hand corner of your browser. When your browser closes, a dialog box appears asking if you want to disconnect from your ISP. Click **Yes**, and you're done.

Sometimes the dialog box doesn't appear. When this happens, double-click on the Internet Connection icon in the System Tray. The Internet

Connection icon is a symbol of two computers located in the lower right-hand corner of your computer screen. This opens the Connection Status box. Click on **Disconnect**, and you're done.

Help for the Reluctant Surfer

Almost every family has one. They come in different shapes and sizes. Some are tall, some are short. Some are young, some are old. For whatever reason, there seems to be one member of every family who either cares nothing about the Internet or is reluctant to try. As hard as you try to get them interested, they may never fully embrace the Internet. But you can help them overcome their reluctance. Here are seven tips for helping the reluctant surfer.

1. Don't push

Nobody likes to do something they don't want to do. Nobody wants to be pushed, cajoled, or coerced. In your enthusiasm, you can pressure the reluctant surfer. Don't. It's the worst thing you can do.

2. Don't minimize their reluctance

There are many reasons why someone is a reluctant surfer. They may see the Internet as something for a different generation. They probably don't see any reason why they should be online. They may be afraid of their lack of knowledge or of appearing a fool. They may be afraid that they'll do something wrong and break the computer. The "bad press" that the Internet sometimes receives causes many to wonder if anyone should be online. There are lots of reasons why someone may be reluctant to try the Internet. Your job is to understand their reluctance.

3. Find out what interests them

On your own, look up some sites and find information that would be of interest to them. Print out the pages to give to them. Don't say, "If you would only learn to use the Internet, you could find this yourself." Instead, say, "I found this on the Internet. I thought you might be interested in it."

When they begin to show an interest, offer to show them some sites online whenever they'd like to see them. When they take you up on your offer, be careful. Don't make the mistake of getting them in front of the computer only to show them what excites *you*. Better yet, don't show them anything that interests you. Show them how to find and do what interests *them*.

4. Go slowly

When you do get them online, don't race through connecting, searching, and moving around the Web. Let them sit in the chair. Let them handle the mouse. Let them type in the commands on the keyboard. Pause and explain everything. If they ask why something happens, tell them (without using "computerese").

5. Make it fun

Stick with what they want to do online. Think of it as leading them on an adventure.

6. Let them set the pace

Don't overload them. If their only interest is E-mail, show them how to log on and send and receive a message. If they're interested in finding information about a hobby, show them how to log on, find some sites, and navigate around those sites. Bookmark some of the sites so they can easily go back to them.

7. Be patient

They may be satisfied with E-mail or with checking the status of their mutual funds. In time, the person who checks E-mail may want to compare airline ticket prices. The family member who checks mutual funds every day will soon want to check out the online versions of the *Wall Street Journal,* *Money Magazine,* or *Business Week.* One day you'll walk through the family room and find them checking sports scores, reading an online book review, or checking out the latest *Precious Moments* figurines.

Well, you've done it. You've done what you might have thought you'd never be able to do. You've logged on to the Internet and even moved between two or three sites. Now that you've gotten your feet wet, it's time to really start surfing.

CHAPTER 12

MOVING AROUND THE WEB

The Internet is a broad, far-ranging environment. With the click of your mouse, you can move from Miami, Florida; to Sydney, Australia; to Seattle, Washington; to London, England. But to get from here to there, you have to know how to move around the Internet.

Eight Ways to Move around the Internet

Opening your browser and dialing your Internet Service Provider connects you to the World Wide Web. Once connected, your browser goes to what's called the *home page*. In the next chapter, I'll show you how to change this page to whichever one you select.

Figure 1 is a screen shot of a typical Web page. This page is the home page of Crosswalk.com. (Remember: The term *home page* can refer to the page your browser opens to when you log on to the Internet or to the opening page of a Web site.) Crosswalk.com is a family-oriented, Christian Web site. In 1997 and 1998, it was named Christian Web site of the year. It's stated purpose is "an Internet Company building Christian community on the World Wide Web." This page is a good example of the eight different ways you can move around the Internet. The first four are on your browser's toolbar. The last four are on the Web page itself.

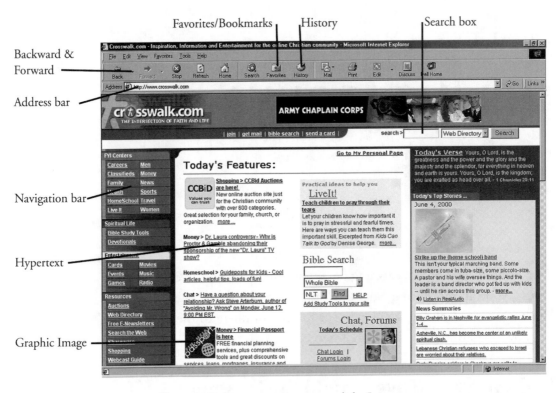

Figure 1. Eight ways to move around the Internet

1. Address Bar

The most obvious way to move from site to site is by way of the Address bar. Right now, the URL or Web address of Crosswalk.com appears in the Address bar. To go to a different Web site, simply enter the new address and click **Go** (or press the Enter key). In the newer versions of both Internet Explorer and Netscape Navigator, you don't have to enter the http://www of the Web address. Your browser assumes this part of the address. So, if you want to go to Focus on the Family, all you need to enter is: family.org. Occasionally, the browser will have trouble with an address entered without the http://www prefix. If that happens, simply add the www before the domain name. In our example, you would type: www.family.org.

As you type a Web address, the auto-complete feature will try to complete it for you. If the address you need appears in the Address bar or on the pull-down menu, just select it and press Enter.

You'll notice the small arrow button on the right end of the browser bar. When you click on it, a menu appears of the most recent sites you've visited. If you forget an address, you can scroll down the list and select the correct address.

2. Back and Forward Buttons

These two buttons are second only to the Address bar as the most used feature of your browser. Get to know them well. They are like the bread crumbs Hansel and Gretel scattered along the path as they wandered into the dark woods. The only difference is that there are no birds in cyberspace to eat your electronic bread crumbs. These two buttons enable you to retrace your steps from page to page during your current Internet session. When you close your browser, this history is cleared.

These buttons are helpful if you're searching for information on a Web site and the link you followed was a dead end. Instead of having to remember the Web address of the previous page, click on the Back button. Each click of the Back button will move you back one page. If the page to which you're returning is three pages back, click the button three times. You don't have to wait for the new page to load before clicking again.

You can play leapfrog with these buttons. Next to both buttons is a small down arrow. Click on this arrow, and a pop-up list presents you with a list of the last few sites visited. If the page you want is four pages back, choose that page from the list and your browser "leapfrogs" over the other three pages. If it's further back than those listed, click on the bottom address. As that page is loading, click the down arrow again for a new list.

The Forward button is grayed-out until you've backed up one or more pages in your current session. Once you've backed up, you can go forward to a page you backed up from by using this button.

3. History Button

Where is that site you visited last Monday that had the chocolate cream puff recipe? You've forgotten the address? Don't worry. The History button contains a list of the sites visited in the last few weeks. In Internet Explorer 5, you can sort them by date visited, by site, or by the most visited. You can change how many days' worth of information is kept in your history by choosing **Tools, Internet Options**. In Netscape, choose **Edit, Preferences**.

4. Favorites or Bookmarks

It won't be long before you develop a list of Web sites that you visit regularly. You can use your browser to keep track of them. In Internet Explorer, they are called *favorites*. In Netscape Navigator, they are called *bookmarks*. In the next section, I'll show you how to set a bookmark.

5. Navigation Bar

To aid your moving around a site, most Web sites have at least one Navigation bar. Crosswalk.com's Navigation bar extends down the left side of the page. Navigation bars can be found across the top of the page, on either side, at the bottom, or in any combination. In this example, you'll find a secondary Navigation bar at the bottom of the page. This second bar is often smaller than the main Navigation bar. Its purpose is to help you move through the site without having to scroll back to the top of the page.

Navigation bars contain hyperlinks that move you from one Web page to another on their site. Sometimes they appear as hypertext. At other times they will be in a Button bar or a series of graphic images. Usually the buttons and graphic images will have one-word or two-word captions showing where they link.

6. Graphic Image

The Internet would be a very dull place if it were all text. Text is important. It carries the ideas and information you're looking for. Nevertheless, colors, pictures, and images make searches more enjoyable. Many of those images serve not only to make a Web site more attractive but also as links to other pages. The right image will tell where it leads you with little, if any, accompanying text. To see which images are links, move your cursor over the images. When the cursor turns to a pointing hand, you're on a link.

7. Hypertext

The highlighted text is called *hypertext*. It is usually colored and underlined. When you click on the text, it takes you to the page suggested by the words in the text. If you look carefully, after you've visited a few pages on a site, the hypertext changes color. This is a navigation aid, showing you pages you've visited and those you haven't.

8. Search Box

Many Web sites today are quite large, containing hundreds, thousands, and sometimes hundreds of thousands of pages. Finding what you need would be impossible without a site search engine. That's where search boxes come in. You use them the same way you use a regular search engine. The only difference is that they usually search only the current Web site.

Saving Your Favorite Sites

Now that you have a handle on moving around the Web, how do you keep track of all the sites you want to return to? You could write them on scraps of paper and tape them to your monitor. After awhile, however, your monitor would look like the community bulletin board at the local grocery store. You could type them into a file in your word processing program. But you'd have to be sure you entered them correctly and then print out an updated list every time you added an address. You could memorize them. Or . . . you can bookmark them.

Bookmarks (or *favorites*) are lists of Web sites you've stored in your browser. When you click on the Bookmark or Favorite button, your browser accesses that list stored on your hard drive.

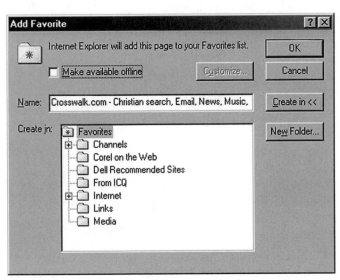

Figure 2. Add Favorite dialog box

To add a Web site to your list, you have to be on the Web site. Choose **Favorites** from the Menu bar, then **Add Favorite** (see figure 2). In the add favorite dialog box, edit the name if necessary, and click **OK**. If you want Internet Explorer to download the page for viewing offline, choose **Make available offline**. In Netscape, choose **Bookmarks, Add Bookmark**.

To return to a book-marked Web site, click **Favorites/Bookmarks** on the toolbar. Click on the desired site from the list.

Before long you will have a long list of bookmarks to search through. It's time to organize them into folders. In Internet Explorer, select **Favorites** from the Menu bar, then **Organize Favorites** (see figure 3). In Netscape, select **Bookmarks, Edit Bookmarks**. In the dialog box, you can create a new folder, delete, or rename your bookmarks.

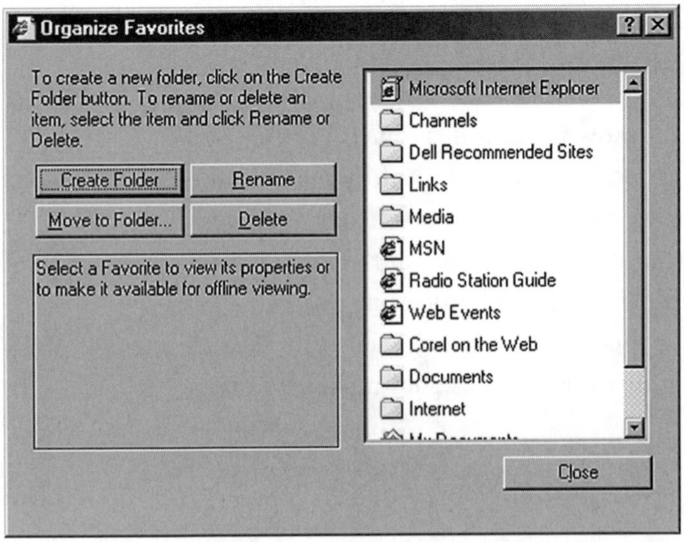

Figure 3. Organize Favorites dialog box

Choose **Create Folder** in the Organize Favorites box. (In Netscape, choose **Files, New Folder** in the Edit Bookmarks box.) Give the new folder a name. Drag all your bookmarks related to that topic into that folder. You can create as many folders as you need. You can even create folders inside folders. For example, I have a folder called Family. Inside it are four folders with each family member's name on one of them. As each family member creates a favorite, they put it into their folder.

Sometimes you'll bookmark a site, and later decide you don't need it. To delete it, reopen the Organize Favorites/Edit Bookmarks dialog box. Highlight the bookmark you wish to delete, and click **Delete**.

Now it's your turn. Put this book down, log on to the Internet, and go to some of your favorite sites. Bookmark the sites, adding them to your favorites/bookmarks list.

CHAPTER 13

CUSTOMIZING YOUR CONNECTION

The first automobiles off the assembly line were painted black. It wasn't long, however, before people began asking for automobiles in different colors. When Henry Ford was pressed to start painting his Model Ts a different color, his reply was, "They can have their car any color they want, as long as it's black."

People are different. How your family uses both the Internet and your browser will differ from how my family does. Both Microsoft and Netscape recognize this truth. With each new version of their browser, they have provided ever more customization options.

Changing the Look of Your Browser

You can hide toolbars, move them around, add and remove buttons or text, and resize the buttons. You can add and delete items on the links or personal toolbar.

Hiding Toolbars

- *Internet Explorer:* Place your mouse pointer over any open section of a toolbar. Right-click to open the pop-up menu. Remove the checkmark from beside the toolbar you want to hide by clicking on it. Repeat the process to reveal the hidden toolbar.

- *Netscape:* Click the vertical tab on the right end of the toolbar you wish to hide. Click the tab again to reveal the hidden toolbar.

Customizing Toolbar Buttons

- *Internet Explorer:* Right-click on the toolbar you wish to customize. Choose **Customize** from the pop-up menu. In the Customize Toolbar dialog box, select the buttons you want to add from the left column. Click **Add** to move the new button(s) to the toolbar. Highlight the new button in the Current Toolbar window and use the Move up/Move down buttons to position it where you want it on the toolbar (see figure 1).

  In the Customize Toolbar box, you can customize how your buttons appear. You can turn button labels on and off and choose large or small icons. Turning off text labels and using the smaller icons gives you more room to view Web pages in the browser window.

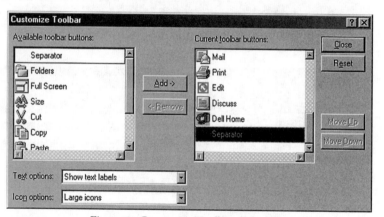

Figure 1. Customize Toolbar dialog box

- *Netscape:* Choose **Edit, Preferences** from the Menu bar. In the Preferences dialog box, choose **Appearance**. Select from among the "Show toolbars as" options.

Moving Toolbars

- *Internet Explorer:* You can move or resize the Address and Links toolbars. To move or resize the Links toolbar, click and hold down the left mouse button on the word Links. With the button depressed, slide the bar to the left, reducing the size of the Address bar and increasing the size of the Links bar. With the button still depressed, drag the bar above or below the Address bar. When you're satisfied with the position, release the mouse button. Follow the same procedure to move the Address bar.
- *Netscape:* Click and hold down the left mouse button on the toolbar tab (the vertical tab on the left end of the toolbar). Drag the toolbar to its new location (see figure 2).

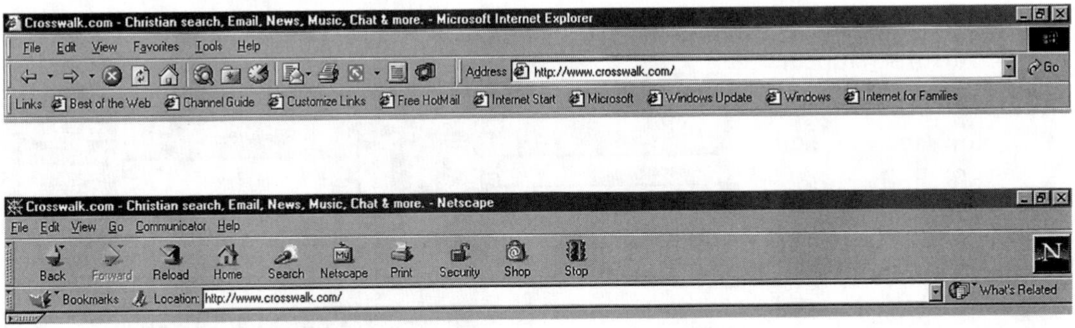

Figure 2. Customized examples of Internet Explorer and Netscape Toolbars

Customizing Links

Both Internet Explorer and Netscape provide a toolbar on which you can place links to your favorite Web pages. In Internet Explorer, the toolbar is called Links; in Netscape, it is the Personal Toolbar. Both toolbars come with a set of shortcuts. You don't have to keep all or any of these. You can add your own to the toolbar. If you have a small group of Web sites that you visit almost daily, this toolbar is the place to put them.

Adding Links to the Toolbar

Adding links to your toolbar works the same in both Internet Explorer and Netscape.

1. Go to the Web page you want to add.
2. Choose the Internet symbol next to the Web page's address in the Address bar. In Netscape, choose the Location symbol next to the Address bar.
3. Drag the symbol to its position on the toolbar. Release the mouse button.

Editing Links on the Toolbar

You edit links slightly differently in Netscape and Internet Explorer.

- *Internet Explorer:* To rename or delete a link, right-click on the link. Select the desired action from the pop-up menu.
- *Netscape:* Open **Edit Bookmarks** by choosing **Communicator, Bookmarks, Edit Bookmarks** from the Menu bar, or **Ctrl-b** from the keyboard. In the Edit Bookmarks dialog box, right-click on the link you want to edit in the Personal Toolbar list. Select the desired action from the pop-up menu.

If you're planning to use the Links bar, consider making it a full-length bar. You can shorten the address window, giving the extra space to the Links bar, or move either to a new location.

Changing Your Home Page

One of the first things you might want to do is change your home page. This is the page your browser opens to every time you log on to the Internet. When you first install Internet Explorer, your home page is the Microsoft Network (MSN). The default home page in Netscape is NetCentral. You can

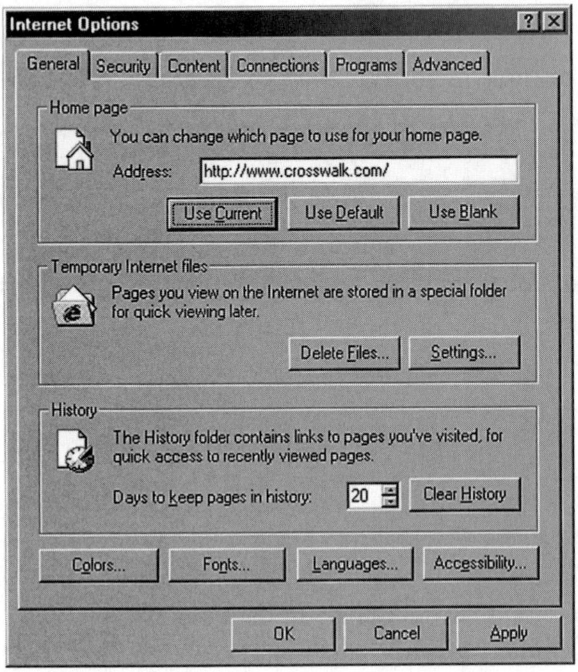

Figure 3. Selecting a new Home page

select any page you want as your browser's home page. It can be a search engine, a comic strip, news, weather, sports or financial site, a devotional site, a thought for the day, or your own Web site. It's up to you.

To change your home page, go to the Web page you want as your new home page. In Internet Explorer, choose **Tools, Internet Options**. In Netscape, choose **Edit, Preferences**. Find the Home page section of the dialog box. Click **Use Current** (see figure 3). The next time you start your browser or click the Home button on the toolbar, you will go to your new home page.

Speeding Up Your Connection

Many factors go into how fast pages load in your browser. The two major factors are the speed of your connection and bandwidth. *Bandwidth* is a technical term for how much traffic there is (the number of people) on the Internet at any time. Today the Internet is like a major highway. At times there are few cars on the road, and you can travel the speed limit. At rush hour, traffic slows to a crawl.

When there are few people on the Internet in your area, information moves quickly. When a lot of people are on at the same time, your connection speed can slow dramatically. High-speed connections (DSL and cable) aren't affected by bandwidth. If you have a standard 56K connection, the speed of connection will be a problem at times. You can do a couple of things to speed up your connection.

Turn off Multimedia Features

If you are looking for information and are not concerned with pictures, graphics, and sound, turn them off. Much of the time spent waiting for Web pages to load is in waiting for the graphics. Text loads quickly.

- *Internet Explorer:* To turn off graphics and multimedia, open the Internet Options box (see figure 4). You'll find that this is the place where you'll make most of the changes to how your browser looks and operates. Select the Advanced tab. Scroll down the list of options to **Multimedia**. Deselect the animations, sound, videos, and pictures options by clicking on them. Click **OK** to apply the changes. Before closing the window, notice the Restore Defaults button. Selecting this button turns on all the options you've turned off.

- *Netscape:* Netscape has a feature called Automatic Loading. When this is on, Netscape automatically loads images, java scripts, and other Web features. To disable this feature, open the Preferences dialog box (see figure 5). Click on **Advanced**. Unselect the "Automatically load images" option. Don't disable style sheets since many newer Web sites use this feature.

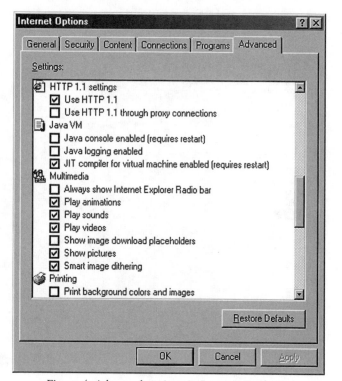

Figure 4. Advanced options in Internet Explorer

Choose the Time of Day

The second thing you can do to speed up your connection is to choose a different time of day to get on the Internet. I live in a small town that has only one local Internet Service Provider. As you can imagine, there are times during the day and evening when I don't try to log on. The first is from 3:00 to 4:00 P.M. Why? School is out and many of those children are arriving home and logging on to the Internet. The other time period is from after dinner to before 9:00 P.M. During this time, moms and dads are checking their E-mail upon arriving home from work, and the kids are doing their homework, playing games, or chatting online with friends. If speed is important, I avoid these times of day. But remember, every area is different. You'll need to match your Internet usage to your lifestyle and the best time of day for your situation.

Another option exists, if you want to pay for it and if it's available in your area. As mentioned in chapter 3, "Selecting Your Connection," the best way to speed up your connection is by using a cable modem or DSL.

As you surf the Internet, you'll discover a way of surfing that's just right for you. Some people never use the Links or Personal toolbar feature; others couldn't do without it. Some turn off the graphics and leave them off; others couldn't imagine surfing the Internet without all the images. That's what's nice about the newer browsers. They offer you the chance to customize them to the way you browse. So go ahead and experiment. Tweak the browser until it fits your style of surfing.

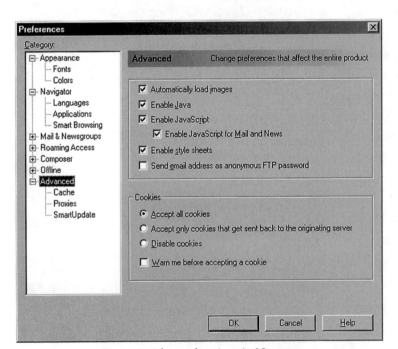

Figure 5. Advanced options in Netscape

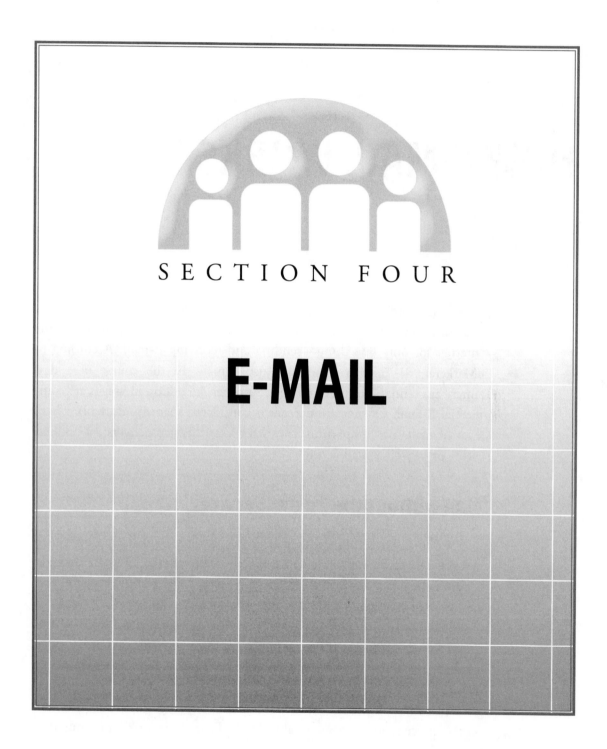

SECTION FOUR

E-MAIL

CHAPTER 14

HOW E-MAIL WORKS

E-mail is the number one activity on the Internet. Some people use the Internet for only one thing—sending and receiving E-mail. According to eMarketer, 81 million Americans use E-mail. In the course of a day, Americans send 2.1 billion messages. Another 7.3 billion messages are commercial E-mail. Of that, 96 percent is considered spam (junk mail). That's a lot of mail. By comparison, the U.S. Postal Service delivers 107 billion pieces of first-class mail a year.[1]

Mail without the Postal Service

Without stamps and envelopes, more messages are delivered by E-mail every two weeks than first-class mail is delivered by the U.S. Postal Service in a year. So how is it possible? How does a message you type on your computer end up on your friend's computer fifteen hundred miles away?

Think of the Internet as a global network of post offices. Typically, your ISP serves as your post office. If you have a free E-mail account through someone like Hotmail or Mail.com, then the Web site acts as your post office.

When I send a letter from my hometown of Clewiston, Florida, the postal service sends it to West Palm Beach. There, it is sorted and routed to its next stop. Depending on its destination, it may travel through several regional distribution centers before it reaches the local post office of the person I've written.

When you send an E-mail message to your friend, the message goes to an electronic version of those big blue steel boxes standing outside the post office. On the Internet they are often called mailhosts, or SMTP servers. SMTP stands for Simple Mail Transfer Protocol. From there your mail is "picked up" and sent to a router. This router reads the "post office" part of the E-mail address and sends it on to your friend's Internet Service Provider.

Once it reaches your friend's "post office," the POP server (Post Office Protocol) sorts it to the right "electronic P.O. box." The P.O. box in this case is your friend's UserID. Unlike regular mail, E-mail isn't delivered "door-to-door." There are only P.O. boxes. Your friend will have to "go to the post office" (by checking his or her E-mail) to receive your message.

How long does this take? Most of the time, just a few seconds.

There are thousands of post offices, with hundreds of P.O. boxes in each post office. For mail to reach the right person, you must use the right name, box number, city, state, and zip. For mail to reach the right person on the Internet, you need the electronic equivalent of their name and address. That is their E-mail address.

Understanding an E-mail Address

An E-mail address has two parts, separated by @ (the "at" symbol). The first part of the address is your user name (see figure 1). If you receive your E-mail through your ISP, then your user name is the same as your UserID. Your user name will be different from your UserID if you have multiple E-mail addresses or use a free E-mail service. The second part of the address is the domain name of your ISP or Web site where you receive your mail. The domain name tells your computer and Internet routers the location of your mailbox on the Web.

ken@internetforfamilies.org

User Name	Separator	Domain Name
ken	@	internetforfamilies.org

Figure 1. Parts of an E-mail address

Understanding Your E-mail Program

Today all browsers have their own E-mail programs. Internet Explorer includes Outlook Express, and Netscape includes Netscape Messenger. America Online has its own E-mail program as well. There are other E-mail programs you can purchase separately. For most people, they're not necessary. Both Outlook Express and Netscape Messenger do a good job of handling mail and keeping track of E-mail addresses.

To open Outlook Express, double-click on the icon on your desktop. You open Netscape Messenger by choosing **Start, Programs, Netscape Communicator** from the taskbar. You can also open your E-mail program from within your browser. If you have Windows 98, you can open your E-mail program from the Quick Launch toolbar next to the Start button on the taskbar.

Figure 2, Anatomy of an E-mail program, identifies the different parts of an E-mail program. You'll notice it is similar in layout to your browser. It's designed to look, feel, and work like its corresponding browser program. Though some of the buttons and menu items are different, the layout is the same.

The Title bar tells you the name of the program. To enlarge it to full screen or reduce it, double-click the bar or click the Resize button just to the left of the Close [X] button.

The Menu bar lists E-mail functions in easy-to-access, pull-down menus. In Outlook Express, these functions are listed under the headings File, Edit, View, Tools, Message, and Help. Netscape's headings are File, Edit, View, Go, Message, Communicator, and Help.

The toolbar contains the most frequently used E-mail commands. All programs share the following: New Message (or New Mail), Reply, Reply to all, Forward, Print, Delete. Other buttons vary by program and by function. The images and captions clearly indicate the function of each button. We will learn how to use these buttons in the following chapters.

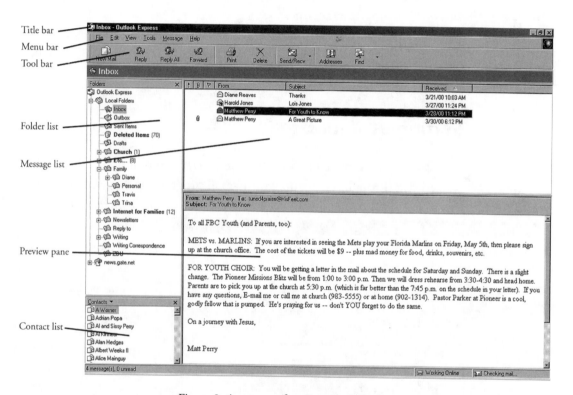

Figure 2. Anatomy of an E-mail program

As you look at the example in figure 2, you'll notice the E-mail program window is divided into several sections. Beginning in the top left and moving clockwise, the sections are Folders, Message List, Preview, and, in Outlook Express, Contacts.

Today's E-mail programs allow you to organize your mail into folders. The Folders pane displays a list of these folders.

The Message List box displays a list of messages contained in the current folder. By default, your E-mail program opens to the Inbox. From this view, you can select or sort your messages. Messages can be sorted in a list here by sender, subject, date, priority, and flagged.

The Preview pane allows you to read the first few lines of a message without opening the message.

In Outlook Express, the Contact list provides an easy place to view those in your Address Book. Double-clicking on a name opens a New Message, addressed and ready for you to type your message.

Setting Up Your E-mail

When you signed up for Internet service, tech support should have walked you through setting up your E-mail program. If they didn't and your E-mail is not working, I suggest you start by calling your ISP's tech support. That is part of the service they provide.

Both browser programs come with a set-up program, often called a Connection Wizard. This program helps you set up your E-mail (see figure 3). When you run this program, it will ask for

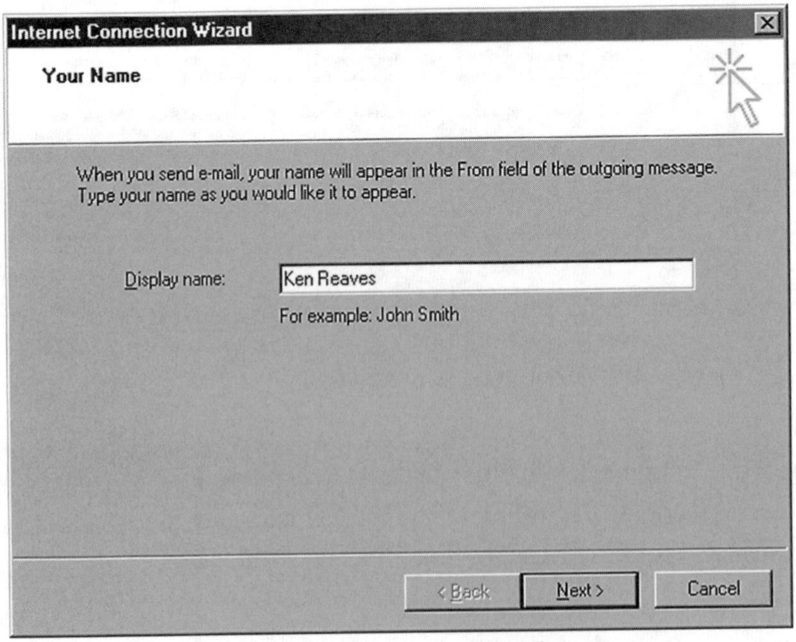

Figure 3. Connection Wizard

four pieces of information: your UserID, password, E-mail address, and E-mail server names. You'll need the names of both your ISP's outgoing and incoming mail servers. The incoming mail server is called a POP server. Its name usually looks something like this: pop.yourisp.com. The outgoing mail server, called an SMTP, typically looks like this: mailhost.yourisp.com. Your Internet Service Provider will provide you with this information. Once you have this information, run the Connection Wizard and fill in the blanks.

With Outlook Express, you can run this program anytime. You will need to run it again if you change ISPs or add E-mail accounts. To change or add settings in Netscape, you'll need to access the Preferences under Edit on the Menu bar.

Testing Your E-mail

Once you've set-up your E-mail, it's time to test it to see if it's working. The easiest way to do this is to send a message to yourself.

1. In the main window, click **New Mail**. This opens a blank mail message.
2. Enter your E-mail address in the To: field.
3. Tab down to the subject box and type: Test Message.
4. Tab again, and type anything you'd like in the message box.
5. When finished, click **Send**.

Depending on how your E-mail program is configured, it may send your message right away or store it in the Outbox. If it's in the Outbox, the folder will be bolded with the number (1) beside it. The number shows how many messages are ready to send. If your message goes to the Outbox, click the Send/Receive button. If offline, your computer will connect to the Internet, send all messages in the Outbox, and check for new messages. If your E-mail program checks messages before sending new ones, you will have to click **Send/Receive** again to check for new messages. If your E-mail is working properly, your test message will appear in your Inbox.

What if it doesn't? Look to see if your message has left your Outbox. If the message was sent but you didn't receive it, wait a few minutes and try again. Typically, messages sent to yourself return instantly. Sometimes heavy usage slows the mail servers.

If after waiting a few minutes and trying again you still do not receive your message, make sure you addressed it correctly. Click on the Sent folder. A copy of your message should be there. Look in the To: field to see if your address is correct. Are both parts of the address there—your UserID and your ISP's domain name separated by the @ symbol? If you're confused about your E-mail address, read "Understanding an E-mail Address" earlier in this chapter. If the address is correct and the message has left your Outbox, then the most likely culprit is the name of your incoming (POP) mail server.

What if the message didn't leave your Outbox? Check to make sure you're connected to the Internet. If you are, try sending it again. If the test message still refuses to leave your Outbox, then more than likely the name of your outgoing (SMTP) mail server is wrong.

In both cases, you will need to check the mail server names you entered when setting up your E-mail program. In Netscape Messenger, choose **Edit, Preferences, Mail & Newsgroups, Mail Servers** from the Menu bar. In Outlook Express, choose **Tools, Accounts**. Select the Mail tab and double-click on your E-mail account and then the Server tab.

For both programs, make sure you have entered the server names correctly, with dots (periods) in the right places. Once you've made any corrections, try again. If your message still fails, try composing a new test message, indicating this as "test message 2." If it still doesn't work properly, call your ISP's tech support.

I've provided another way for you to test your E-mail. On my Web site, Internet for Families, I've set up an autoresponder. Send a test message to the following address: test@internetforfamilies.org. When your E-mail reaches this site, it will send you an automated reply. The message looks like this:

You've reached the E-mail test site for Internet for Families. This test shows that your E-mail is working properly.

If you haven't visited the Internet for Families Web site yet, let me encourage you to do so. You'll find it at the following address: www.internetforfamilies.org.

If you aren't receiving the free monthly newsletter, called *Internet for Families Ezine,* you can subscribe to it by sending an E-mail message to: subscribe@internetforfamilies.org. Put the word "subscribe" in the subject box. This newsletter arrives in your E-mail box every month. It is filled with helpful information, Web sites, and tips.

If you have any comments or questions, you can reach me at comments@internetforfamilies.org.

Go ahead, try it. And next time you're on the Internet, stop by and check out the Internet for Families Web site.

CHAPTER 15

SENDING AND RECEIVING E-MAIL

Now that you've set up your E-mail program, you're ready to let all your friends know you're online. Gather all those E-mail addresses people have given you. We're going to learn how to send, receive, reply to, and forward E-mail to all your friends.

Composing E-mail

Composing an E-mail message is as simple as counting to five.

1. *Open a new message by clicking on the appropriate toolbar button.* Your E-mail address is automatically added in the From: field. You won't see your return address in Netscape Messenger until the message goes to the Unsent Messages folder. If you have more than one E-mail address, in Outlook Express you can select the one you want to use by clicking on the drop-down arrow.

2. *Enter the address of the person to whom you are sending the message in the To: field.* If the person you're sending the message to is in your Address Book, the auto-complete feature will attempt to select the right person as you type his or her name. Once that person's name appears, tab to the

next field. If the person is not in your Address Book, complete their address here.

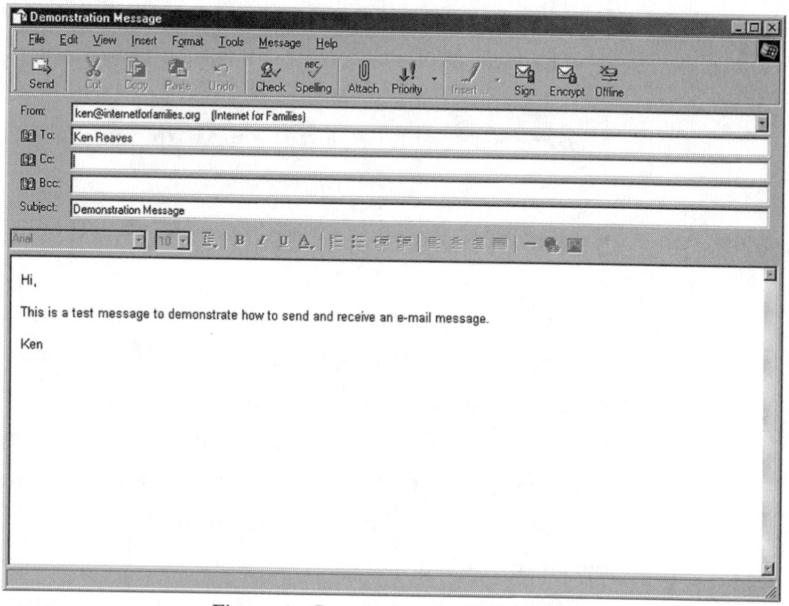

If you want to send your message to more than one person, type a semi-colon (;) or a comma (,), depending on your system, and a space after each address.

Do the same in the Cc: (carbon copy) and the Bcc:

Figure 1. Composing a new message

(blind carbon copy) fields. (If the Bcc: field isn't visible in Internet Explorer, choose **View, All Headers** in the New Message window.) Addresses entered in the To: and Cc: fields will be seen by everyone who receives your message. Addresses entered in Bcc: fields are hidden from all who receive the message. When sending messages to a group of people, use the Bcc: field as a courtesy and to protect the privacy of others.

3. *Add a subject.* Add a two-to-four-word description of your message in the subject field. This helps those who receive your message know what it's about. Later, it also helps them find your message quickly from all they've received.

4. *Type your message.* Type your message just as you would in any word processing program. In the next chapter you'll learn how to jazz up your message using stationery, colors, and different fonts. (See figure 1 for a sample E-mail message.)

5.   *When finished, click* **Send**. That's all there is to it. You've just sent your first E-mail. Well, not quite. If you're working offline, your E-mail went to your Outbox (Outlook Express) or your Unsent Messages folder (Netscape Messenger). It will be sent the next time you check your mail.

Sending and Receiving E-mail

When you're ready to send your messages and check for new ones, click the appropriate button on the toolbar. If you're not online, your E-mail program will connect to the Internet, send any unsent messages, and check for new messages. New messages are stored in your Inbox. If your Inbox is not open, you can see how many new messages you have in the Folder panel. The Inbox will be bolded. The number beside the Inbox indicates the number of unread messages.

You can set your E-mail program to send E-mail immediately or to send it only when you check for new mail. There are advantages and disadvantages to both. Sending mail immediately means composing your E-mail messages while connected to the Internet. When you click **Send**, the message is sent immediately. If you're not connected to the Internet, then the first time you click **Send** your E-mail program will dial up the Internet and send the message. Sending messages immediately means you don't mind tying up your phone line while you compose each message.

I recommend composing messages offline. This leaves your phone line free for calls. You can write messages at your leisure. You can stop to throw a load of clothes in the washer or play catch with your son. When finished writing, click the button to send all your unsent messages at one time. If you have unsent messages when you close your E-mail program, it will ask if you want to send messages now. Click **Yes**, and your program will connect to the Internet, send your messages, disconnect, and close; click **No**, and your messages will remain in the Outbox until you check for new messages.

To change Outlook Express settings, choose **Tools, Options** from the Menu bar. Click the Send tab. To compose offline, remove the check from the box next to the "Send messages immediately" line. If you want to send messages immediately, make sure this box is checked. If you are using Internet Explorer 5, you'll want to make sure the box next to the line "Send and receive messages at startup" on the General tab is not checked (see figure 2). If this box is checked, every time you open your E-mail it will attempt to connect to the Internet and check your mail.

You change these settings in Netscape Messenger by selecting **Edit, Preferences, Offline**. Choose **Ask Me** in the Startup State box and **Do not send my unsent messages** from the When Going Online box (see figure 3).

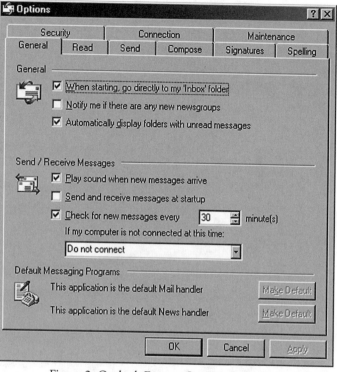

Figure 2. Outlook Express Options dialog box

Reading Your E-mail

Once you've downloaded your mail, it's time to read it. Don't make the mistake of trying to read your messages in the Preview pane. This window, located on the bottom right side of your E-mail program, allows you to read the first few lines of each message. You can read the entire message in this window, but if the message is long, this is not an easy thing to do. Also, you can't open attachments from the Preview pane.

Unread messages appear in bold in the Message List pane. To open a message, double click on it. This opens the E-mail in a new window (see figure 4). Opening a message makes it easier to read. From the Message window you can reply, forward, print, delete, open attachments, and move back and forth among your messages.

To print a message, click **Print** on the toolbar. If you don't want to keep the message, use the Delete button. This moves your message to the Delete, or Trash, folder. This folder works like the Recycle Bin on your desktop. It saves deleted messages until you empty it. If you delete the wrong message, you can drag it back to your Inbox. When you finish reading your messages, close the Message window.

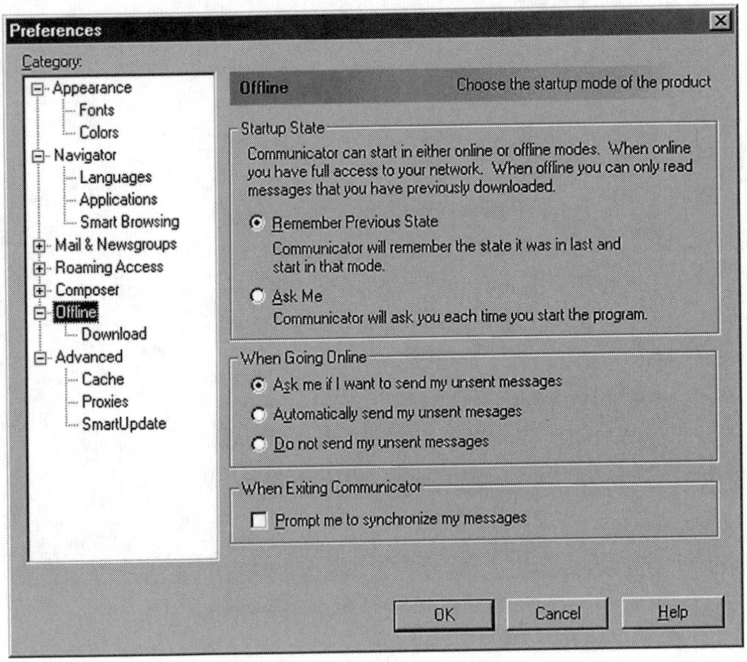

Figure 3. Netscape Messenger preferences box

Replying to E-mail

Sometimes you will want to reply to a message someone sent you. There are two ways to reply. Highlight the message in the Message List window and click **Reply** on the toolbar. Or, with the message open, click **Reply** from the Message window toolbar. Both open a Reply Message window (see figure 5). Notice that the message is already addressed and the cursor is positioned for you to begin typing your reply. You'll also notice the original message appears in the window below your reply. This is helpful because the person receiving your reply doesn't have to remember what they originally wrote. Type your reply and click **Send**.

Notice there are two different Reply buttons. The Reply button sends a message back to the person who sent you the original message. The Reply to All button sends a copy of your message to everyone who received the original message.

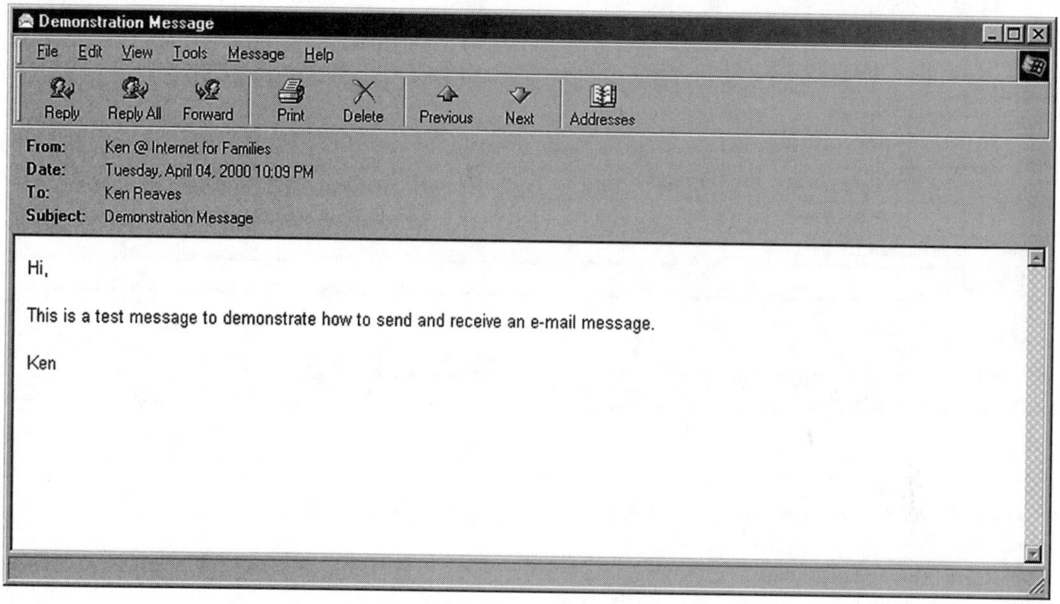

Figure 4. Received Message window

Forwarding E-mail

Forwarding a message sends a copy to others not on the original list. When you click **Forward**, a new message window opens just as it does when replying. The only difference is that the To: field is blank. Enter the address(es) of those to whom you want to forward the message. Add a note to the message if desired, and click **Send**.

Please set your browser to forward E-mail in the body of your message, not as an attachment. An E-mail message that's been forwarded numerous times as an attachment means having to open numerous message windows to the original message. If you receive an E-mail with multiple attachments, do your friends a favor: don't compound the error. Block the part of the message you want to forward by holding down the left mouse button while dragging it across the text. With the text highlighted, Click **Edit, Copy** from the Menu bar. Open a new message and paste the copied text into the New Message box.

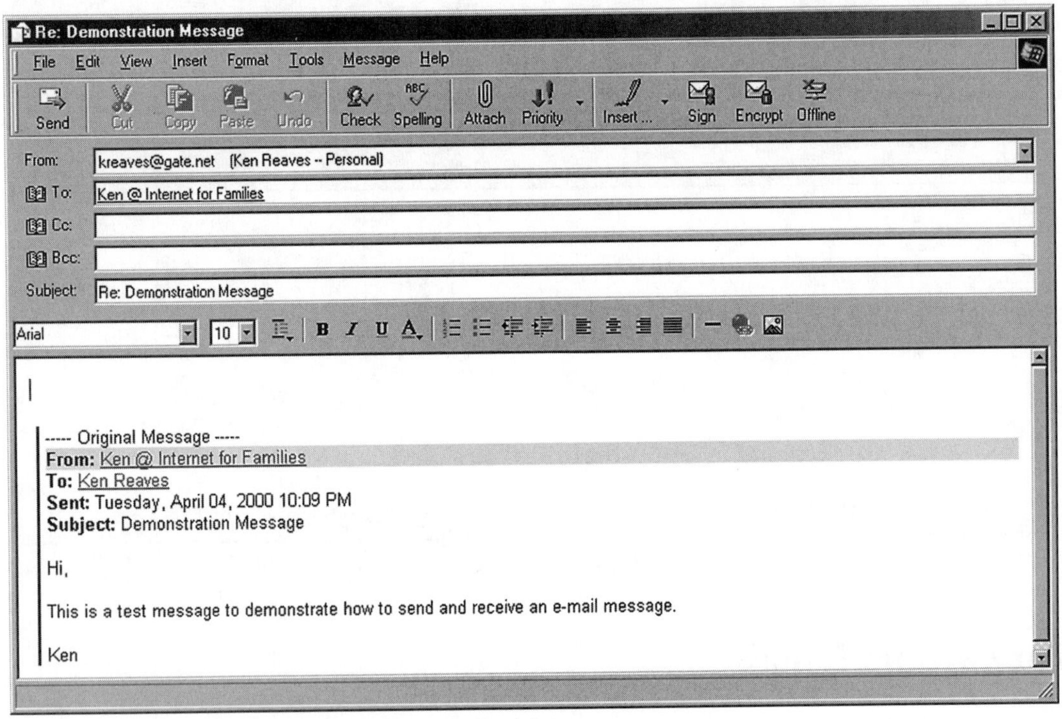

Figure 5. Replying to a message

Quick Reference: E-mail Toolbar

Button	Function	Outlook Express	Netscape Messenger
New Mail	Opens a New Message window	Yes	Yes, called "New Msg"
Reply	Opens a Reply Message window addressed to the original sender	Yes	Yes
Reply all	Opens a Reply Message window addressed to all who received the original message	Yes	Yes
Forward	Opens a New Message window with original message included so it can be forwarded to a new recipient	Yes	Yes
Print	Prints current E-mail message	Yes	Yes
Delete	Deletes current message or group of messages	Yes	Yes
Send/Receive	Sends all messages stored in Outbox and retrieves any new messages	Yes	Yes, called "Get Msg"
Address	Opens the Address Book	Yes	Click **Communicator, Address Book**
Find	Searches for a specific message	Yes	Click **Edit, Find,** or **Ctrl-F**
File	Files message in folder you select	No, must drag message from List window to the folder in the Folder window	Yes
Next	Moves to the next unread message	No, up and down arrows found in Read Message window move you between messages	Yes

CUSTOMIZING YOUR E-MAIL

There's more to E-mail than sending and receiving messages. Today's E-mail programs let you express your personality. You can jazz up your messages with symbols, colors, fonts, stationery, and signatures. If you have a scanner, you can scan and send your preschooler's latest masterpiece, a family photo, or a newspaper article describing the game-saving tackle your son made last Friday night to anyone in your family. If you have a digital camera, you can send photos to grandparents every week (if it's OK with them). Get your creative juices flowing, and let's get started.

Netiquette

Before we get to the fun stuff, let's talk about a few do's and don'ts of E-mail.

- Don't SHOUT. TYPING IN ALL CAPITAL LETTERS IS CON-SIDERED SHOUTING. It's hard to read and is considered rude. If you need to emphasize a message, use quotes, exclamation points, or italics.
- Don't flame. If someone upsets you, don't respond with an angry E-mail. All you accomplish is offending someone, and you might start

a flame war. A flame war is where people attack one another other with angry, hostile E-mail messages. Remember, there is a person on the other end of that E-mail. You probably know very little about what's going on in their life. You might have misunderstood something they wrote. Give them the benefit of the doubt. And take Jesus' counsel: "Turn the other cheek."

- Don't betray a confidence. Assume that all E-mails are private conversations, unless otherwise noted.

- Don't automatically choose Reply to All. Everyone may not want to know what you think. Reply only to those who need your message.

- Don't forward every cute saying, story, or site to everyone in your Address Book. Do ask if they would like to receive them.

- Don't send an attachment unless the receiver wants and is expecting it.

- Don't automatically forward virus alerts or chain letters. Take five minutes to check them for truth and accuracy. Your friends will appreciate your not wasting their time.

- Do be brief. Whenever possible, keep your messages short and to the point.

- Do use short, easy-to-read paragraphs. It's very difficult to read long run-on paragraphs.

- Do proof and spell-check messages before sending them.

- Do use the blind carbon copy (Bcc) field. If you E-mail a group of people, keep their E-mail addresses private by using the Bcc field.

- Do use the right format. Today's E-mail programs use HTML by default. This format allows you to send messages with color, fonts, stationery, and more. Some people have older browsers and E-mail programs that cannot handle HTML. If you send them an HTML-formatted message, they'll see lots of meaningless characters. The message will be difficult or impossible to read. Send their messages using plain text.

Follow these simple rules, and everyone in your Address Book will appreciate you. You'll save yourself and them needless headaches and lots of time.

Jazzing Up Your Messages

Now, let's turn our attention to the fun stuff. E-mail can be rather dull. The printed word lacks emotion and personality in the visual format of computers. Fortunately, E-mail program manufacturers and creative individuals have developed some unique ways for us to express our individuality with E-mail.

Communicating Emotion

It's hard to communicate emotions with plain text. Words alone can be misunderstood. Something said "tongue-in-cheek" could be read as a sarcastic remark. Creative folks have created acronyms and emoticons to help us communicate our feelings. Acronyms are words formed from the first letter of each of the words in a phrase. The term *emoticon* is a combination of the words *emotion* and *icon*. Using letters and symbols on the keyboard, people have created a whole series of "faces" that communicate emotion. Tables 1 and 2 give lists of common acronyms, emoticons, and their meanings.

Table 1
Common Acronyms

BTW	By the way
EOL	End of lecture
FYI	For your information
IMHO	In my humble opinion
IMO	In my opinion
IOW	In other words
LOL	Laughing out loud
OTOH	On the other hand
ROTFL	Rolling on the floor laughing
TTFN	Ta ta, for now
TYVM	Thank you very much

Table 2	
Common Emoticons	
:-)	Smiling
8o)	Person with glasses smiling
;-)	Wink
:-(	Sad, frown
:'-(	Crying
:-O	Surprised, uh-oh
:-&	Tongue-tied
:-D	Big smile
<;-|	Dunce, dumb
:-@	Shouting

Typing with a Crayon

Well, not quite. You can't write your E-mail messages with a crayon, but you can "color" your E-mail messages. To create a jazzed-up message, open a new message. The default setting for E-mail is HTML. If for some reason it's set to plain text, you can make HTML your default by changing it in the Options or Preferences dialog box. Figure 1 identifies the common format buttons in your E-mail program.

There are two ways to apply formatting to your text. You can format it as you go. Or, you can enter your text, then highlight portions of the text and format it. Figure 2 is an example of what you can do with the

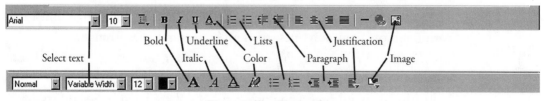

Figure 1. Text Format bars

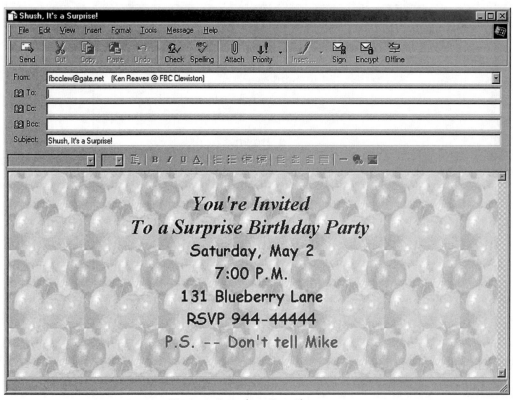

Figure 2. Jazzed-up E-mail message

formatting options. You'll find step-by-step instructions for creating an E-mail invitation in chapter 35, "Fun Family Activities."

Text Formatting: You can choose different fonts, colors, sizes, and emphases (italic, bold, underline) to communicate your message. When selecting fonts, realize that not everyone will have the same fonts on their computer as you do. If you select a font your friend doesn't have, his or her E-mail program will try to match it with one that is close. This can create some interesting lettering on the other end. When you change fonts, stay with the more common ones, such as Arial and Times Roman.

Paragraph Formatting: You can format your text using numbered lists, bulleted lists, indents, and justification. Paragraph formatting functions as it does in any word processing program. Numbered and bulleted lists create easy-to-read outlines. The Increase and Decrease Indent buttons shift the left margin of your paragraph.

Graphic Formatting: You can insert a horizontal line to divide segments of text, add a link to a Web page, or insert a photo or graphic image. You can add a background image to your E-mail. In Outlook Express, it's called Stationery. To access it, click **Format, Apply Stationery**. You find it in Netscape Messenger by choosing **Format, Page Colors and Properties**. With either program, you can also use your own images.

Signatures: Signing Your Messages

You can't actually sign them, but you can add a closing block of text to any or all of your E-mail messages. This text is called a *signature*. Your signature can include your name, address, phone number, a quote, or any other information you'd like.

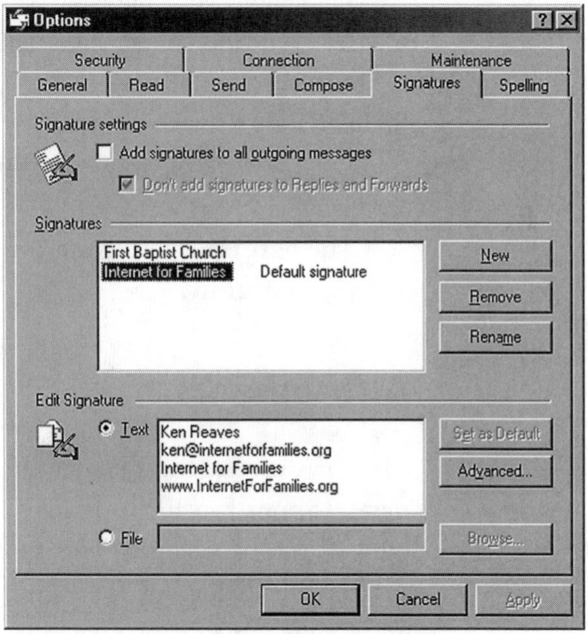

To create a signature in Outlook Express:

1. Open the Options dialog box **(Tools, Options)**.
2. Choose the Signatures tab (see figure 3).
3. Click **New** to add a signature.
4. Enter your text in the Edit Signature box.
5. When finished, click **OK** or **Apply**.

Figure 3. Creating a signature

If you have more than one signature, give each a descriptive name. Choose one as your default. If you want your signature added to all your messages, choose **Add signatures to all outgoing messages** at the top of the Signature tab. If you send a lot of messages to the same people, you might not want your signature on every message. Instead, add your signature manually by clicking the Signature button on the New Message toolbar.

To create a signature in Netscape Messenger:

1. Open Notepad by choosing **Start** from the Windows taskbar, then **Programs, Accessories, Notepad** (in Netscape, you have to create your signature using Notepad).
2. Type the information you want in your signature.
3. Choose **File, Save**, then name your file and save it to your hard drive. By default, your file is saved in the My Documents folder.
4. In Netscape, open the Preferences dialog box, and choose **Mail & Newsgroups, Identity**.
5. Click the Choose button.
6. Double-click on your signature file. Click **OK**.

The next time you create a new message, Messenger will automatically add your signature.

Attachments

You can send text files, pictures, graphics, and small programs as attachments to your E-mail. To attach a file to an E-mail, click on the Attachment button (the paperclip). Find the file on your hard drive using the Insert Attachment dialog box (see figure 4). When you find the file, double-click on it. The name of the attachment appears in the Attachment box. Finish your message. When ready, click **Send**.

To open an attachment sent to you, double-click on it. The Open Attachment Warning box will appear (see figure 5). You will be asked to choose between opening the file or saving it to disk (hard drive). If you save it to disk, the default location will be the Windows desktop. You should always save Microsoft Word files and programs to disk. Then scan them with your antivirus program before opening. You don't need to scan plain text attachments or graphic images. Always err on the side of caution. If you're unsure of the source of the attachment, save it to disk and scan it before opening.

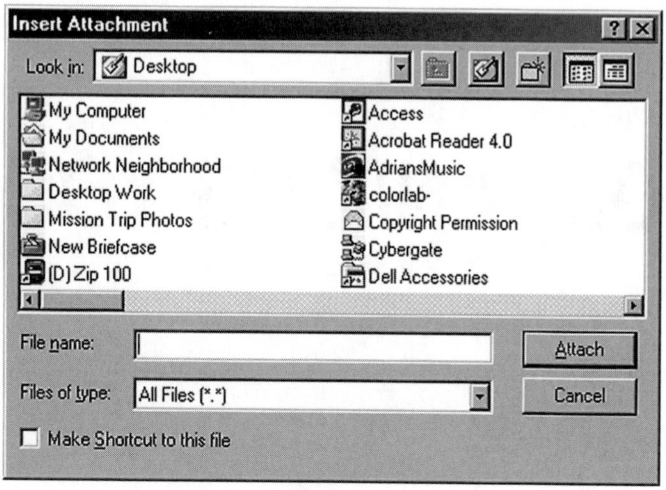

When sending an attachment, be sure the person you are sending it to is expecting it. This is especially important if it is a large attachment. A large attachment can take some time to download, so arrange with them when to send it.

Figure 4. Adding an attachment

Also, limit the size of your attachments. As a rule of thumb, the largest file you should send is 500KB (kilobytes). Even then, smaller is better. If possible, break very large attachments into two or more E-mails sent over a period of time.

Now it's your turn. Let your creative juices flow. Jazz up your E-mail. Then send it to yourself or a friend. You can do it!

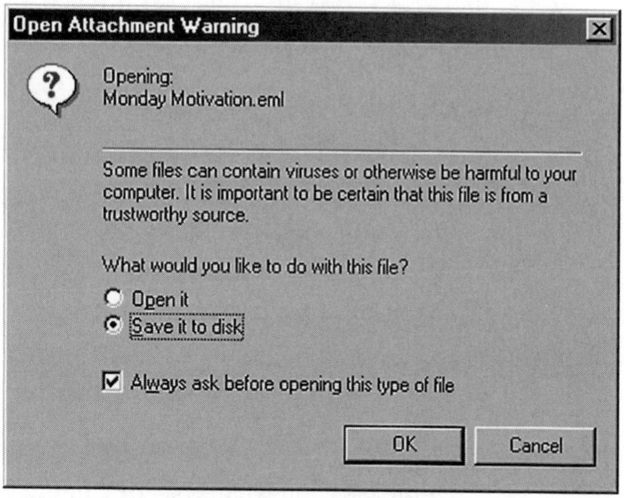

Figure 5. Open Attachment Warning box

CHAPTER 17

ORGANIZING YOUR E-MAIL

At first, a scrap of paper and your Inbox will do for organizing E-mail addresses and messages. After subscribing to a few newsletters, a newsgroup, receiving E-mail from numerous friends, and getting a daily supply of junk mail, that piece of paper and your Inbox will no longer be enough. You'll need to get a handle on all that mail. Your E-mail program provides tools for helping you organize it.

Using Your Address Book

Your Address Book provides a quick and easy way to save E-mail addresses. It even helps cut down on typing mistakes that would prevent your messages from being delivered.

Opening Your Address Book

Open your Address Book by clicking the appropriate button on the toolbar or the Menu bar (see figure 1). (It's found under **Communicator** in Netscape, and **Tools** in Outlook Express.) Your Address Book has both a Menu and Button bar. Below the Button bar is a Search box. Type a name here to find it quickly. Below the Search box are two panes. The left pane displays a list of groups and files where addresses are organized. The right pane displays a list of those in your Address Book. Double-click on a name in the right panel. The dialog box displays all the information you've stored about that person.

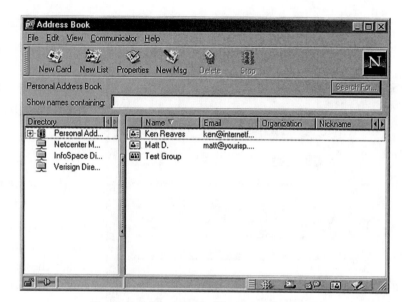

Figure 1. Address Book (Netscape Messenger)

Entering Names into Your Address Book

To enter a name manually into your Address Book, choose **New Card** from the Button bar. In the Contact box, sometimes called Properties box, enter the person's name and E-mail address (see figure 2).

Use the additional fields and tabs to enter other information about the person. There are places for work and home addresses, phone numbers, and Web page addresses. There's even a place to add additional information that doesn't fit the supplied fields.

You can quickly add someone to your Address Book in two ways. In the Message List pane of your E-mail program, right-click on the message from the person you wish to add. In the pop-up menu, choose **Add Sender to Address Book**.

A second way to quickly add someone to your Address Book is from the Message window. After reading a message and before closing the Message window, double-click on the name in the From: field. Add any additional information. When finished, click **OK** to add. Using one of these two methods eliminates address mistakes.

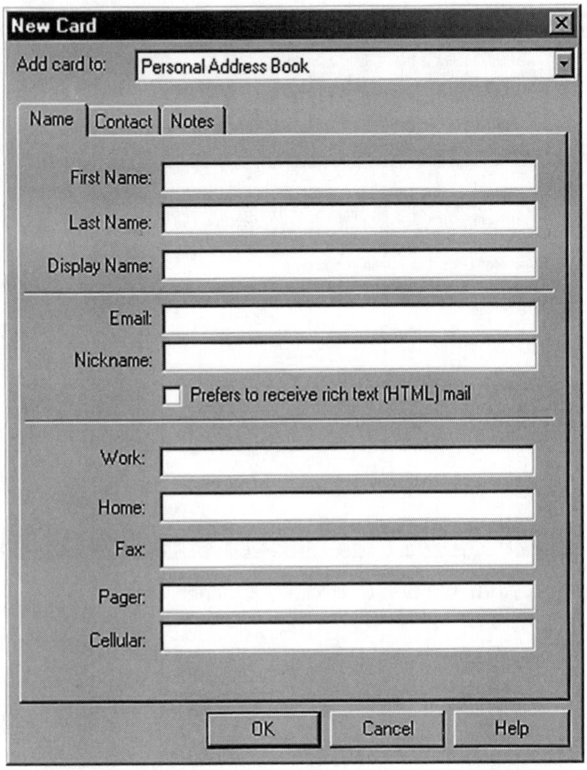

Figure 2. Entering Addresses (Netscape Messenger)

Organizing Your Address Book

Sorting Names in Your Address Book

You can quickly sort the names listed in your Address Book by clicking on the Name or E-mail title bar above the contact list. Clicking the Name bar sorts your contacts by first or last name and in ascending or descending order. Click the bar until they display in the order you prefer. (Tip: When searching for a contact using the search box, be sure to type the name the way it is displayed in the list.) Clicking the E-mail Address bar sorts your contacts by E-mail address in ascending and descending order. For other sorting options, choose **View, Sort By** on the Menu bar.

Creating Groups or Mailing Lists

Now that you have people in your Address Book, you can organize them into groups (Netscape calls them lists). For example, you can create separate groups for Sunday school class members, coworkers, family members, or those with the same hobby interest. You can add people to more than one group. A Sunday school class member could also be a member of a project group at work. Once you've created a group, you can send E-mail to everyone in the group by entering the name of the group in the Address field.

To create a group, open the Address Book. Choose **New Group** from the File menu or click the appropriate toolbar button. In the dialog box, give your group a name (see figure 3). Now you're ready to add names to your group. In Netscape, begin typing the names. The autocomplete feature will try to complete the name for you. If it's a new person, type in their name and E-mail address. They will be added to your Address Book.

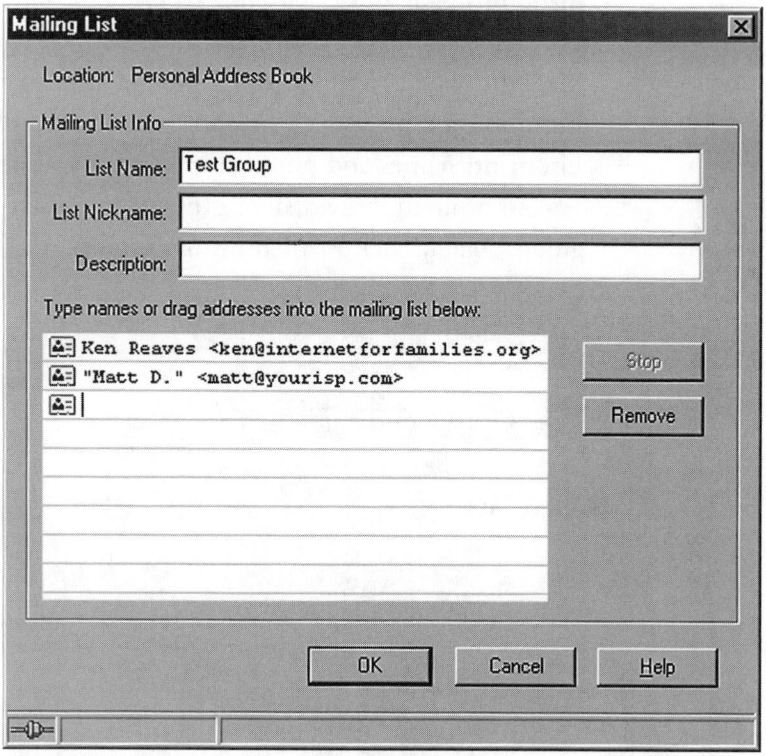

You can add names to a group in Outlook Express in one of three ways: (1) Enter the person's name and E-mail address in the fields provided for that purpose. Persons added in this manner appear only in the group list and not in the master list of addresses. (2) Click **Select Members** to add people already in your Address Book. (3) Click **New Contact** to add a new person to the group and to your Address Book.

Figure 3. Creating a new group (Netscape Messenger)

To remove a name from a group, open the group by double-clicking on it. Highlight the name on your group list. Click **Remove**.

When finished, the new group appears in the left pane of your Address Book. If it doesn't appear, click on the small plus sign (+) next to your personal identity. If you have more than one group, they will all appear in alphabetical order.

Printing Your Address Book

Outlook Express makes it easy for you to print all or part of the information in your Address Book. To print the entire Address Book, click the Print button. In the Print dialog box, set the Print range to **All**. Next, select the Print Style. Memo prints all the information in a person's record. Business Card prints only business information plus phone numbers. Phone List prints names and phone numbers only. When ready, click **OK**.

To print an individual or group record, first highlight the individual or group. Again, click **Print** from the toolbar. In the Print dialog box, make sure the Print range is set to **Selection** (see figure 4). Next, choose the Print Style. Click **OK**.

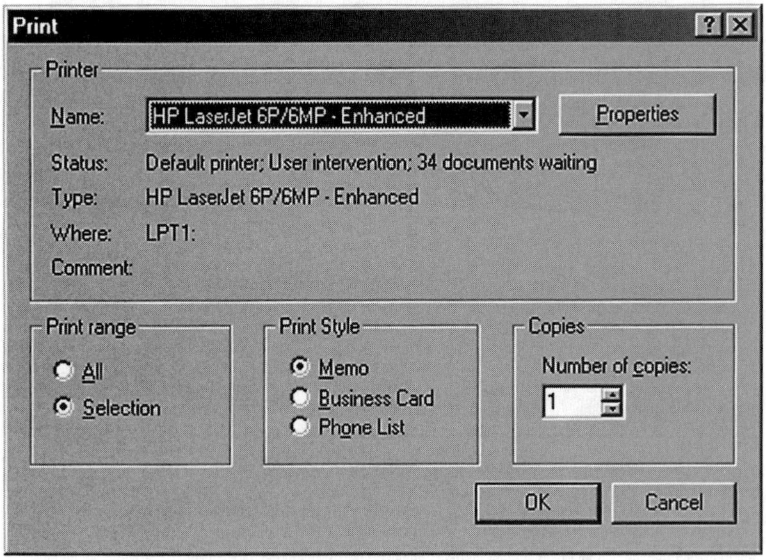

Unfortunately, there isn't an easy way to print your Address Book in Netscape. You must first create a file using the Export command. On the Menu bar, select **File**, then **Export**. In the dialog box, name the file "myaddresses." Select tab-delimited format.

Figure 4. Printing your Address Book

From the **Save as type**: pull-down menu, open and print the file, which is usually saved in the My Documents folder on your hard drive, using any word processor program. You might have to "clean up" the file by adjusting your tab settings before printing.

Filing and Sorting E-mail

It won't be long before your Inbox is crammed full of messages. If after reading a message you don't need to save it, then delete it. Still, there will be an ever-growing list of messages in your Inbox. What do you do with them? You file and sort them into folders.

Creating Folders

Folders allow you to organize your messages for easy retrieval. Messages from your Sunday school class, coworkers, or a hobby group can be sorted into different folders. Each member of your family can have his or her own folder(s).

To create a new folder, do the following:

1. Select **New, Folder** from the File menu or right-click the Local Folders icon in the Folder pane. If you are creating a subfolder, right-click on the folder where the new one is to be located.
2. Give your new folder a name in the dialog box (see figure 5).
3. Before closing the dialog box, make sure the folder is located in the proper place.
4. Click **OK**.
5. Repeat this process every time you need to create a folder.

Moving Messages

Once you've created the folders in which to store your messages, you can move your messages by dragging and dropping them. To drag and drop a message, highlight the message by left-clicking on it in the

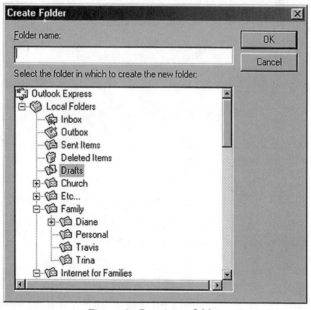

Figure 5. Creating a folder

message box. Hold down the left mouse button on the message and drag it to the desired folder. When the folder is highlighted, release the mouse bottom and the message is moved.

You can also move messages by right-clicking on them and selecting **Move** or **Copy** from the pop-up menu. To move more than one message at a time, hold down the **Ctrl** key while selecting the messages with your left mouse button. Then move them as you would a single message.

Sorting Automatically

Dragging and dropping messages into folders is fine if you receive only a few messages a day. If you receive a lot of messages, dragging and dropping isn't practical. There is an easier way. You can create filters to automatically sort messages into folders. Then whenever you check your E-mail, your E-mail program automatically sorts your messages according to the filters you've created. If there isn't

New Mail Rule   **? X**

Select your Conditions and Actions first, then specify the values in the Description.

1. Select the Conditions for your rule:

☑ Where the From line contains people
☐ Where the Subject line contains specific words
☐ Where the message body contains specific words
☐ Where the To line contains people

2. Select the Actions for your rule:

☐ Move it to the specified folder
☐ Copy it to the specified folder
☐ Delete it
☐ Forward it to people

3. Rule Description (click on an underlined value to edit it):

Apply this rule after the message arrives
Where the From line contains 'ken@internetforfamilies.org'

4. Name of the rule:

New Mail Rule #1

[OK   ]   [Cancel]

Figure 6. Creating a filter

a filter, the message goes to your Inbox. Folders with unread messages appear in bold, with the number of unread messages listed beside the folder.

To create a filter:

1. Highlight the message in the Message List box.
2. In Outlook Express, choose **Message, Create Rule from Message, New**

from the Menu bar. In Netscape, choose **Edit, Message Filters, New**.

3. Enter the necessary information to create the filter. In most cases you will use a name, E-mail address, or subject to sort your messages (see figure 6).

4. Select the folder where you want to file the message.

5. Give your filter a name and click **OK** when finished.

Now, whenever you receive a message that matches your filter, your E-mail program will automatically move it to the correct folder. You can create as many filters as needed. To turn a filter off, remove the checkmark beside the filter name. To turn it back on, replace the checkmark. Use the up and down buttons to change the order of which filters are to be applied first to a message.

You can use message filters for more than sorting. You can set filters to forward messages, delete unwanted mail, flag mail as important, and mark mail as read.

> **Five Steps to Defeating Spam**
>
> 1. Use your E-mail filters to block unwanted messages.
> 2. Don't respond to spam. All you're doing is letting the sender know your E-mail address is real.
> 3. Use a free E-mail address to subscribe to newsletters and newsgroups.
> 4. Forward the spam to any legitimate Internet domain you find in the return address. For example, if the return address reads, getrich@yourisp.com, then forward the message to abuse@yourisp.com. Legitimate ISPs have policies against spam. You can also forward it to the Network Abuse Clearing House (www.abuse.net).
> 5. If all else fails, use an antispam program. Most are either freeware (free to use) or shareware (must pay a small fee). Spam Killer, Spam Slammer, and Spam Hater are three of the more popular programs.

Dealing with E-mail Abuse

Yes, there is junk mail in cyberspace. Because E-mail is free, and because it's so easy to send thousands of messages at once, unethical and immoral marketers of all types now pitch their "products" using E-mail. Often called "spam," junk mail includes get-rich-quick schemes, advertising, and unsolicited pornographic offers. You can use filters to block such unwanted E-mail.

Don't Be Part of the Problem

If you've ever sent the same letter to more than a few people, you didn't include the name and address of everyone who was going to receive that letter on each envelope. It would be considered offensive. Yet, people often think nothing of pasting ten, twenty, thirty, or forty E-mail addresses into the To: and Cc: fields for all to see. I have a personal policy that I don't include E-mail addresses in the To: or Cc: field unless there's a compelling reason to do so. Many cases of junk E-mail can be traced back to a careless use of the To: and Cc: fields. Here are a few tips to protect yourself and others from spammers.

1. Don't include lists of E-mail addresses in your forwards. It's a spammer's dream come true.
2. Refrain from using the Forward and Reply to All button. Don't forward every quote, story, or tidbit of information you receive. Some may enjoy it, but not all those you send it to want it or have time to read it. Set up a special group of those who like to receive all your forwards. Give your group a special name, like Tim's Tidbits or Mary's Musings.
3. Check out any virus alert or chain letter before forwarding it. If it proves to be false, send a polite note back to the person sending it to you, letting them know it's false and where they can find the information about it. Don't pass it on.
4. If it's too good to be true, it is. Delete it.
5. If it can't be verified, delete it.
6. If it's too way out, delete it.

To block junk E-mail, look for a pattern in the messages you're receiving. Since spammers often use false E-mail addresses, look for a pattern in the subject line. If the subject line includes the words "Get Rich" or "hot girls" or "ADV," you can easily block these by creating a filter. Instead of creating a filter to sort messages, you're going to tell your program to delete the message.

1. Highlight the offending message.
2. Open the filter dialog box and select **New**.
3. Choose **Subject** from the rule box. Enter the specific word or words you want to filter.
4. Choose **Delete** as the action you want taken.
5. Give your filter a name and click **OK** when finished.

You will probably need to create more than one filter. If you find you are receiving junk mail from a specific address or domain, then create a filter to block that particular domain. Unfortunately, because E-mail is free, spam can become a problem. Check the side bar on page 131 for ways you can cut down on the spam you receive.

CHAPTER 18

E-MAIL FOR THE ENTIRE FAMILY

In the children's classic *Goldilocks and the Three Bears,* each bear has its own chair, bed, and bowl of porridge. If the story were written today, each member of the bear family would have its own E-mail address.

Your family has more than one member in it. As each of them gets online, it won't be long before everyone is sending and receiving E-mail. You can choose to have all that mail pour into one E-mail address, or you can set up separate accounts for every member of the family.

What Is Free E-mail?

As the name indicates, free E-mail accounts cost you nothing. Most make money on the advertising that appears on your screen when you check your mail online or on the messages left in your E-mail box by "content providers." A few businesses, like American Express, provide free E-mail accounts for their customers.

You will lose some features with free E-mail. Most require you to access your E-mail online. You cannot check it using your browser's E-mail program. You must compose and send messages online, and keep your Address Book on the Internet. You cannot automatically forward your free E-mail to your local Internet Service Provider. There are often limits to the size of attachments and the number of messages you can receive. Messages are stored on the Internet, not on your computer. If there is a lot of traffic on the Internet, checking your mail can become a time-consuming task. It's harder to monitor your kids' E-mail if their mail is on the Internet.

Some free E-mail services will add features for a fee. Fees vary from one dollar per feature per month to ten dollars a month for a full-featured E-mail program. Of course, when you have to start paying for it, it's no longer free, is it?

There are some advantages. You can check your mail from any computer, even while on vacation or away on a trip. You can have the program check for E-mail on your home Internet Service Provider. Every member of your family can have an E-mail account. You can set up separate accounts for newsgroups, thus protecting your privacy. There are free E-mail accounts that do forward E-mail to your ISP account. And, of course, it's free.

Selecting a Free E-mail Account

It seems that everyone today is offering free E-mail. Search engines, major Web sites, Microsoft, Netscape, banks, and many online businesses offer free E-mail. Some computer manufacturers offer you free, limited Internet access and E-mail accounts when you buy a computer from them. Larger Christian Web sites offer free E-mail. There are even companies that offer nothing but free E-mail.

Before you sign up for a free E-mail service, check with your Internet Service Provider. Some offer a family plan that includes multiple E-mail addresses. If they don't, or if they don't offer enough for your family, then you'll need to find a free E-mail service.

Check to see if your bank, credit card, or other company with which you do business offers free E-mail accounts. In many areas of the country, you can sign up for a free E-mail account with Juno. You don't have to have Internet access to open a Juno account; you need only a modem and special software provided by them. They have two levels of service. The basic service is free. With it, you can receive only plain-text E-mail. Juno Gold provides for attachments and HTML-formatted E-mail.

Table 1 explains common free E-mail features. Table 2 lists a number of the more popular free E-mail services.

Table 1 Free E-mail Features	
Feature	**Function**
Forwarding	Automatically forwards E-mail from your free account to your home or office E-mail account
POP	Allows you to download your mail from their servers using your E-mail program
Consolidation or Retrieval	Retrieves messages from other E-mail accounts (like your home ISP) so you can view them online from any computer
Filtering	Filters E-mail for spam or personal filters you create
Autoresponder	Automatically responds to all E-mail with a message when you're away
Daily Reminders	E-mail messages to remind you of birthdays, anniversaries, and other special events or appointments

Table 2 Free E-mail Web Sites	
AmExMail	www.amexmail.com
Bigfoot	www.bigfoot.com
CCNmail (Crosswalk)	www.ccnmail.com
Hotmail	www.hotmail.com
Iname.com	www.iname.com
Juno	www.juno.com
Mail City	http://mailcity.lycos.com
Net@ddress	www.netaddress.com
Yahoo! Mail	www.yahoo.com

Which One Is Right for Your Family?

Don't be anxious to sign up for the first free E-mail service that appeals to you. The following five questions will help you decide which free E-mail service is right for your family.

1. What features do you want with your free E-mail? Consult Table 1 for an explanation of the most common features.
2. Do you want to be able to monitor your kids' E-mail? If you do, you'll need to select an E-mail that forwards mail to your home ISP. If you have children, I highly recommend you use a free E-mail service that forwards E-mail.
3. How much personal information do you want to give out? You will have to give some information. I gave the same information for all the accounts I set up. Therefore, the only personal information they have is mine; they have no information on my kids or my wife. I also read the privacy policy carefully to find out how they planned to use the information that I gave.
4. How reliable is the service? Ask a few people who use the service, and then test it yourself. Before creating new accounts for every member of your family, create just one. Use it for a few weeks. If you're using a forwarding account, send yourself test messages from your home ISP and see how long it takes for them to be forwarded back to you.
5. If the service you chose must be accessed on the Internet, how slow or fast is it? Most free E-mail services earn their money from advertisements. Advertisements are graphic images and can take a long time to download. Try checking your E-mail at the times of day your family is most likely to want to check their mail.

Setting Up an Account

Once you've selected a free E-mail service, it's time to set up your account. Every company does it a little differently. Generally the process is simple and straightforward. The order may change, but it will include the following steps. Typically, you'll be asked to fill out a form providing your name and other personal information. This information is often used to develop a profile of all the users of that service. Marketing creates profiles of the average users of their service. They then use the information to attract advertisers.

Next, you'll select a UserID or user name. This can be anything you like. It doesn't have to be the same as your UserID with your ISP. Have three or four options available in case your first choice is taken. If it is, the registration program may offer you alternatives based on your original choice and/or your name. You can select one of those or try a different one. For the sake of privacy, especially with your kids, you might ask them to pick an online name that has nothing to do with their real name.

Once you've selected a UserID, you'll be asked for a password. You'll have to enter it twice to make sure you typed it correctly the first time.

Finally, you'll select the options and features you'd like to use with the free E-mail service. Carefully read all the "check boxes." You might sign up for a whole group of newsletters and advertisements if you're not careful.

Setting Up Your E-mail for Multiple Accounts

If you selected a Web-based E-mail service, there is nothing for you to set up in your E-mail program. You will use their Web site to compose, send, and receive E-mail, and to store addresses. You can use part of the following instructions to be able to send E-mail from your E-mail program, with your Web-based free E-mail account as the return address.

You will want to create separate accounts or users so that as each family member sends mail, it goes out with their own E-mail address. With E-mail arriving to your Inbox from two, three, four, or more different addresses, you'll want to create filters and folders to sort all that mail. You will also need to set up accounts if you've signed up for a free E-mail service that uses a POP address. A POP address allows you to use your E-mail program to download your mail directly from your free E-mail Web site without having to forward it to your home E-mail address. If your free E-mail is a POP address, you'll need to print out the information concerning how to configure your E-mail program.

The following instructions are for creating separate accounts using free E-mail that is forwarded to your home E-mail address.

Outlook Express

To use Outlook Express with your free E-mail address, you'll have to create accounts for each new address. This way you can send E-mail using Outlook Express instead of having to log on to the free E-mail Web site.

Creating an Account. Generally, there are six steps to follow in setting up new E-mail accounts in Outlook Express.

1. Choose **Tools, Accounts** from the Menu bar.
2. Start the Internet Connection Wizard by choosing **Add, Mail** in the Internet Accounts box.
3. The Connection Wizard will ask for your name as you want it to appear in the From: field, the free E-mail address, and your incoming and outgoing mail server address. These will be the same as those listed with your home ISP E-mail address. Since you are forwarding E-mail to your home address, the account name and password will be the same as your home ISP.

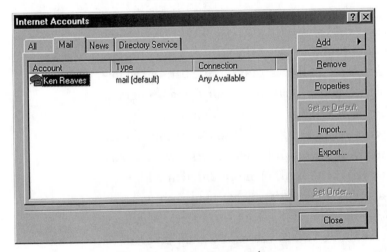

Figure 1. Internet Accounts box

4. When finished, the new account will appear in the Internet Accounts box under the Mail tab (see figure 1).

5. Double-click on the new account, opening the Properties box. Remove the check in the "Include this account when receiving mail" box (see figure 2). Since your home mail account checks your local mailbox, it's not necessary to check twice.

While you have the Properties box open, look at the information on the General tab. Here you can change the name of the account or the name that will appear on all outgoing E-mail.

6. Click **OK** and then **Close** to accept the changes and close both the Properties box and Internet Accounts box.

Repeat this process for every free E-mail account you have. Now you'll be able to send mail from your machine using your free E-mail account.

The final thing you'll want to do is set up filters and folders for each person. This will sort their mail into their personal folders. Check the previous chapter for help with sorting E-mail.

Sending Messages. To send a message using your new E-mail address:

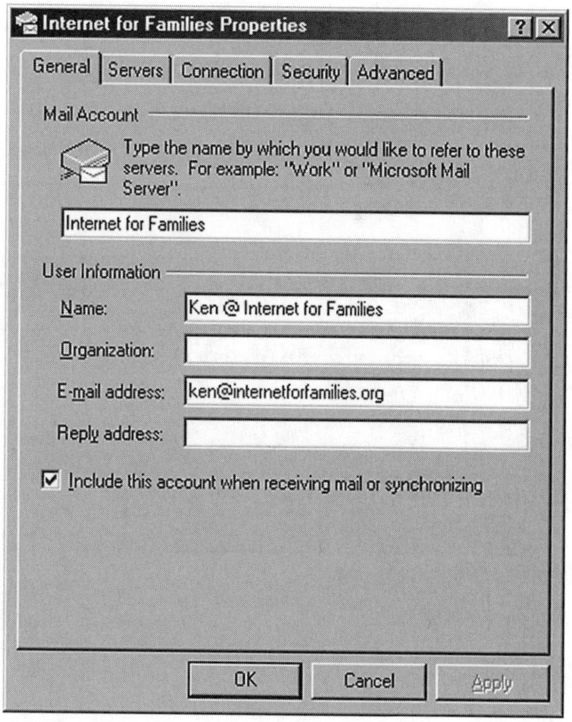

Figure 2. Account Properties box

1. Choose **New Message**. Notice there is now a drop-down arrow on the far right side of the From: box. Your default E-mail address appears in this box.

2. Click on the arrow and choose your new address from the list.

3. Enter the address of the person to whom you're writing in the To: field.
4. Add a subject and your message.
5. Click **Send** when finished.

Netscape

Creating an Account: To set up multiple accounts in Netscape, you have to create separate user profiles. Before creating a new profile, you must close Netscape.

1. From the Windows taskbar, select **Start, Programs, Netscape Communicator, Utilities, User Profile Manager**.
2. Read the information in the Profile Manager dialog box (see figure 3). Click **New** to start the Profile Wizard.
3. Follow the steps to create a new profile. When prompted for an E-mail address, use your free E-mail address. Use the same SMTP and POP addresses as for your home E-mail address.
4. Make sure to use the person's name for whom you are setting up the new profile.
5. When done, click **Finished**.

Repeat this process for every member of your family. Creating a new profile enables each member of the family to have his or her own bookmarks, E-mail account, and other personal settings. When someone

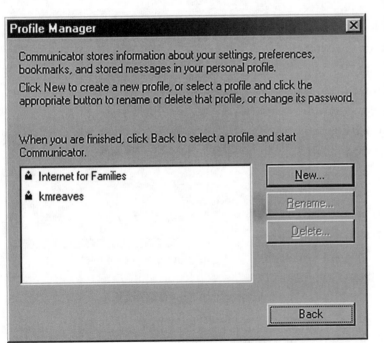

Figure 3. Netscape Profile Manager

opens Netscape, they are asked to select a profile (see figure 3). All the information and settings are then opened. If you wish to change users during a session, you must close Netscape and reopen it with the new user profile.

Sending Messages: To send a message with your new profile:

1. Double-click the Netscape icon on your desktop.
2. Choose your new profile from the Profile Manager box that appears as Netscape opens.
3. Open Netscape Messenger, and send and receive messages as before.

CHAPTER 19

DELIVERING INFORMATION TO YOUR DESKTOP

Pick a subject—any subject. Pick a hobby, a political issue, a field of science, a moral or ethical issue, an obscure topic, a style of music, a field of literature, or a support group. Somewhere in cyberspace there is a group of people talking about it—in a newsgroup or by way of a mailing list. There might even be an electronic newsletter published on the subject.

Mailing Lists

The terms *mailing lists* and *newsgroups* are often confused. Mailing lists are E-mail groups, while newsgroups require a special news reader to read and post to the group. When you subscribe to a mailing list, E-mail messages are sent to your E-mail address. All of these messages will be on the designated topic. If you're on a gardening mailing list, then the discussion will be about dirt, flowers, weather, fertilizer, etc. A scrapbooking mailing list will share ideas about supplies, scrapbook layouts, and preserving photos.

Finding the Right Mailing List

There are a number of mailing list directories on the Internet. You can also find mailing lists by using a regular search engine. In a regular search engine, use Boolean search functions or the advanced search feature to find mailing lists you're interested in. For example, to find mailing lists on gardening, you would enter the words: "gardening" AND "mailing list." For more information on advanced searches, see chapter 22.

Subscribing and Unsubscribing

When you find a mailing list of interest to you, follow the subscription instructions carefully. You will soon receive a confirmation message. This message will contain information about posting messages to the group and unsubscribing information. Save this message so you'll know how to unsubscribe from the mailing list when you want to do so.

When you're ready to unsubscribe, find the confirmation message you received when you subscribed. Again, follow the directions carefully. You will receive an automated reply when you've successfully unsubscribed from the group.

Joining the Discussion

There are two ways to respond to a mailing list message. You can reply to the person who posted the original message or post to the whole group. Use the Reply button to send a message to the person who wrote the original message. Send your E-mail to the mailing list address to post to the whole group.

Newsgroups

Newsgroups are electronic bulletin boards where people post and read messages on a given subject. There are tens of thousands of newsgroups on the Internet. The largest collection is on Usenet, but many organizations manage their own newsgroups. Some of them are public; others are private.

Newsgroups provide for lively discussion. Monitored newsgroups have someone who checks messages for relevance before posting them. Unmoderated groups are more loosely organized and are policed by group members. Typically, you can post anything to an unmoderated group, but you run the risk of being flamed by others if it doesn't apply to the purpose of the group.

One word of caution: Newsgroups are open to abuse. This is especially true of unmoderated groups. If you decide to subscribe to a newsgroup, follow the newsgroup tips carefully.

Setting Up Your Newsgroup Reader

Newsgroups use a file format called NNTP, Network News Transport Protocol. To subscribe and read newsgroups, you must configure your E-mail program's newsgroup reader. If a newsgroup folder appears in the file folder pane of your E-mail program, then the newsgroup reader was configured when you initially set up your E-mail. If not, open the Connection Wizard in Outlook Express, or the Preferences box in Netscape. Use these tools to configure your newsgroup reader. Contact your Internet Service Provider if you don't know the name of your ISP's news server.

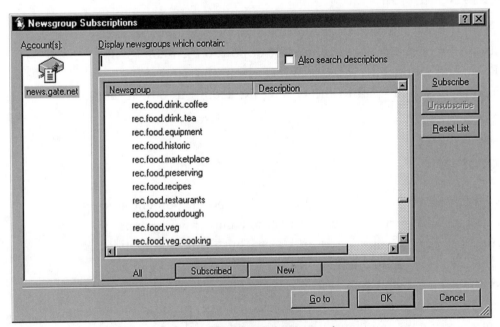

Figure 1. Newsgroup Subscriptions box

When you've finished creating your newsgroup account, a dialog box will ask if you want to download the newsgroup list. Click **Yes**. You'll need this list to find the group(s) of interest to you. You can manually download the list when you tell it you want to subscribe to a group.

Finding the Right Newsgroup

With more than fifty thousand newsgroups on the Internet, your Internet Service Provider cannot provide you access to all of them. To open the newsgroup list, start your E-mail program and open your newsgroup reader. Open the Newsgroup Subscriptions box by clicking on the newsgroups button (see figure 1). Click the All tab to display a list of newsgroups available through your ISP.

Table 1 Top-Level Hierarchy Names	
Label	**Meaning**
comp	Computers
humanities	Humanities
k12	Kindergarten through high school students and teachers
misc	Miscellaneous—topics that don't fit anywhere else
msn	Microsoft Network
news	News, current events
rec	Recreation, sports, hobbies, the arts
sci	Science
soc	Sociology, both social interest and socializing
talk	Ongoing discussions on a variety of subjects
alt	Alternative (stay away from these)

You can search for newsgroups by title or sometimes by description. Newsgroups are organized into a hierarchy. The top-level hierarchy sorts newsgroups by subject (see table 1). The second and following hierarchy levels, each divided by a dot, narrow the groups' focus. For example, newsgroups beginning with

- comp.graphics host discussions on the use and creation of computer graphics, art, animation, and images;
- rec.gardens are for those interested in gardening;
- rec.running will interest those who like to run for sport, enjoyment, or exercise;
- rec.arts.books are for all the book lovers out there;
- sci.math deal with mathematics; and
- misc.kids.computer are for those interested in the use of computers by kids.

Alternative (alt) newsgroups are set up by individuals. Many of the newsgroups on the alt hierarchy deal with immoral and illegal issues such as drugs, sex, evil, and computer hacking. Alt groups are not the only place to find such groups. So, if you're going to subscribe to a newsgroup, be very careful.

Subscribing and Unsubscribing

Once you find a newsgroup that interests you, you'll need to subscribe to it. To subscribe, highlight the newsgroup name in the All pane and click **Subscribe** (see figure 1). An icon will appear beside the name, indicating you've been successfully subscribed. To see the newsgroups you've subscribed to, click **Subscribed**. Click **OK** to save changes and exit the subscription box.

To unsubscribe from a newsgroup, open the Newsgroup Subscriptions box. Click the Newsgroup button. Open the Subscribed tab and highlight the newsgroup you wish to unsubscribe from. Click **Unsubscribe**. Click **OK** to save changes.

Joining the Discussion

To read newsgroup messages, start your E-mail program. In the Folders pane, click on the newsgroup you want to read. Your E-mail program retrieves a list of messages, displaying them in the Message List pane. Scan the subject headings, highlight a message that interests you, and read it in the Message pane. To open the message in its own window, double-click on the message in the Message List pane. You move through the messages the same way you do when reading your E-mail.

You will find three different types of postings to a newsgroup. Posts, also called Messages, are on a new subject. Follow-up Posts, or Follow-up Messages, are messages others have contributed to the original message. Some messages receive many follow-up posts; others receive none. Binaries are graphics, video, and program files. They are often divided into a number of sections and have to be reassembled. (Caution: I do not recommend downloading files from newsgroups. There are a lot of pornographic and illegal images posted to newsgroups. Also, it's very difficult to scan program files for viruses.)

To add your own message or follow-up message, click the newsgroup to which you want to post a message. Click **New Message** and a window will open similar to the New Message window for E-mail. Type your message and click **Send**. (Note: Postings to newsgroups take longer than sending and receiving E-mail.)

You can reply to the person posting a message by selecting the Reply button. Type your message and click **Send**. Your message will be sent to the individual, not the group.

Mailing List and Newsgroup Tips

Keep the following in mind when subscribing and posting to any mailing list or newsgroup.

- Use a free E-mail address. This helps maintain your privacy. Mailing lists and newsgroup E-mail addresses are easy pickings for spammers.

If your free E-mail address begins to get spammed, you can drop it and open a new one.

- Use a nickname instead of your real name. If you're a woman, pick a "gender neutral" nickname. This prevents unwanted passes that occur in some newsgroups.

- Don't subscribe to more than three or four newsgroups or mailing lists at a time. You will quickly be overwhelmed by the volume of messages you'll receive.

- Learn to manage these messages using the built-in features of your E-mail program.

- Read any FAQ (Frequently Asked Questions) file or message before posting. As the name implies, these files will answer most of the questions you might ask about a particular group.

- Be careful what you post to a newsgroup or send in a mailing list message. A lot can be inferred about a person by what they write. Plus, whatever you write is archived somewhere on a computer.

- "Listen" for at least a week before you join the discussion. This will help you understand the type of people who are part of the group. After reading the messages, you might decide the group or list is not for you.

- Don't post "Me, too" or other annoying messages that waste people's time.

- Don't get involved in a "flame war" or discussions that are negative in tone or illegal in nature.

One last note: Newsgroups can be rather wild and rough places. Some are very good, but many are not. You may need to search through many groups before you find one you're comfortable with. Moderated groups tend to be the best. Even then, the content posted is determined by the moderator's ethics and morals, not yours.

There may be a need to subscribe to a newsgroup, but do so with caution. I do not recommend newsgroups at all for kids.

Electronic Newsletters

Electronic Newsletters, Ezines, are electronic forms of the old postal newsletter. Unlike the old postal newsletter, almost all Ezines are free. Like mailing lists and newsgroups, there are newsletters on just about any subject you can imagine. Some are formatted with plain text. Others are sent using HTML. Some offer a choice of plain or HTML formatting. Newsletters are published daily, weekly, biweekly, or monthly. They are sent directly to your E-mail box.

Unlike mailing lists and newsgroups, you cannot post a message to everyone who receives the newsletter. Newsletters are basically one-way communication tools. The author composes the newsletter and sends it to you. Newsletters are sent using the blind carbon copy or a special program that hides all the E-mail addresses. This protects your privacy.

Finding the Right Ezine

Like mailing lists, there are Web directories listing hundreds of newsletters (see table 2). You can search for a specific Ezine or browse the list by subject. Each Ezine is listed with a brief description and information on how to subscribe.

The first place to look for newsletters is on the sites you frequent. These are the sites that interest you. Many of them, especially the larger sites, will have at least one newsletter associated with them. Larger sites will often offer more than one newsletter—each on a different subject addressed on the Web site. The newsletters you find will relate to the subjects covered by that Web site. For example, you won't find a gardening newsletter on IBM's Web site.

Often, you'll first hear about a newsletter from a friend. They might even forward a copy to you. Most newsletter authors encourage forwarding of their newsletters to increase interest. My newsletter, *Internet for Families*, receives most of its subscribers by word of mouth or by people visiting my Web site (internetforfamilies.org).

Table 2 **Where to Find Mailing Lists and Newsletters**		
Name	**Types of Lists**	**Address**
Deja	newsgroups & mailing lists	www.deja.com
eGroups	mailing lists & Ezines	www.egroups.com
Christian E-mail Service Mailing Lists	mailing lists	www.christianemailservice.com
Internet for Christians	Ezines & mailing lists	www.gospelcom.net/ifc/mail/view
Liszt	mailing lists	www.liszt.com
Reference.com	newsgroups & mailing lists	http://reference.com

Subscribing and Unsubscribing

Newsletters vary in how you subscribe to them. Many Web sites provide a subscription box, where you fill in your name and E-mail address. If the site has multiple newsletters, you then select the ones you want to receive. On others, you are instructed to send an E-mail message to a specific address. Usually there are specific instructions on what you need to put in the subject field or the body of the E-mail. It is important that you follow the instructions exactly. Often a software program is used to manage the newsletter, and it is sensitive to the messages it accepts.

Most newsletters will have both subscribing and unsubscribing information at the bottom of every letter. To unsubscribe, follow the author's instructions.

Pick a subject—any subject—and you'll find lots of great newsletters. If you're looking for a few newsletters to get an idea of what's available, check out the list in appendix 2. There I've listed a variety of different newsletters.

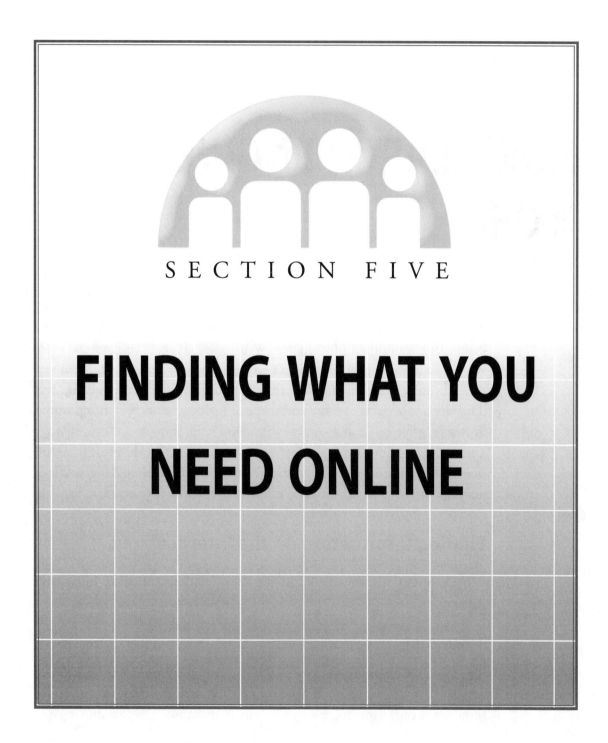

SECTION FIVE

FINDING WHAT YOU NEED ONLINE

CHAPTER 20

HOW SEARCH ENGINES WORK

As of July 1999, the Internet contained more than 200 million Web sites comprising more than 800 million Web pages.[1] Forget the haystack here; we're talking about trying to find a needle somewhere in the state of Kansas.

Fortunately, search engines can help you find what you're looking for. They are not perfect. The size and scope of the Internet makes it impossible at this time for one search engine to catalog it all, though some are trying. Understanding how search engines work will help you get the most from the ones you choose to use. Before we look at search engines, however, let's examine some other ways to find information on the Internet.

Finding Information on the Internet

There are six ways you can go about finding information on the Internet.

1. Browsing

Some people approach the Internet the way they approach shopping in a mall. They start at one end and browse their way through every store. At some stores they stop long enough to look in the window before moving on.

At others, drawn by something they see, they go in for a closer look. If they find something they like, they might be in that store for hours. When you browse the Internet, you're casually moving from site to site. You're not looking for anything in particular, but if you find something you like, you'll stop on that Web site and stay awhile.

2. Everyday Life

Web addresses are everywhere. They are more common than phone numbers on billboards and advertisements. You see them in newspapers and magazines. Someone at work, at church, or in the neighborhood tells you about a site he discovered last night. Your sister in Washington state E-mails you an address. You hear a site mentioned on the radio, or you see one on television. Some of the best sites you'll find are those you hear about offline.

3. Links

Graphic images, hypertext, advertisement—every Web site contains both internal and external links. Internal links connect you to related pages on the same Web site. External links take you to a different, but related, Web site. If you find some information you're searching for on one site, some of the links on that page should take you to additional information.

4. Site Search Engine

Most Web sites of any size have a search engine. A site search engine searches only the Web site it's on. Without such a search engine, you would have difficulty finding information on a site as small as fifty pages. On sites ranging into the hundreds of thousands of pages, a site search engine is essential.

5. Go Command

This is a shortcut to a keyword search. Instead of going to a search engine to begin your search, you start by typing a keyword into your browser's Address bar. For example, let's look up sites for building kites. In the Address bar, type: go kites, then click **Enter** on the keyboard. Your browser will open to the default search engine with a list of possible Web sites on kites. (Note: You can change your default search engine using the Internet Options or Preferences box.)

6. Web Search Engines

The Go command is a quick way to get a set of search results from one search engine. But there are hundreds of search engines on the Internet. As mentioned earlier, no single search engine has been able to index the entire Web. The largest, AltaVista, has indexed 140 million Web pages. That's not even one-fourth of the entire Web. Though there is some overlap in the larger search engines, each also has its own unique content. Depending on how much information you need, or how obscure the search subject, you'll need to learn how to use a number of search engines.

How Search Engines Work

Think of a search engine as being like the index in the back of a book. When you're looking for information on a subject, you turn to the index and use a keyword to look for a list of pages where the information might be printed. You then turn and scan those pages until you find what you need.

You do basically the same thing with a search engine. A search engine is a giant electronic index to millions of Web sites scattered across the Internet. When you enter your keyword, the search engine returns a list of sites where that word is used. Most sites rank the results according to which ones best match your search request. Each result will have a brief summary of what is on the Web page. As you scan the results, you'll click on the links to the sites you want to investigate further.

Search engines use different techniques to find and index Web sites. Some use people to do all the searching and indexing. Many use small programs, called spiders, that "crawl around" the Internet looking for new Web sites. When the program finds one, it "reads" the title, meta (hidden) tags, and other information off the Web pages and sends it back to the search engine. The search engine then uses sophisticated software to evaluate and index the site according to the information received. Many use a combination of both humans and software to index the Internet. Most search engines allow webmasters to submit their site to the search engine by filling out an information form.

Types of Search Engines

There are four basic types of search engines. Web search engines are stand-alone search sites that attempt to index as much of the Internet as possible. Crosswalk.com, AltaVista, Ask Jeeves, Excite, LookSmart, Lycos, HotBot, and Yahoo are examples of Web search engines.

Today, many of these search engines have transformed themselves into Web portals. They have tried to become the Wal-Mart of the Internet. They offer free E-mail, online shopping, discussion groups, online games, news, weather, sports, entertainment, travel bookings, and more. It is all with the hope of keeping you on their site longer—viewing more of their ads, purchasing more of their products—so that they can make more money. This isn't all bad. In many ways, this is how the Internet remains free.

Specialized search engines are smaller, focusing on a particular field, subject, or group. There are search engines devoted to science, education, newsgroups, Ezines, job hunting, Christianity, the arts, kids, and more. Examples include: Ask Jeeves for Kids, Yahooligans, Ezine.com, and Net/SEARCH at Christianity Online.

People finders are search engines that help you find information about a person. Such information includes E-mail address, phone number, and street address. Some people finders help you search for lost family members, old college roommates, service buddies, fraternity and sorority members, and professionals in any field. Electronic yellow pages catalog businesses, both on- and offline.

Metasearch engines are a hybrid form of Web search engines. A metasearch engine doesn't have its own database that it searches. When you perform a search in a metasearch engine, it polls anywhere from three to as many as a few dozen Web search engines. It then combines the results and presents them to you in a similar form as a Web search engine would. Metasearch engines include: Dogpile, MetaCrawler, and Savvy Search.

Family-Friendly Search Engines

Typically, search engines catalog everything they find on the Internet. They index the good and the bad. Search for the word *doll* and you'll find doll collectors, toy stores that sell dolls, and another kind of doll you don't want anything to do with. If you have blocking/monitoring software and/or are using a family-friendly ISP, most (if not all) of those undesirable "hits" will be blocked. You can safely use most search engines.

In the past year a few search engines have seen the proverbial "writing on the wall." They realize that if they want to attract and keep families coming back to their site, they need to be sensitive to the concerns of families. Today there are a number of family-friendly and kid-friendly search engines. These search engines do a better job of evaluating content and either filtering it or refusing to post offensive sites. Here are a few family-friendly search engines that I frequent.

AltaVista is one of the largest search engines. It has more than 140 million Web pages indexed. The context is updated every twenty-eight days. AltaVista has an optional "family filter" that you can set. When set, this filter blocks search results containing pornography, hate, violence, gambling, drugs, and alcohol. AltaVista provides two levels of blocking. "All except Web pages" filters image, video, and audio searches only. The "All" choice filters all searches, including Web pages. You can even report offensive pages that have slipped through their filters. Once you've set the filter, it's password-protected and can't be turned off except by someone who knows the password. Because of its size and the family filter, AltaVista is a good place to start almost any search.

LookSmart advertises itself as a family-friendly search engine. According to its press releases, it doesn't accept pornographic advertising, nor does it catalog "adult-themed" Web sites. Because definitions of "adult-themed" differ, you and I might find some objectionable sites listed. It would be nice if they had a family filter as a second level of protection. It limits, but doesn't filter, all other types of sites families would find objectionable. If your access is filtered, it will serve to block any questionable sites still listed.

Both Lycos and the GO Network have optional family filters. Lycos' SearchGuard functions similarly to AltaVista's filter. It is password-protected, so your child can't tamper with it. GOguardian lacks a password and is toggled on and off by the click of a button.

When you find a search engine you like, look to see if it offers a family filter. If it does, set it. Then direct your family to these search engines.

Crosswalk.com is a Christian Web site offering a filtered search engine. There are no filters to set; it does it for you. Because this is a Christian organization, I have found I can trust their results. It uses the Searchopolis search engine. It may not be as comprehensive as one of the secular sites, but it is growing. The more popular it becomes, the faster it will grow.

There are other Christian search engines, but they are more specialized in their search. Their purpose isn't to catalog the Web but to catalog Christian Web sites. If you want to compare new car prices, you need to go to a secular search engine. If you are looking for a new devotional to start your day, then use a Christian search engine.

Kids' Search Engines

There are a number of search engines just for kids. Because they are for kids, their content is geared for that age group. Kids' search engines focus on providing research and homework help, as well as providing a list of

Table 1
Search Engines to Get You Started

Family-Friendly Search Engines (Filtered)

AltaVista	www.altavista.com
Crosswalk	www.crosswalk.com
GO Network	www.go.com
LookSmart	www.looksmart.com
Lycos	www.lycos.com
Searchopolis	www.searchopolis.com

Standard Search Engines

About.com	www.about.com
Ask Jeeves	www.aj.com
Excite	www.excite.com
Yahoo	www.yahoo.com

Metasearch Engines

Family Friendly Search	www.familyfriendlysearch.com
MetaCrawler	www.metacrawler.com

Kids' Search Engines

AOL NetFind Kids Only	www.aol.com/netfind/kids
Ask Jeeves for Kids	www.ajkids.com
Searchopolis	www.searchopolis.com
Yahooligans	www.yahooligans.com

Christian Search Engines

Cross Search	www.crosssearch.com
Goshen	www.goshen.net
NetSEARCH	www.christianityonline.com
The Best of the Christian Web	www.botcw.com

sites that interest kids. The two most popular kids' search engines are Ask Jeeves for Kids, and Yahooligans. We will discuss these search engines in chapter 23 "Homework Helper."

Unfortunately, there aren't any youth search engines. Teens, especially when they reach the eighth grade, have to turn to regular search engines for help in finding information. In some ways, teens are more vulnerable to certain influences and temptations presented by the Web. It's important that you direct them to filtered search engines and use some form of filtered access.

This brings me to one last thought. Those who run search engines may not share completely your moral, ethical, and spiritual values. For example, we don't watch or permit *The Simpsons* in our home. Nor would I want my family interested in the Spice Girls or MTV. Other adults and parents see nothing wrong with these. Family-friendly search engines are just that—family-friendly. That doesn't mean they are mistake-proof or share your values completely. You still need to be involved in what your kids are doing online.

CHAPTER 21

SEARCH BASICS

Enough talk. You know how a search engine works. You know the difference between the types of search engines. And you have some idea of where to start. So . . . start.

As you begin searching the Internet, don't try to use a wide variety of search engines. Each search engine is a little different in both how it searches and how it reports its results. Instead of frustrating yourself by jumping from one search engine to another, select two or three to learn well. Once you've mastered both the basic and advanced searches in them, select a new search engine to master and add it to your search arsenal.

The first time you log on to a search engine, read the Help page. This page provides important tips on how to use that search engine. Taking a few moments to read this page will save you a lot of time and frustration.

Mastering Internet searches means mastering the lingo. *Keywords, phrase searches, Boolean operators, wildcards, more-like-this, URL searches*—these are terms you need to know if you're serious about finding good information fast. The reason is simple: The better you build your search query, the better the results.

Learning how to use search engines is the first step in mastering Internet searches. You must also know what to do with the search results.

Did you find what you were looking for? If not, why not? Are there other terms you can try? Should you narrow or broaden your search? Should you use the advanced search feature?

Searching is part knowledge and part experience. It's knowing how to do a search. But it's also knowing which search engine to use and what words or phrases will return the best results. This only comes from experience. There is no substitute for just doing it.

Basic Search

In this chapter, we're going to start with a basic search. A basic search uses a keyword or words. Often, this is where you'll begin. You'll pick a keyword, select a search engine, and initiate a search. Scanning the results, you'll decide if you've found what you need or if you must refine your search or move on to an advanced search.

1. Select a Search Engine

Determining the best search engine is often a matter of experience and preference. I typically start with one of four search engines. If it doesn't produce what I'm looking for, I turn to the other three. If I still haven't found what I'm looking for, I may try others. The exception to this rule is when I'm not sure which search engine will produce the best results. Then I often use a metasearch engine. We'll look at those in the next chapter.

With experience, you'll learn that some search engines are better with certain topics. Others, because of the human hand behind the software that reviews and catalogs sites, typically return fewer results but higher quality results. Sometimes it comes down to which ones you feel most comfortable with.

Which search engines should you begin learning to use? It's up to you. But you can't miss with any of those recommended in the previous chapter.

For our example, we'll use AltaVista because it is a family-friendly search engine. Open your browser, log on to the Internet, and enter the address to AltaVista's home page, www.altavista.com (see figure 1). (First try entering altavista.com. Your browser should recognize the address and add the http://www automatically.)

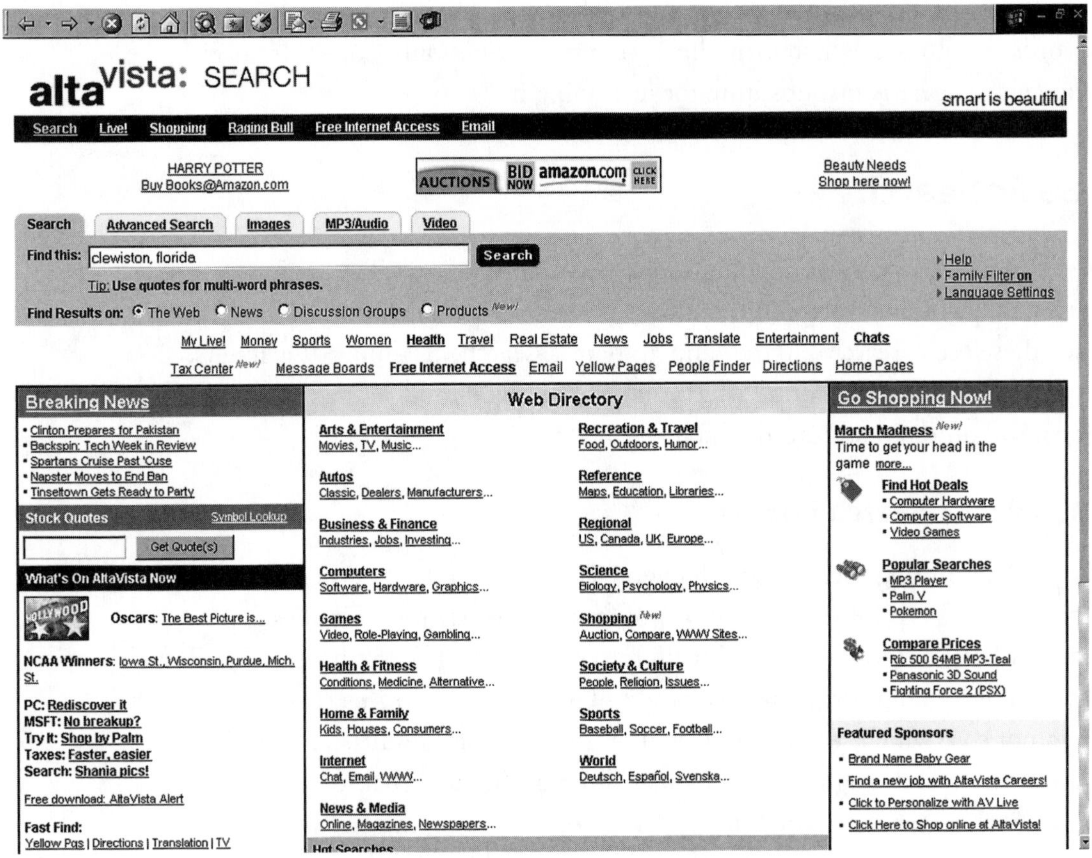

Figure 1. AltaVist home page

2. Enter a Keyword

Find the search box and enter the keyword. When selecting your keyword, try to pick the word or words that will narrow your search to the desired results. For example, if you enter the word "fishing," AltaVista will return almost five million hits. Searching for "bass fishing" returns a little more than 27,000 hits. Adding the word "Okeechobee" (which, for all you nonfishermen, is a popular bass lake in South Florida) produces only sites talking about bass fishing on Lake Okeechobee.

In our example, we're going to look for the small town of Clewiston, Florida. In the search box, type: Clewiston, Florida (see figure 2). Click **Search** to initiate the search. When you type a city and state, the search engine assumes you are looking for a city.

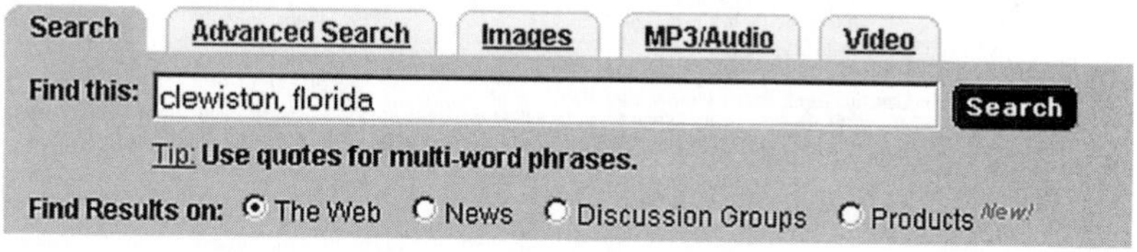

Figure 2. Search Box close-up

3. Scan the Results

On the first two pages, you'll find links to restaurants, churches, city hall, businesses, weather, fishing, and personal Web pages (see figure 3). If this were a real search, you'd scan the results for the information you needed.

Here's something for you to try. Pick another search engine and do the same search. (Don't pick LookSmart; it shares the same search technology as AltaVista.) Compare results. Which sites appeared in both search engines? Which sites were unique to the second search engine? How did they organize the results? Which was easier for you to use? (Why did we search for Clewiston, Florida? That's where I live.)

Saving What You Find

Now that you've found the information you were looking for, what do you do with it? How do you save it? You have five options for saving what you find.

1. Print It

All the information on the Internet is copyrighted. Even if the page you're viewing lacks a copyright, it is still copyrighted by law. You can,

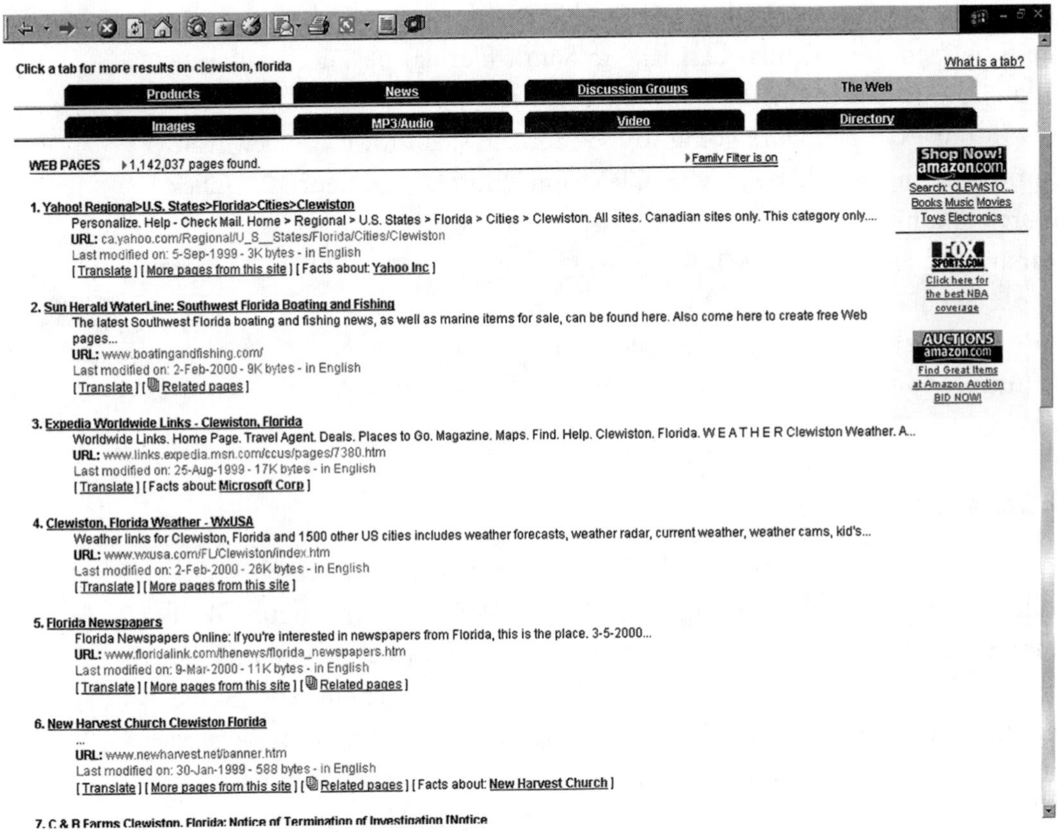

Figure 3. Search results

however, print a page for your use. This is beneficial if you're doing research, homework, or planning a vacation.

To print, click **Print** on the browser's toolbar. Or choose **File, Print** from the Menu bar.

2. Bookmark It

If you plan to return to the Web site often, bookmark it. To create a bookmark, choose **Favorites** or **Bookmarks**, then **Add**. (For more information on bookmarks, see chapter 12.)

3. Create a Shortcut on Your Desktop

Another option is to save a link on your desktop. Use this feature if you're doing research and need to reference a site repeatedly over a short period of time. Once you've finished your research, delete the shortcut from your desktop. To create a shortcut in Internet Explorer, drag the Internet icon on the left side of the address in the Address bar to the desktop. Or, choose **File, Send, Shortcut to Desktop** from the Menu bar. In Netscape, drag the bookmark icon next to the word *Location* on the toolbar.

4. E-mail the Web Page or Link

If I'm working at home and I need a Web site at the office, or vice versa, I use this helpful feature. With it, I can send the Web page address or a copy of the page to my other address. If I run across a site my son might enjoy or one my daughter needs for school, I send them the link by E-mail. I've also used this feature when helping someone else find information. To E-mail the page, choose **File, Send, E-mail link** or **Web page** from the Menu bar.

I usually don't send the entire page, for two reasons. First, it can create a large file to send and download. Most of the time the file contains only the text and not the images. If the person needs more than the text, they will still have to log on to the Web site. It's faster and easier to send the link. Second, some people have trouble receiving HTML files. It's best to send them plain-text E-mail and simply include the link.

5. Save the Web Page to Your Hard Drive

The latest browser versions allow you to save the entire Web page—graphics and all—to your hard drive. Then it can be viewed offline at your leisure. Saving the Web page places it in either a separate folder on your desktop or in the My Documents folder on your hard drive. Be sure to note where your browser saves the page. Once saved, clicking on the shortcut opens your browser and loads the page from your hard drive. When you're finished viewing saved pages, delete or drag them to the Recycle Bin. To save a page to your hard drive, choose **File, Save As** from the Menu bar.

Common Problems

Speling. Speeling. Spelling: Typographical errors and misspelled search words are the number one reason for failed searches. Keep a dictionary handy and proof your typing. If you are searching for biographic information, know how to spell the person's name.

Don't use plurals: Dolphin is better than *dolphins. Church* is better than *churches.* If you use the plural, search engines will overlook pages that have the singular.

Not specific enough: If you're looking for information on the New York Yankees, don't search for "baseball." That is far too broad a search. "Yankee" isn't specific enough, either. Searching for "Yankee" would return hits on the Civil War, Broadway musicals, sailing ships, books, and baseball teams.

Wrong words or too specific: Yes, you can be so specific that your search returns few, if any, hits. If you're looking for bass fishing on Lake Okeechobee from Clewiston, Florida, don't try to enter all that information. Try one of the following combinations: "fishing Clewiston, Florida," or "bass fishing Okeechobee."

Use the three-strike rule: If you don't find what you're looking for in the first two or three pages of hits, then change your search or change search engines.

It's your turn now. Give it a try. What is your favorite hobby or sports team? What information can you find on your hometown? Pick a search engine, select a keyword or words, then scan the results. Try a different search engine and see what results are the same and what is different.

CHAPTER 22

ADVANCED SEARCHES

The basic search is a good way to get started. However, after a few of these searches, you'll realize that unless you're doing a very general search, it's not the best way to find information quickly. Fortunately, there are tools and techniques to target your search more effectively.

Refining Your Search

Sometimes your initial search proves too broad and returns too many hits to be useful. To return more useful results, you will need to refine your search. Refining your search is simply narrowing it, using your initial search results as the new starting point. Before going further, ask yourself why you didn't get the results you wanted. Did you misspell a search term? Are there other keywords you could have used? If you answered yes to either of these questions, rerun your search. If you get closer but still haven't found what you need, use one or more of the following techniques.

Search the Recommended Site

Sometimes search engines pull a Web page that just doesn't seem right. You wonder how that page ended up on the list. Sometimes it's a mistake, but often the information you need is somewhere on that Web site—you just have to look a little further for it. If the site appears promising (perhaps you're searching for Windows 98 tips and it returns a page from *PC Magazine),* then search the site before returning to the search engine. If the site has a site search box, use it.

Those who build and manage search engines want you to be successful using their site. If you're successful, you'll come back. That is why they always seem to be tinkering with their site. Most search sites offer tools to help you find what you need if you're not successful the first time. Each search engine approaches this process differently. Most will have at least one of the following ways to refine your search.

Use the Recommended Related Searches

Along with search results, many search engines try to help you find what you need by offering related searches. Each site does this differently. AltaVista returns a list of related searches at the top of the Results page. If any of the recommended searches are closer to what you're looking for, click on the link. Excite includes a link under each search result, called "Search for more documents like this one." Selecting this option returns a new list of sites based on the one closest to your initial search.

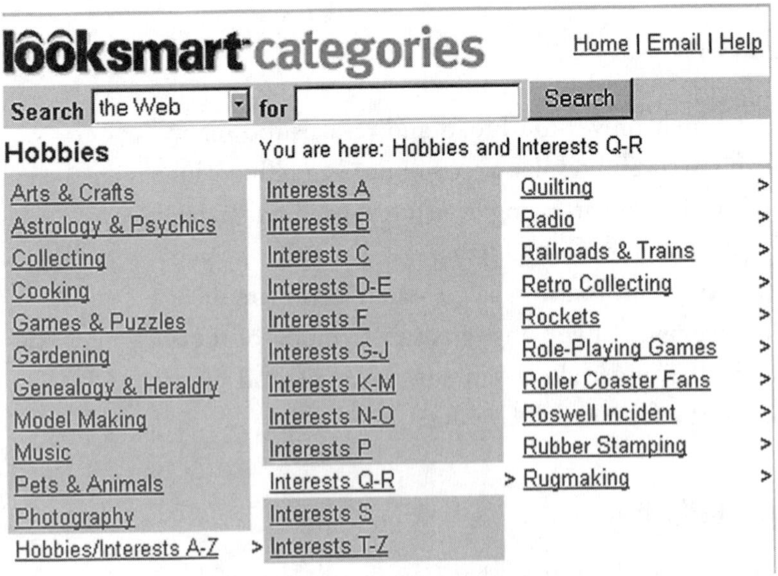

Figure 1. Directory search

Search Specific Categories

Search engines like Yahoo and LookSmart have a directory or topic structure. You can search the entire site or narrow your search by selecting a specific category. When you search these sites, they recommend categories, grouped by subject, that might relate to your search (see figure 1). Browse or narrow your search to one of these categories.

Advanced Search Techniques

Refining your search is a way to quickly narrow your initial search when it returns hits close to what you're looking for. Using advanced search techniques can also quickly narrow your search, returning accurate search results the very first time. There are two ways to use advanced search techniques. You can learn to use specialized search terms, or use the advanced search page of each search engine.

Specialized Search Terms

Using search terms allows you to narrow or expand your search as needed. Use wildcards to expand your search on a general subject. For instance, typing in the word *lock* with an asterisk (lock*) searches for all forms in which the word appears. Results would include *lock, lockbox, locker, locking, locks, locksmith,* and *Lockheed* (the airline manufacturer). You can also use the question mark to perform the same search (lock?).

Use Boolean logic or operators to narrow your search and thereby return more accurate results. Boolean logic was named after the man who invented it, George Boole. It allows you to set up relationships between words in a search. Having problems with bugs in your garden? Try the following search: Type: gardening AND insects AND NOT weeds.

Boolean operators allow you to string words together in your search. This enables you to exclude or include documents containing specific words. Here are some examples of how you use Boolean operators.

AND—A search using "flowers AND gardening" returns sites where both words appear on the Web page. All types of gardening sites that talk about flowers are included.

OR—A query using "flowers OR gardening" returns sites containing either word. Search results would include: vegetable gardens, flower gardens, general gardening sites, silk flowers, FTD Florist, and more.

NOT—A search using "flowers NOT gardening," returns Web sites containing the word "flowers" but not the word "gardening." This eliminates all gardening sites and returns primarily florists and sites selling books on flowers. Another way to frame a "not" search is to use AND NOT.

PHRASE—The old way of framing a phrase query was to type: PHRASE(flower gardening). Most search engines now allow you to use quote marks ("") around the phrase. Typing "flower gardening" tells the search engine to look only for documents using the specified phrase. In our example, our search would return only those sites using the phrase "flower gardening."

You can also string more than one operator together. For example: flowers AND gardening AND Canada. This would return sites on growing flowers in Canada. You could exclude Canada by searching for: flowers AND gardening NOT Canada.

In some search engines you can substitute symbols for the standard Boolean operators. For a list of these, see table 1. Use these symbols in place of the Boolean terms. For example, instead of "flowers AND gardening," type: "flowers + gardening."

Not all search engines use the same search terms. Some prefer the math symbols instead of the text terms. Even if they do use the same terms, they may apply them differently. Save yourself some frustration by learning how each site applies search terms.

In most search engines you do not have to capitalize your Boolean terms. However, doing so makes it easier for you to differentiate between search words and operators.

Table 1 Specialized Search Terms		
Term	**Meaning**	**Example**
AND	Looks for pages having both words	fishing AND Florida
OR	Looks for pages having either word	fishing OR bass
NOT or AND NOT	Looks for pages having the first word but not the second	fishing NOT bass fishing NOT Florida
PHRASE( )	Looks for pages that have the exact phrase	PHRASE(bass fishing) (fresh water fishing)
"" Quote Marks	Same as Phrase Search	"bass fishing"
+	Same as AND	fishing+Florida
-	Same as NOT	fishing-bass
* ?	Wild card (searches for all forms of a word)	fish* fish?

Specialized Search Pages

Most search engines have advanced search pages (see figure 2). These pages are designed to help you get the most out of the search engine. Not all search engines share the same features, but they all have some of the following: the ability to search for sites by language, type of site, and date posted; simplified Boolean searches; custom filters; and subject categories.

An advanced search page may support searching for meta words. *Meta tags* are text you normally don't see when you view a Web page. *Meta words* are the keywords included in the tags that identify the page and its content to search engines. Often these meta words are more accurate than a basic search because they are the words the site author uses to describe his Web site or page. The two most common types of meta word searches are domain

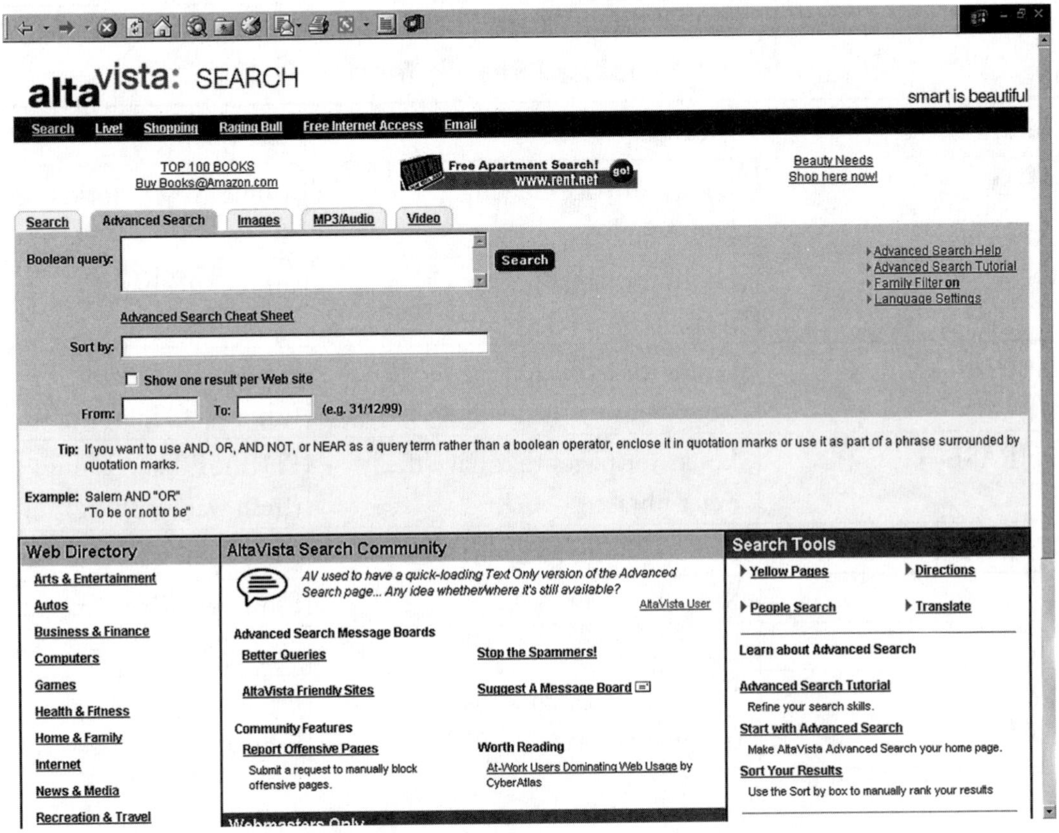

Figure 2. Advanced search page

and title searches. Domain name searches restrict the search for information to one Web site or domain. Title searches examine all the words the author uses in the title meta tag. These searches can be combined with Boolean operators on the advanced page to narrow your search further.

A link to the advanced search page is usually located next to the search box. A few search engines don't offer an advanced search page. In the following example, we're going to search for information on John Newton, the author of "Amazing Grace." In our search, we're not interested in midi files (digital music files that can be played on a computer). We also are looking only for pages posted in the last two years.

On the AltaVista advanced search page, enter the following in the

Boolean search box: John Newton AND Amazing Grace AND NOT midi. In the date box, add the date range: 1/1/97 and 12/31/99. Click **Search**. The results include a link to a British museum in Newton's hometown, two Web sites devoted to Newton, and the lyrics to "Amazing Grace."

Metasearch Engines

If you have no idea which search engine to use, then consider using a metasearch engine (see figure 3). On the surface, a metasearch engine looks like any other search engine. That's where the similarity ends. These search engines do not catalog sites themselves. Instead, they poll other search

Figure 3. Metasearch page

Pro **Bass Fishing** The Complete Professional Bass Fisherman'
  Infoseek: Tips from professional bass fisherman, links, chat, and more.
  DirectHit: Pro **Bass Fishing**, The Complete Professional Bass Firhermans resource. Featuring the Lake reports, Free Boat Llsting service, Live Chatroom, Message boards, links and more.
  Google: ...Tucker's Bass 2000 Florida **Bass Fishing** Photo Gallery Boats...
  1000. http://www.probass.com/ (Infoseek, Direct Hit, Google) | More Results Like This

Bass Fishing Home Page
  Infoseek: The **Bass Fishing** Home Page is the world's #1 site for information on **Bass Fishing**. Site includes fishing reports, articles, tactics, message boards, boating info, stories, and much more.
  DirectHit: The **Bass Fishing** Home Page is the world's #1 site for information on **Bass Fishing**. Site includes fishing reports, articles, tactics, message boards, boating info, stories, and much
  Google: ... BASS FISHING HOME PAGE Advertising makes the BFHP possible --...
  867. http://www.wmi.org/bassfish/ (Infoseek, Direct Hit, Google) | More Results Like This

bass fishing guides fishing trips texas mexico alaska
  WebCrawler: Wildgoose.com © **bass fishing** guides texas lake fork freshwater fishing guides saltwater fishing guides outdoor adventure guides and outfitters fly fishing guides fly fishing outfitters fly fishing lodges texas lake huites mexico alaska canada south carolina georgia alabama mississippi arkansas oklahoma new mexico lake huites new brunswick colorada new york louisiana tx al ca sc ga ms ak...
  DirectHit: **bass fishing** guides fishing trips texas mexico alaska brazil **bass fishing** outfitters fishing lodges mexico fishing lodges lake fork lake aqua milpa lake huites lake baccarac el
  Google: ...Dealers Fishing Fishing Lake Fork **Bass Fishing**, Lake...
  826. http://www.wildgoose.com/fishing.htm (WebCrawler, Direct Hit, Google) | More Results Like This

BassAngler.Com
  Excite, DirectHit: BassAngler.Com is the site for **bass fishing** articles, information and discussion.
  635. http://www.bassangler.com/ (Excite, Direct Hit) | More Results Like This

Kevin's **Bass Fishing** Site
  Excite: Best **Bass Fishing** Site on the net! **Bass Fishing** Resources, **Bass Fishing** Information, **Bass Fishing** News, **Bass Fishing** Tips, **Bass Fishing** Articles, **Bass Fishing** Message Boards, **Bass Fishing** Everything!
  DirectHit: Best **Bass Fishing** Site on the net! **Bass Fishing** Resources, **Bass Fishing** Information, **Bass Fishing** News, **Bass Fishing** Tips, **Bass Fishing** Articles, **Bass Fishing** Message Boards, Bass
  Google: ...techniques! HOT LINKS Hundreds of **Bass Fishing** Links! REPORTS Post...
  523. http://www.bassfishin.com/ (Excite, Direct Hit, Google) | More Results Like This

Figure 4. Metasearch results page

engines for answers to your query. Most metasearch engines include the major search engines, like AltaVista, Excite, Lycos, and Infoseek. Others include smaller, specialized search engines.

Metasearch engines do simple searches best. This is because advanced searches differ among search engines. Metasearch engines accept Boolean searches with mixed results. Most metasearch engines do not do an exhaustive search. Instead, they poll the top 10 to 100 hits from each search engine. The results are combined and posted.

One of the nicest features of most metasearch engines is the way they display search results (see figure 4). Each search result will include the name of the search engine from which the result was pulled. On a list of ten search results, you might have results from five different search engines. If more than one search engine returned the same site, both engines are listed. As you scan the list, look for a pattern in the results. See if most of the hits come from one or two search engines. If they do, you might want to jump to that search engine and look for more results using the basic or advanced search.

Specialized Search Engines

There are hundreds of specialized search engines. There are search engines for business, employment, sports, science, research, education, Christianity, Usenet, computers, medicine, libraries, and Ezines. There are even search engines for search engines. Appendix 2 lists some specialized search engines and where you can find others. There are two unique search engines I'd like to mention here.

Ask Jeeves and Ask Jeeves for Kids are natural-language search engines. Instead of using keyword and Boolean operators, you type in your question. For best results, you need to give some thought to how you word your question. Ask Jeeves uses skilled researchers to categorize information and identify the types of questions people ask. If Ask Jeeves can't find a match in its data bank, it submits your question to five other search engines. Ask Jeeves will even check your spelling.

About.com is not your traditional search engine. It uses people to build directories of information on various subjects. If you're not quite sure where to go to find what you need, About.com can point you in the right direction. One of the helpful features of About.com is that if you can't find what you're looking for, you can E-mail the person handling that subject.

It's your turn. Now that you know how to use advanced search features, try them. Go to one of the search engines you've been learning to use and perform an advanced search. If you don't have any idea what to search for, select two or three terms and try different combinations. For example, you might use the terms: *tiger, cat,* and *football.* Some of the combinations you could use are: tiger AND football; tiger NOT cat; "tiger football." (Note: With the exception of proper names and places, don't capitalize your search words. Some search engines are "case sensitive." Capitalizing the words would cause those search engines to look for sites only where the word is capitalized. By typing it using lowercase letters, it searches for occurrences of the word in both upper- and lowercase.)

CHAPTER 23

HOMEWORK HELPER

Let's be honest. You didn't spend two thousand dollars on a pile of silicone, copper, plastic, and glass to play arcade games. You didn't invest that much money to write letters and design your own note cards. (Two thousand dollars would buy a lot of greeting cards.) Nor did you buy it to get up-to-the-minute sports scores (ESPN), stock market news (MSNBC), or to listen to music (radio and CDs). You invested in a computer, printer, software, and Internet access to help your kids with school.

On the Internet, you can find help with homework, current events, term papers, science projects, and scholastic test preparation. You can even correspond with experts in various fields. Help ranges from online reference works, databases, specialized Web sites, and E-mail correspondence.

How to Begin

Before using a site, familiarize yourself and your child with what's offered at some of the more popular homework helper sites. Start with those listed in this chapter and in appendix 2. You'll save time later by going directly to the sites most likely to help.

Next, with an assignment in front of you, sit down and define what information you need. List all the places where you think you can find the information. What sites do you already know about? Will a homework site be the best place to start? If so, which one? Should you start with a reference site offering almanacs, dictionaries, and encyclopedias? If your assignment concerns current events, start with news sites. Should you start with a search engine? What keyword(s) or phrase should you use? Be specific but not so specific that your search returns few, if any, relevant results.

Places to Begin

For the student looking for help on the Internet, resources fall into four broad categories. The two most common sites you and your child will turn to are homework sites and search engines. Also useful, however, are reference and specialized sites.

Homework Sites

Homework sites won't do your kids' homework for them; however, they do provide a directory of sites listed by subject. These directories point your student to sites where they can find needed information. Many sites offer help according to grade level. Typically, they divide their help between elementary school, middle and high school, and college. Often these sites contain the word *homework*, as in: Homework Central, Homework Helper, Homework Help, and Homework Center.

Many homework sites have volunteers who assist students with questions. These volunteers include teachers, scientists, and college students. On most sites your child can search for previously answered questions or post their own question. If you E-mail or post a question to a bulletin board, you'll have to wait one to three days for an answer.

Most homework sites are free, but some offer access to larger databases or services for a fee. Fees range from ten to fifty dollars a year. Before signing up for such a service, make sure your child needs it. With a little experience and work, you can probably find much of the same information elsewhere on the Web.

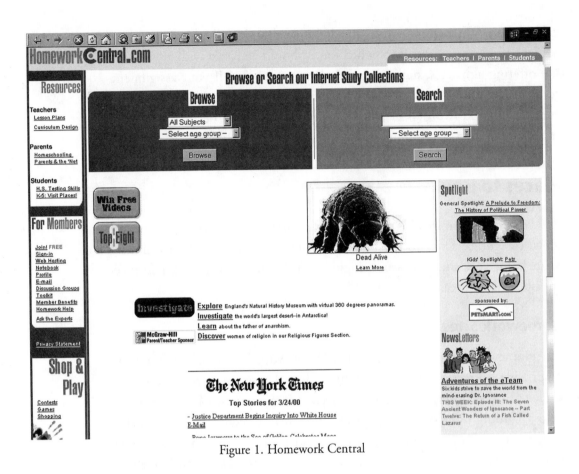

Figure 1. Homework Central

Search Engines

Some homework sites, like Infoplease's Homework Central (see figure 1), are actually specialized search engines, collecting and cataloging only those sites most likely to help students. In addition, there are search engines designed for children. These include: Ask Jeeves for Kids, Yahooligans, and AOL's "Ask a Teacher" (keyword: homework). Older students may want to use a filtered search engine, like AltaVista Family Filter, GO Network, Searchopolis, and Crosswalk.

Ask Jeeves for Kids is the most popular question-and-answer search engine (see figure 2). Type in your question and get back the answer and links you need.

Enter a question at Homework Helper, check what type of reference materials you want to search—magazines, maps, books, newspapers and news wires, TV and radio, pictures—and receive an annotated list of resources.

A little-known site is The Learning Network on the *New York Times* Web site. This site contains three annotated lists of helpful Web sites—one for parents, one for students, and one for teachers. When you don't know exactly where to start your search, this is a good place to begin.

Reference Sites

Reference sites include encyclopedias, almanacs, dictionaries, and grammar helps. Reference sites offer short, concise articles on various

Figure 2. Ask Jeeves for Kids

subjects. Some, like Encarta and the Encyclopedia Britannica Web site, offer full access if you are willing to pay a membership fee. Others offer full access if you own a CD or printed version of their materials. Again, before paying, make sure your child needs what is offered.

Specialized Sites

In addition to homework sites, there are sites specializing in individual subjects. You'll find links to many of the better ones on the homework sites. As you use these sites, you'll find some more helpful than others. Have a math question? Go to Ask Dr. Math. Need help on how to do a research project? Check out Researchpaper.com (see figure 3). If chemistry is your

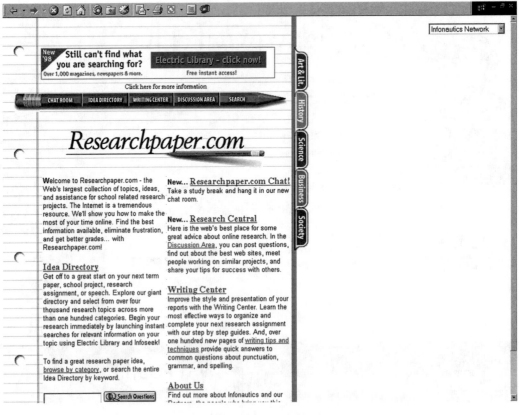

Figure 3. Researchpaper.com

need, there's Chemfinder and Chemical Elements.com. There are specialized sites for science project ideas; SAT, ACT, and PSAT test prepping; human anatomy; dissecting a virtual frog; maps; presidents; NASA; and more.

If you need a place to begin, start with the nine homework sites listed in the "Where to Begin" sidebar. For a more extensive list, see homework and reference sites in appendix 2. If you want some practice, take the Homework Challenge found in the sidebar.

Don't forget to bookmark the useful sites. Create a separate folder called "Homework" to hold your children's bookmarks.

Where to Begin

Homework Central	www.homeworkcentral.com
Homework Helper	www.homeworkhelper.com
Homework Help	www.startribune.com/education/homework.shtml
Infoplease Homework Center	www.infoplease.com/homework/index.html
Researchpaper.com	www.researchpaper.com
StudyWeb	www.studyweb.com
AOL NetFind Kids Only	www.aol.com/netfind/kids
Ask Jeeves for Kids	www.ajkids.com
Searchopolis	www.searchopolis.com

Documenting Online Information

Note cards and footnotes are still an essential part of research, even in the computer age. Properly documenting online information is as important as documenting traditional information sources. Currently, there is no single authority on how to document online resources. However, there does seem to be a general consensus among college and reference sites as to what is correct. Before using these suggestions, your student should ask his teacher. If no instructions are given, here is a recommended style.

In creating a footnote or bibliography, you will need the same basic information you would from a book or periodical: author, article title, date posted or last updated (if given), and the title of the complete work. In addition you will need the URL (Web address), the name of the Web site, and the date the information was accessed. The name of the Web site isn't always needed, but it is good to have. Sometimes the Web site name and the title of the completed

Homework Challenge

Pick a search engine and see if you can find the answers to the following five questions. Be sure to save the answer to each one and the Web site where you found it.

1. What is the official Space Shuttle Web site?
2. Define the term *aerobic?*
3. Where would you find information on deer ticks?
4. What is the population of Equador?
5. What is the atomic symbol and weight of zinc?

work are the same. Teach your student to look for and record all necessary information before leaving the Web site.

I suggest you have your child print out a copy of the information he or she is using. Most browsers will print the title of the page, the Web page address, and the date accessed on the document. If this information doesn't print, have your child write it (and any other bibliographical information needed) on the printout. He or she will need it for documenting purposes or if needing to return to the site.

The following is an example of an article citation from the Internet:

Reaves, Ken. "Finding the Right Internet Service Provider." Internet for Families, 19 November 1999. www.internetforfamilies.org/tips/isp.htm (22 November 1999).

When citing an E-mail message, include the author, subject line, E-mail address, date of message, and date of access (if different). When referencing an E-mail from a friend or acquaintance, omit the E-mail address, inserting the words *personal E-mail* in place of the address.

- Reaves, Ken. "Eliminating Spam." ken@internetforfamilies.org (10 November 1999).
- Jones, Mike. "Another Hoax E-mail," personal E-mail (11 November 1999).

Citing Web pages and E-mail are the most common forms of citation you and your kids will use. The format is a little different for referencing FTP, Gopher, Usenet, images, and other electronic media. For more information on citing these resources, check out the following Web sites:

- "Style Sheets for Citing Internet Resources: MLA, APA, Turabian" was written by Janice Walker of the University of South Florida. Her style sheet was adapted by the UC Berkeley Teaching Library Internet Workshops. It is endorsed by the Alliance for Computers and Writing. www.lib.berkeley.edu/TeachingLib/Guides/Internet/MLAStyleSheet.html.
- Library and Information Science: Citation Guides for Electronic Documents. This site offers examples and links to other style guides on the Internet. www.ifla.org/I/training/citation/citing.htm.

Don't Forget the Library

I spent many afternoons browsing the musty shelves of the public library in the small town where I grew up. I learned a lot about the subject I was studying, but I learned more than that. I learned how to do research. I learned to ask for help when I was stuck. I learned persistence, when finding what I was looking for wasn't as easy as I first thought. I learned how one subject related to another by exploring other books around those I researched. I discovered facts, truths, and ideas unrelated to my topic because I was forced to read entire chapters and books. By investing time in the library, I learned to love books, reading, and learning.

The library is still the best place for in-depth research. You don't find many four-hundred-page books on the Internet. Neither will you find many out-of-date books, complete copies of scholarly journals, rare maps, or photos on the Internet.

On the other hand, the Internet excels at current information. It may be in the form of text, sound, video, or graphics. The Internet also excels at connecting you with others who know. It is surprising how many busy experts will respond to a simple E-mail written by your child. My son has had scientists as well as corporate officers respond to requests for information. Then again, sometimes the person who responds is simply an individual who turned an interest or a hobby into a lifework.

Three Cautions

1. Don't wait until the last minute. When I was in school, the temptation was to wait until the last minute, grab an encyclopedia, read the related article, and write a paper from memory. Nowadays, it's easy to succumb to the temptation of using the Internet as a shortcut to the hard work that goes into doing a paper well or procrastinating and then use the Internet to "bail you out."

2. Avoid information overload. The Internet makes it easy to find a lot of information quickly. Before you know it, however, you can print out half a ream of information. The real challenge is to find accurate information quickly. Be selective. Pick only the best sources. Print what you need, and leave the rest in cyberspace.

3. Parents: Don't do the work for your children. Although it may be easier to hop online, type in a few keywords, find the sites, and even print out the information, that's not your job as a parent. You should be a coach. Encourage them. Let them sit down at the computer and do the tough research. Look over their shoulder and guide them through a search as they master a new skill, but don't do it for them. It's their homework, not yours.

> ## Where to Find the Answers to the Homework Challenge
>
> 1. Kennedy Space Center
>   www.ksc.nasa.gov/
> 2. Merriam Webster Online
>   www.m-w.com
> 3. Start with Ask Jeeves
>   www.aj.com
> 4. CIA World Fact book
>   www.cja.gov/cia/publications/fact-book/index.html
> 5. Chemical Elements.com
>   www.chemicalelements.com

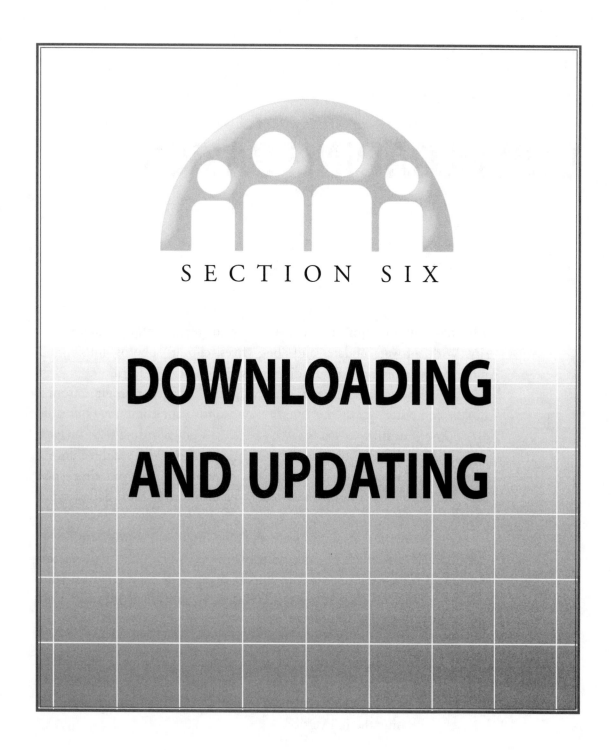

SECTION SIX

DOWNLOADING
AND UPDATING

CHAPTER 24

DOWNLOADING BASICS

Downloading files from the Internet is no longer an option—it's a necessity. With software updates and "bug" fixes, clip art, photos, music, and more available online, downloading is a skill you need to learn.

Downloading is the process of moving a file, image, or program from a distant computer, across the Internet, and onto your computer. Actually, every time your browser loads a Web page, it is downloading files, images, and sometimes small programs from the Internet. You don't see these downloads because they are done in the "background." When you clear your cache or Temporary Internet Files folder, you are deleting those downloaded files.

One of the most attractive features of the Internet is all the "stuff" you can find and download. The most obvious reason you'll want to download a program from the Internet is to update or upgrade a program on your computer. But there are many other reasons to download files and programs. Here are some examples:

- You're doing research and there is a PDF (Portable Document Format) file you need.
- You want to download a trial version of a software program before purchasing the full version.

- Your daughter finds a free graphic image she wants to use on a party invitation.
- Your son wants to download a browser plug-in (a small program that runs inside another program) so he can play games with his friends online.
- You find a free program that will help you organize your baking recipes.
- You want to order and download a program directly from the Internet, saving both time and money.

How It Works

Downloading from the Internet requires a special protocol, called FTP or File Transfer Protocol. This protocol enables your computer to request and receive files and programs from another computer on the Internet. It wasn't long ago that you needed a separate program to download files. Today, however, both Internet Explorer and Netscape have built-in FTP support. You also use FTP to upload files to the Internet.

When you request a download, your computer negotiates an FTP connection with the remote computer. Once connected, you are asked where you want to save the file on your hard drive. The computer then takes over and begins sending the file or program across the Internet. As with a Web page, the file is divided into small data packets so it can be easily transferred. Your computer notifies you when the download is complete.

Downloading a file can take anywhere from a few seconds to a few hours. How long it takes depends on the size of the file and the speed of your connection. The larger the file, the longer it will take to download. The faster your connection, the faster your file will download. A 28.8K connection takes twice as long to download the same file as a 56K connection. The time of day also influences how long it takes. If you're trying to download at a busy time of day, your download will take a lot longer than if you choose a time when fewer people are online.

What's Available

If it can be packaged into a file, image, or program, it can be downloaded across the Internet. Downloads fall into three broad categories.

1. Software Programs and Utilities

Software programs range from trial versions that have built-in time limits, to full commercial versions. Utilities are small programs designed to add features to other programs or to stand alone and perform specific actions. Some utilities are very small; others (like virus scanning programs) are large.

Another group of programs is called *freeware* or *shareware*. These programs are produced by individuals who then make them available on the Internet. Freeware programs are free. (There may be an optional registration fee upgrading you to a more powerful version or tech support.) Shareware programs are like freeware, except there is a registration fee. Typically, you can use them free for a set period of time before you must register or remove them from your hard drive.

2. Multimedia

You can find a lot of free multimedia files on the Internet. These include graphic images, photos, video, sound and music files, and electronic presentations. Some companies sell multimedia files across the Internet. With the emergence of MP3 and writeable CDs, you will be able to purchase music by your favorite artist across the Internet. Once downloaded, you can listen to it on your computer, or, with the right equipment, record it on a CD.

3. Text

You can download and print entire books, training manuals, booklets, newsletters, tech support documents, and other printed items from the Internet. Many of these are PDF files. The Portable Document Format was created by Adobe. To view and print these files, you'll need the free Adobe Acrobat Reader (see chapter 27). With the latest generation of Microsoft and Corel Office products, you'll see more and more documents shared on the Internet. Using these programs, you can publish to HTML (the format used by the Web) and make these files available on the Internet.

Where to Find

It is easy to find downloadable files on the Internet. There are Web sites devoted to making freeware and shareware programs readily available. Banner ads promote software and graphic images. Most large Web sites offer downloads from their site or link you to sites that do. Search engines provide links to all types of downloads.

Online companies, like Beyond.com and Outpost.com, sell full versions of software programs for you to download. Most software manufacturers will provide ways for you to purchase and download software directly from them or through an online software company. Software manufacturers also provide "bug" fixes and free updates for software you already own. Often these same companies offer free templates, images, macros, and plug-ins to enhance software you already own.

The problem is not in finding sites that offer downloads; it's in finding the particular download you want or need. If you're looking for software updates or upgrades, always start with the software manufacturer's Web site. When looking for other types of downloads, start with the Web sites that deal with those types of downloads. If looking for utilities, freeware, or shareware, start with reliable Web sites such as C/Net and ZDNet. If searching for graphic images and photos, start with software and magazine publishing sites. Go to entertainment and music sites for video and music. If these sites don't have downloads, they probably have links to sites that do. These sites will be legitimate sites.

Don't forget search engines. When searching for free downloads, don't use the words *download, images,* or *music.* Those words are too broad—your search will produce hundreds of thousands of hits. Instead, be as specific as possible. If you're looking for free Christmas graphics, search using those words. If you're looking for music, specify the style of music and type of file. For example, you might search for: music AND jazz AND midi. This will return a list of jazz music sites that have midi files on them.

The Ten Commandments of Downloading

Downloading can be hazardous to your computer's health if you don't follow some simple guidelines. It can also be hazardous to your own health if you have to lose sleep reformatting a crashed hard drive. If you follow the ten commandments of downloading listed here, you should be safe.

1. I will back up my computer regularly, and before and after any major downloads.

It's rare, but you could download and install a file that crashes your system. If you download from an unsafe site, you could download a virus with the file. You never want to crash your computer, but if it happens, you'll be glad you backed up your data. (For more information see chapter 4, "Maintaining Your System.") Remember, a computer can crash anytime. Regular backups protect your data.

2. I will run ScanDisk and Disk Defragmenter regularly.

Again, we talked about this in chapter 4. To start these programs, choose **Start** from the taskbar, then **Programs, Accessories, System Tools**. At the very minimum, you should run ScanDisk at least once a week; Disk Defragmenter, once a month. If you have Windows 98, use the Maintenance Wizard to schedule these maintenance procedures at recommended intervals.

3. I will be as familiar as possible with the sites from which I download.

Only download from sites you trust. You'll want to download from sites that guard against viruses in their files, protect any information you give them, and provide only the latest in software. Often major companies contract out their downloads. If you were sent (by a link) to a different site to download a file, you can trust it.

4. I will download only what I need.

It's easy to go download crazy—downloading every interesting file, image, sound bite, or program you find. If you're not careful, however, you can quickly fill your hard drive. Plus, the more freeware and shareware you download and install, the greater the chance you'll "hit a bump," where one program doesn't work well with another one.

5. I will keep my virus protection software up-to-date and running properly.

If you have any questions, read chapter 9, "Protecting Your Computer." Make it a habit to scan a file before opening it. Some people feel this is overkill, but it takes only a few moments to open your antivirus software and tell it to scan the desired file.

6. I will always read the download instructions before I download.

Every site is different. Even if you've downloaded from a site before, the procedure can change. Always read the download instructions.

7. I will always save downloaded programs to the disk.

When you start a download, Windows asks if you want to save it to disk or open and run it from the remote server. Downloading and then running the file later is safer. If you get disconnected or something goes wrong with the connection, you might have half a program installed on your computer. This could cause problems. Even if it installs properly, you might have to reinstall the program later. If you didn't save it to disk, you'll have to download it again.

8. I will scan all downloaded files for viruses before opening.

Most virus protection programs scan as you download files. Make sure your program is set to do so. Even then, a virus could get through. Saving the file to disk allows you the opportunity to scan it again before opening. If you download from reputable sites, you probably don't have to worry about viruses. But it doesn't hurt to be careful. If anything goes wrong in the installation process or after installing, you can rule out viruses in the download as one source of the problem.

9. I will purchase and learn to use a good uninstaller program.

Never try to remove a program from your hard drive by merely deleting the program folder. Programs scatter files all across your hard drive and make changes to key system files. Many provide built-in uninstallers. Unfortunately, they don't always remove all the files and folders and restore your computer to the way it once was before the program was installed. To remove programs effectively, you need an uninstaller program.

10. I will respect and observe all copyright laws.

If something is printed, drawn, recorded, programmed, or created in any way, it is copyrighted. This is true even if there is no copyright notice. The very act of creating it makes it copyrighted, according to federal law. Therefore, if you want to use it, you must have copyright permission.

The copyright notice is located somewhere on the Web page, usually in a text file accompanying the download or in the EULA (End User License

Agreement). The notice tells you what you can and cannot do with the downloaded file. Please read this notice and abide by its limitations.

Copyright law also extends to information and pictures on a Web page. If you plan to use information found on someone's Web site, you need to seek permission from the author or webmaster.

There are two exceptions: Generally, you can download or print something from the Internet for personal use; and in a school setting, there are exceptions for educational use. In all other cases you must seek copyright permission.

To secure copyright permission, send a message to the author, webmaster, or other individual listed on the Web site. Include the author's name, title, and where the item can be found. In the case of the Internet, supply the URL. Explain how you plan to use the information and indicate the number of copies you wish to produce. Be sure to provide your name, address, phone number, and E-mail address. These permission guidelines apply to books, magazines, tapes, and all other recorded or printed items. For more information, there are a number of Web sites you can visit.

- United States Copyright Office   www.loc.gov/copyright
- University of Virginia   www.virginia.edu/~urelat/
  Guide/PartII-9.htm
- Copyright Law in the Computer   www.mame.gen.ml.us/profdev/
  Age (Michigan Association for   mame25/handouts/copyright/
  Media in Education)   index.htm

Downloading images, files, and programs from the Internet can be fun—if you abide by these guidelines. Now that you understand what downloads are, let's look at how you actually download files and images.

CHAPTER 25

DOWNLOADING FILES AND IMAGES

In the last chapter, we looked at how downloading works; why you want to download images, files, and programs from the Internet; and some very important considerations for when you download. In this chapter, I will walk you through the process of actually downloading both a file and a graphic image. We will use the download page on the Internet for Families Web site.

Downloading a File

Most of the time you'll be downloading files from the Internet. A file can contain a complete program, a single program file, a software fix, a text document, or an image. Once you've learned to download a file, you can download just about anything from the Internet.

Downloading files and images is a simple process if approached correctly. I've broken the process into four steps.

1. Create a folder for your downloaded file

Before downloading a file for the first time, create a special downloads folder on your hard drive. This will help you keep track of your downloads. When you keep them in one place, you'll always know where to find them.

To create a downloads folder, open Windows Explorer. Make sure you are on the C drive by highlighting it in the folders' window. Choose **File, New, Folder** from the Menu bar. Name the new folder: My Downloads. Close Windows Explorer.

Now, every time you download a file, you'll save it to your My Downloads folder. You'll never lose a download again. Whenever you need to find a downloaded file or image, you'll know exactly where to begin looking.

2. Find the file you want to download

For our example, we'll download a file from my Web site. You will have a choice of two or three files. It doesn't matter which one you select.

Before you can download the file, you first have to locate it. Point your browser to the Internet for Families Web site. The address is www.internetforfamilies.org. On the home page you can find the file in either of two ways.

First, you can search for it using the search box. In the search box, type: download. Click **Search**. Check the results for the link to the downloads page.

Or you can use the Navigation bar to move through the site and find the downloads page. The downloads page is located in the Family Fun section. Follow the Family Fun link to the downloads page.

3. Read the download instructions

Before you download the file, read the instructions. On this page they are quite brief. It's important to get into the habit of reading instructions before you begin a download. The download instructions will tell you if you must register before you download or if there are any special steps unique to the site. Even if you've downloaded from a site before, the procedure might have changed. It pays to reread the information.

4. Download the file

Select the file you want to download by clicking the hyperlink. Sometimes you'll download the file directly from the description page. At other times you will be directed to another page. On some larger sites, such as Microsoft, you'll be sent to a third party's Web site for the actual download. If you're given a choice of sites from which to download, select the site geographically closest to you.

When you click the download link, the File Download box appears (see figure 1).

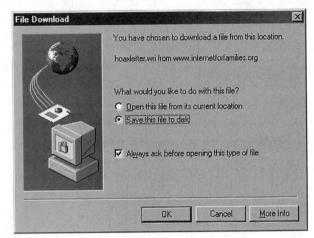

Figure 1. File Download box

Choose **Save this program to disk**, and click **OK**. Always save downloaded files to the disk. Make sure the "Always ask before opening this type of file" box is checked.

When the Save As window appears, use the Navigation bar to move to the My Downloads folder. Double-click the folder to open it. Begin the download by clicking **Save** (see figure 2).

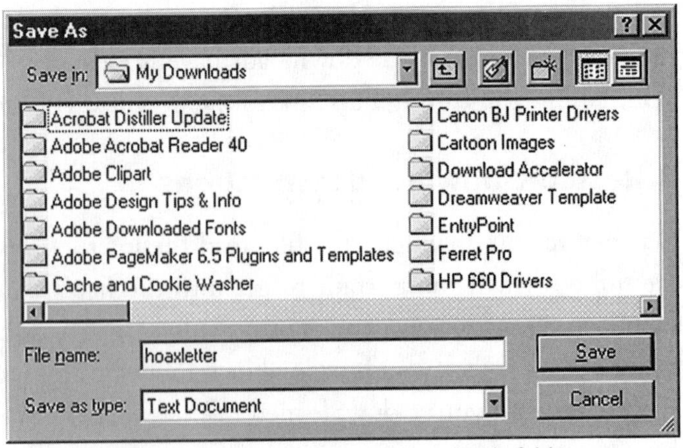

Figure 2. Saving file to My Downloads folder

The File Download box reappears, giving you the status of your download. Windows will notify you when the download is complete (see figure 3). In the next chapter, we'll learn how to install and uninstall downloaded programs.

Downloading an Image

There are two ways to download an image. You can download it as a file or use the Save As command to save it. The site and the type of image file will determine how you will need to download the image. Image files other than JPEG and GIF are downloaded as files. JPEG and GIF image files are file formats used on the Internet. Depending on the site, individual files in these formats can be downloaded using the Save Picture As command in Internet Explorer or the Save Image As command using Netscape.

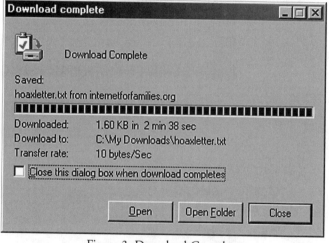

Figure 3. Download Complete

Downloading an Image as a File

To download images as a file, follow the same procedure you used to download other types of files. (Use the directions given in the previous section.) Remember the following when downloading an image as a file:

1. The file may be in a zipped format, requiring you to "unzip" or uncompress it before you can use it. (See the next chapter for details on installing files.)
2. Always put the file on your hard drive in a place where you can find it later. I suggest you create a folder called Graphic Images in the My Downloads folder that you created for downloaded files.

3. If you are downloading a single image and the name of the image file doesn't tell you what it is, change it. For example, change "332af.tif" to "elephant.tif"—or whatever name best describes the image. When renaming the image, don't change the extension. The extension is that which appears after the dot. Most image files will have one of the following extensions: BMP, TIF, WPG, WMF, JPG, or GIF. These extensions tell your software programs that it is an image file.

Before reading further, try to download an image as a file. On the Fun and Free Downloads page of the Internet Families Website, you'll find two images to download as files. Follow the above procedure for downloading files and download either or both of these images.

Downloading an Image Using the Save As Command

GIF and JPEG images can often be downloaded using the Save As command. In this example, we'll download an image found on our site's Downloads page. Follow these steps:

Figure 4. Save Picture As

1. Read the download and copyright instructions.
2. Preview the images by scrolling through them.
3. Place your cursor on the image you wish to save and right-click with your mouse. Choose **Save Picture As** from the pop-up menu (see figure 4).
4. When the Save Picture box appears, select where you want the image saved and the name of the image.

Retrieving Saved Images

Open Windows Explorer from your program list and go to the folder where you saved the images. Or open your word processor or other publishing program and use the Insert or Add Image command to find your saved images.

Organizing Your Downloads

There are two common problems people run into with downloaded files. First, they forget where they saved them. Second, because file names are often cryptic, they forget which file is which. Both problems are easily solved if you take the time to organize your downloads. Organizing your downloads also allows you to reinstall them if necessary.

Earlier in this chapter I recommended a six-step method for downloading. The first step was to create a folder on your hard drive called My Downloads. Inside that folder you will want to create different folders for each download. Often the name of a file reveals little about the contents of the file. Do you have any idea what the ar40eng file is? I did the day I downloaded it, but not six months later. However, because it's in a subfolder named Adobe Acrobat Reader 4, I know what file it is. If I ever need to reinstall Adobe Acrobat Reader, I'll be able to find it quickly.

To create a subfolder, double-click on the file you want to download. Before clicking **Save** to start the download, create a subfolder inside the My Downloads folder. Click on the Create New Folder button. Rename the folder, giving it a descriptive name. Press **Enter** to save the change. Double-click on the new folder to open it. Click **Save** to start the download.

Saving files to disk in an organized manner provides another benefit. There are times when you need to reinstall a program. It may be because you are upgrading to a new computer or hard drive, or perhaps the program isn't working properly. If you've saved your downloaded files, you can reinstall them at any time.

When archiving downloads, you don't have to keep them on your C drive. If you have a large hard drive, it's probably partitioned—divided into two or three sections. Each section has a drive letter. For example, a 10 gigabyte hard drive might be divided into a C, D, and E drive. If your hard drive is partitioned, store your downloads on another drive besides C. This provides more space for programs that typically install to the C drive.

If you haven't already tried downloading a file or two, do it now. You can't hurt anything. Go to the Internet for Families Web site and give it a try.

CHAPTER 26

INSTALLING AND UNINSTALLING

In chapter 25 we learned the four steps to successfully downloading a file. This chapter will cover the three steps to installing that file or program. Once you've found and downloaded the files you want, they need to be installed. Software updates and patches, complete programs, templates, and macros (for programs like Microsoft Word) all need to be installed before you can use them.

Nowadays most software manufacturers routinely post patches, fixes, and updates to programs on the Internet. This is convenient for both the manufacturer and you. The manufacturer saves production and handling costs; you get the updates you need quickly and easily. Plus, you save time and money.

After we learn how to install a program, we'll look at how to uninstall it. Many software companies provide trial versions for you to test before investing money in a new program. Others allow you to try a full version of the software for a limited time. When the trial period is over, the program shuts down. These trial versions must be uninstalled. Also, you will occasionally find that you no longer need or use a particular program. If that's the case, uninstall it to save space on your hard drive.

Installing a File or Program

Installing a file or program is a three-step process.

1. Check the download for viruses

Most antivirus programs autoscan files as they are downloaded. To make sure it is set to scan automatically, open your antivirus software and see if the autoprotect or autoscan feature is enabled. If it is not, enable it. Depending on the settings, this feature will scan files as you download them. If you need help, consult the online help file in your antivirus program.

Viruses can sometimes slip through the download process. For example, your antivirus software may not be able to detect macroviruses or other viruses hiding in E-mail attachments until you try to open the attachment. The only way to check it is to manually scan the file. It might be considered a little paranoid to rescan a download, but why take chances? It takes only a minute to scan a file manually. It can take hours to remove a virus once it's unleashed on your system.

To scan a file for viruses, find the downloaded file on your hard drive. If you created a My Downloads folder, or something similar, open Windows Explorer and change to the folder. Find the file you want to install and right-click on it. Select the virus scan option from the pop-up menu. Your virus scan software will scan the file and report the results. If the file is virus-free, you're ready to install. If the file contains a virus, follow your virus software's recommendations for removing the file and virus from your hard drive.

2. Unzip the file

Files you download from the Internet are in what is called a compressed format. A compressed program is like a can of frozen orange juice. The manufacturer has removed the water, making it cheaper to package, ship, and store. When you're ready to use it, you open the can, pour the contents into a container, and add water.

Those who post files and programs on the Internet do the same. (In fact, almost all programs you buy are compressed, even those on CDs or diskettes.) They have removed the programming-equivalent of all the water from the program. Making them as small as possible makes it easier and quicker for you to download them from the Internet. Once you've downloaded the file, you have to "add water." You have to expand the program to its full size.

Downloaded files come in two compressed formats. Some files are self-extracting. You identify these files by the EXE extension on the end of the file name: go4it.exe. All EXE files are program files. They have a built-in program that uncompresses them automatically. You simply double-click on the file to start the installation process.

Other compressed files are called zip files. You identify them by the ZIP extension, as in go4it.zip. These files do not have a built-in extraction program. They require a program such as PKZip or WinZip to open them.

Zip Programs	
Aladdin Expander	www.aladdinsys.com
PKZIP	www.pkware.com
NetZip Classic	www.netzip.com
WinZip	www.winzip.com
Zip Free 2000	www.pepsoft.com

There are a number of freeware zip programs on the Internet, or you can invest in a more elaborate one. If you plan to download many files from the Internet, you'd be wise to invest in a retail version. Five top programs are listed in the sidebar.

Note: In Windows 95, 98, and 2000, common file extensions are typically hidden. To identify what type of compressed file you have, look in the Type column in Windows Explorer. An EXE file is identified as an application in the Type column. A Zip file will say ZIP in the same column. Most Zip files will be represented by an icon, shaped like a file folder held by a C-clamp.

To extract the files from a Zip file, double-click on the file. This opens the Zip program (see figure 1). Many zip programs provide a list of the compressed files contained in the downloaded file. Before installing the program, I recommend you open and read the Readme file. Typically, this file contains the latest installation instructions, specifications for the type of computer the program will run on, and any known problems and solutions. When you're ready to install the program, click **Extract** (or the equivalent) and select the location where you want the files saved on your hard drive. In most cases, it's best to save them to the recommended location (see figure 1).

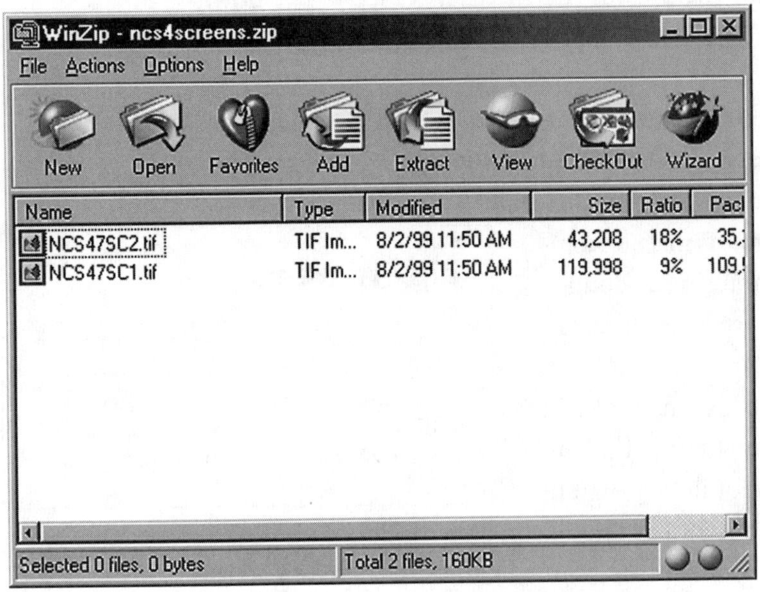

Figure 1. Zip program

3. Install the file

There isn't a standard way to install a downloaded file or program. Most, but not all, EXE programs install themselves as they uncompress. Some EXE and all ZIP files save the uncompressed files in a folder on your hard drive. (This is usually a temporary file that you can later delete.) To install them, follow the installation instructions that come with the program. After you have extracted the files, go to the folder where they were stored. Double-click on the set-up icon to install. Follow the installation instructions as you would for any other program.

Caution: When installing a program, remember to disable your antivirus software before installing. Antivirus software can sometimes interpret the installation procedure as a virus.

Read the Readme files that come with the program. Readme files often contain general information on the program, tips on how to install and use it, and information on any common problems. Even when you purchase a program at a store or by mail order, it's a good idea to read the Readme file. The Readme file will contain the latest information about the program. It will be more current than the information in any accompanying documents.

Uninstalling a Program

Today's programs install files in many different folders on your hard drive. Typically a program creates a folder containing most, but not all, of the files related to the program. Other files will be stored in secondary folders or in the Windows and Program folders. Most programs make changes in the Registry. The Registry is the brain of Windows 95, 98, and 2000. It tells programs where to find their different parts and how to relate to other programs. The program creates a set of shortcut icons on the Start menu and perhaps on the desktop and system tray.

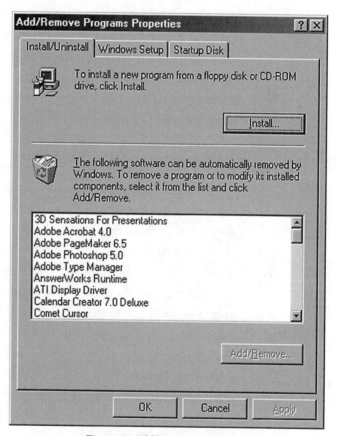

Figure 2. Add/Remove Programs

Removing a program by simply deleting the program folder doesn't work anymore. If you try this method, you'll remove only part of the program. Other files will remain scattered in other folders. If you try to remove those parts, you might delete a file shared with another program. The results would range from a minor headache to a major catastrophe. You do have three other options.

1. Use the program's built-in uninstall program

Many programs contain their own uninstall program. When run, this small program reverses the installation procedure. These programs are not perfect, however. They can leave part of the program on the hard drive or delete a file shared with another program.

2. Use the Add/Remove Program feature of Windows

The second way to remove a program is by using the Add/Remove Program feature built-in to Windows. To use this feature, choose **Start** from the taskbar, then **Settings, Control Panel**. Double-click on **Add/Remove Programs** icon. When the Add/Remove dialog box opens (see figure 2), select the program you wish to uninstall from the list. Click **Add/Remove**. One caution: This doesn't work for all programs.

3. Use an uninstaller program

The best way to uninstall a program is to use a specially written uninstaller program. Typically, an uninstaller program does a better job of cleaning up your hard drive and removing all of a program than a program's built-in uninstall feature. Uninstall programs examine your hard drive, looking for folders, files, and shortcuts that a built-in uninstaller program leaves behind.

These programs do more than uninstall a program; they help keep your programs working properly. They do this by examining the Registry and comparing it to the programs on your hard drive. If an uninstaller program finds problems it can "fix," it will. Today's uninstaller programs can be used to move programs from one drive to another. They can help you find lost space on your hard drive by finding unneeded files and removing them.

There are many good uninstaller programs on the market. Two of the best are Clean Sweep and Uninstaller. Each uninstall program is slightly different, so before using one, read its enclosed manual or online helps.

Installing and using software you find on the Internet is fun and exciting. This is especially true when you tap into the exciting world of multimedia. That's the focus of our next chapter.

CHAPTER 27

MULTIMEDIA PLUG-INS

The Internet without multimedia is like trying to enjoy the Super Bowl by reading about it in the newspaper instead of watching it on television—no audio, no video, no animated graphics, no virtual reality. At one time, the Internet was all text. Today the Internet is a multimedia-rich environment. Your browser, however, is designed primarily to handle text. Multimedia plug-ins fill the gap between text and multimedia.

What Are Plug-Ins?

Plug-ins are small programs that work with your browser, enabling you to enjoy all the Internet has to offer. Once installed, these small programs sit on your hard drive until needed. When a site calls for a certain plug-in, the plug-in runs, enabling you to enjoy all of the Web site.

Plug-ins fall into five broad categories—sound, video, animation, 3D/virtual reality, and utilities. Sound or audio plug-ins enable you to listen to music, concerts, speeches, sermons, commentary, news clips, and more. Video plug-ins allow you to see what you're listening to. Static graphics turn into animated images, and plain text turns into moving text with the help of animation plug-ins. Virtual reality and 3D plug-ins transform two-dimensional images into three-dimensional recreations of everything from parks and museums to worlds that exist only in a pro-grammer's imagination. Utility plug-ins allow you to access information that you might not otherwise be able to receive.

Some plug-ins do more than one job. For example, the RealPlayer plug-in handles both audio and video. Shockwave combines audio with animated graphics.

How Do I Know What I Need?

Typically, a Web site will tell you what plug-in you need. Most sites provide a link to where you can download it if you need to do so. Often, the best approach to plug-ins is to have a collect-as-you-go attitude. When you find an audio, video, or animation that you can't see or hear, then it's time to download the plug-in.

You'll need far fewer plug-ins if you use Internet Explorer. This is because Microsoft has added ActiveX controls to its browser. ActiveX controls take the place of many plug-ins and install directly into your browser. When you arrive at a site requiring an ActiveX control that you don't have, a pop-up window notifies you. You then have the option of installing the control. The pop-up window will have a certificate symbol telling you what the control is, who designed it, and if it is "digitally signed," assuring the control hasn't been tampered with. Some people don't like adding these controls to their computer because of security issues. If you are comfortable with who created the control, then click **Yes** to install it. ActiveX controls are installed to their own file on your hard drive.

Four Plug-ins You Will Want

There are four plug-ins almost everyone needs to have. These four will allow you to access much of the multimedia on the Internet.

1. RealPlayer

RealPlayer and Jukebox enable you to listen to and watch audio and video files. Multimedia files are quite large. If you have to download the entire file before viewing, you're in for a long wait. That's where streaming audio and video come in. Streaming audio/video allows you to begin listening and watching soon after the download begins. When you request a file to listen to, RealPlayer opens (see figure 1) and begins receiving the file from the Web site. Once RealPlayer collects the first few seconds of the file in a buffer, it begins to play the file. As you listen, RealPlayer continues to receive the file from the Internet. This buffer, a few seconds' delay, enables you to listen to the file without interruption. The buffering isn't perfect, but unless the feed is live, you will not miss any of the broadcast. With RealPlayer you can listen to live radio broadcasts;

Figure 1. RealPlayer

concerts; and sports, news, and/or television broadcasts. You can even continue using your browser while listening.

Jukebox is a separate plug-in that enables you to download and listen to MP3 files. MP3 is a newer audio file format, offering CD quality music. To play an MP3 file, you must first download the file to your hard drive. Then double-click on the file, opening the player. The controls are like those on a CD player. Select **Play** and the music starts. MP3 files often contain a picture of the CD cover; information about the musicians, song-writer, and others; and sometimes the notes and lyrics.

There is much pirated music on the Internet; you need to stay away from it. At the same time, there are many legitimate sites where you can download MP3 music. If you find something you like, depending on the site, you can purchase single songs or the CD in MP3 format. These files can then be played on your computer or with an MP3 player. You can find RealPlayer and Jukebox at Real Network's Web site (www.real.com).

2. Shockwave and Flash

Macromedia makes a number of programs that provide full graphic animation. Shockwave combines audio, animation, and text into a unified multimedia presentation. Shockwave is used in online teaching presentations, animated presentations, interactive Web sites, and online games. Once installed, it runs within your browser, giving life to the Shockwave files found on more and more Web sites.

Flash is another plug-in, similar to Shockwave and also made by Macromedia. Like Shockwave, it enables you to view animated graphics made with Macromedia Flash. Once installed, both Shockwave and Flash plug-ins will update themselves automatically. You can find both plug-ins at www.shockwave.com.

3. QuickTime Player

QuickTime is an Apple program that originally ran on Macintosh computers. Today it runs on both Macs and PCs. QuickTime is very popular with video and animation creators. Though it is an older technology, it is considered the standard for video on the Internet. QuickTime has one major drawback: you have to download the entire file before you can play it.

The Quick Tour and Tutorial video presentations that come with many software packages today often require QuickTime. So before you download it, check your Program menu to see if it's already installed. QuickTime is available at www.apple.com.

4. Adobe Acrobat Reader

As you browse the Internet, you will come across files requiring the Adobe Acrobat Reader. These are files written in Portable Document Format (PDF). People use a variety of programs to create documents—Microsoft Word, WordPerfect, Quark, and Adobe PageMaker, just to mention four. However, if you don't have the same program and printer (with the same fonts, images, and settings) as the person who created the files, you won't see them the same as they do. They will be different. A PDF file, viewed or printed using Adobe Acrobat Reader, will look exactly like the original file created on the author's computer.

Adobe Acrobat Reader is a must for reading online software and computer manuals, journal and magazine articles, Tip sheets, brochures, and even books. The IRS publishes all their tax forms and manuals to the Internet in PDF format. No longer do you have to go to the post office or library to get a copy of a form. Simply log on to the IRS site (www.irs.gov) and download it. You can download Adobe Acrobat Reader from Adobe's Web site: www.adobe.com.

EntryPoint

EntryPoint, formerly called PointCast, is an example of another type of plug-in. It's not one of the four "must haves" for being able to view multimedia content. It's more of a utility. It is a program that gathers information from different places on the Internet and delivers it to your computer.

If you need a way to keep up-to-date on headline news, stock prices, sports, and weather information, EntryPoint does the job. EntryPoint is a toolbar that sits on the top or bottom of your desktop (see figure 2). The bar has a customized ticker, delivering news, stocks, sports, and weather information. One mouse click provides access to maps and directions,

Figure 2. EntryPoint

yellow pages, people finders, search engines, and more. Like all software, EntryPoint is constantly evolving. If you're interested in this type of program, check it out online at www.entrypoint.com.

How Do I Find Them?

As I mentioned previously, if you run across a file that you can't see or hear, the Web site will often provide a link to where you can download the plug-in for it. Both Netscape's and Internet Explorer's Web sites have lists of plug-ins for their browsers. There are even Web sites devoted to collecting plug-ins. The fastest way to find a plug-in is to type the name into a search engine and go to the plug-in creator's Web site.

Installing Plug-Ins

Once you find the plug-ins you need, you'll need to download them. I suggest you create a folder on your hard drive called Browser Plug-ins. If you created the My Downloads folder as suggested in chapter 25, then put this new folder inside it. When you download a plug-in, choose the Save to Disk option and store it in its own folder inside the Browser Plug-in folder. Organizing your plug-in downloads this way helps you remember which ones are installed. If you ever need to reinstall a plug-in, you can find it easily. (If you need additional help downloading, see chapter 25, "Downloading Files and Images.")

Unfortunately, some plug-ins don't give you the option of downloading to your hard drive. They install themselves directly into your browser. This isn't the best method because if you reinstall or upgrade your browser or have to reinstall the plug-in, you have to go through the download-install procedure again. Some plug-ins require you to restart your computer after installing. This means logging off the Internet, shutting everything down, restarting, and relogging on to the Internet. If the plug-in gives you a choice, always opt for saving it to disk. This gives you a backup. Installing from the hard drive is quicker and easier than from the Internet.

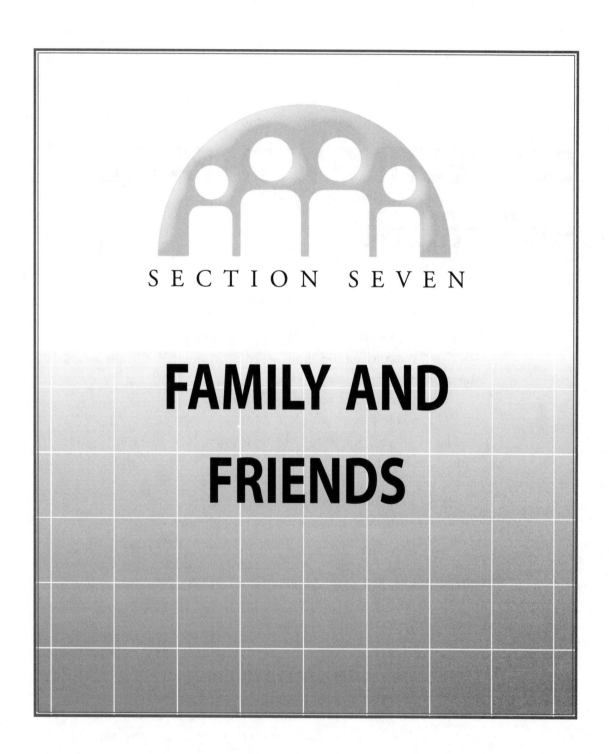

SECTION SEVEN

FAMILY AND FRIENDS

CHAPTER 28

CONNECTING WITH FAMILY AND FRIENDS

Hello," Sue answered as she picked up the phone.

"Sue?" the voice on the phone asked uncertainly. "Is this the Sue Martin who attended Florida State in 1955?"

"Why, yes it is," she replied. "Who is this?"

"This is Jane Jones."

"Jane . . . Jane Jones, my old roommate? How did you find me? It's been . . . what, forty . . . no, forty-five years!" Sue nearly shouted into the phone.

"Why, I found you on the Internet."

"On the Internet? I don't even have a computer."

Keeping up with family and friends is one of the reasons many people get online in the first place. In this chapter, you'll learn how and where to look for people. Not only can you find others who are online, but you can find people who don't even have Internet access. They may not even have a computer.

Connecting with Others Online

Nowadays it seems that almost everyone has an E-mail address. With free services like Juno, you don't need Internet access to benefit from having an E-mail account. And with computers becoming more and more available at work and in schools, libraries, and community centers, you don't need your own computer to have E-mail. This means more and more people are online, making it easier to find and stay in touch with family and friends. But how do you find them?

Sometimes people forget the most obvious way to get a family member's or friend's E-mail address: Ask them! Don't laugh; some of you hadn't thought of that either—at least not while you were talking to them. We get so busy during the day that we forget to ask for someone's E-mail address until we have a need for it later. Get in the habit of asking your friends for their E-mail addresses. Most people, especially people you know, will be more than happy to give it to you. Remember, though, that if they give you a workplace E-mail address, you need to ask what they can receive. Keep such E-mail messages short.

Do you send Christmas cards? Maybe you include a family newsletter in your card, as we do. If so, include your E-mail address. You can even include a business card with your name, address, phone number, and E-mail address. On the back side, you might want to print a reminder: "Would love to hear from you; please E-mail us." (You can find blank business card stock at any office supply store and can create a nice business card in just a few minutes by using the templates that come with most word processing programs.)

But why wait until Christmas? The next time you send a note, include your card. While you're at it, make a few extra business cards and put them in your wallet or purse. When you see a friend or family member, give them a card. If they can't remember their E-mail address, ask them to E-mail you. When they do, add them to your E-mail address book. (See chapter 17 for help with this.)

Another way to get someone's E-mail address is to ask a mutual friend for it. This works well if the mutual friend has E-mail. If they do, send them a note asking for the address you need. Ask them if this friend will mind them sending you their address. If they have your friend's address and send it to you, always make sure you preface your first E-mail to your mutual friend with a note inquiring whether it's OK to E-mail them. Sometimes people don't want their E-mail addresses passed around. Perhaps their only E-mail address is at work, or they access their E-mail only once a week from the library.

Finding People Online

What if you don't have a mutual friend or you don't see someone often enough to ask for his or her address? Just as there are search engines to help you

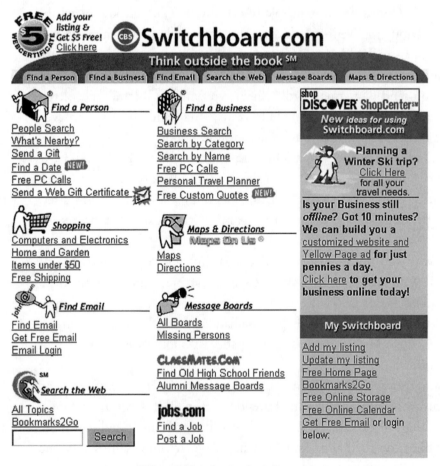

Figure 1. People search engine

find information on any subject you're interested in, there are search engines to help you find people. These specialized search engines are called directories or people finders. Today, most major search engines have their own set of directories or have created a partnership with another directory service (see figure 1).

Using a directory is similar to using a search engine. Instead of entering a keyword or phrase, enter the person's name. Because so many people share the same name, most directories ask for additional information in order to narrow the results. The most common information requested is their state of residence. Once you've entered the information you have, the search engine will return results.

If you don't find someone on the first try, don't get discouraged. Make sure you spelled the name correctly. Use a first initial instead of a first name. Try entering variations of the first name. For example, you won't find me by searching for "Kenneth," but you will if you search for "Ken." Use any advanced search features on the site. If you've lost track of the person, try an adjoining state or see if the search engine will search without a state. Note: You may end up with a long list of results to look through.

Like search engines, there isn't a single directory that contains a list of everyone online. Some directories rely on people registering themselves. Others collect names and addresses from various sources. If you don't find what you need, have patience and try again using a different directory (see table 1).

If you are looking for an old college roommate, army buddy, or service group, there are special directories to help. Your success depends a lot on

Table 1
People Finders

InfoSpace	www.infospace.com
Switchboard	www.switchboard.com
WhoWhere?	www.whowhere.lycos.com
Yahoo! People Search	http://people.yahoo.com

Table 2
Specialized People Finders

ClassMates.com	www.classmates.com
Planet Alumni	www.planetalumni.com
About.Com Military Locators	http://usmilitary.about.com/business/usmilitary/msub13.htm

the school from which you graduated or the group you were part of together.

To search for a college roommate, start with your college Web site. If the alumni office doesn't offer an online directory, E-mail them. Ask if they keep a list or recommend a specific directory for looking for old classmates. If you were in a fraternity or sorority together, start there. The same advice goes for high school classmates and service buddies. There are a few specialized directories that offer help (see table 2).

Finding People Who Aren't Online

A person doesn't have to be online for you to find them. "White pages" are online directories similar to the phone book you have stuffed in the kitchen drawer. Depending on the directory, you can search for E-mail address, mailing address, and phone number.

Some people finders, such as AnyWho, allow you to do a reverse look-up. If you have someone's phone number, you can use it to find their full name and address. Once you've found this information, search again for their E-mail address.

Finding and Making New Friends

There are lots of ways to find and make new friends online. Many larger Web sites strive to build community among their visitors by hosting chat rooms. These chat rooms are online coffeehouses. You can sit and "listen" by reading the discussion, or "add your two cents" by entering into the conversation on your keyboard. Joining a mailing list can also lead to an online friendship, or you can use an online pen-pal service to find someone with similar interests.

One word of warning: people are not always what they seem online. They can pretend to be anyone they want to be on the Internet. To protect your privacy and safety, always follow the guidelines found in section 2, "Family-Safe, Family-Friendly."

Finding Businesses Online

Some of the people finders have business listings. There are other Web sites, often called "yellow pages," that are business directories (see figure 2 and table 3). The two most popular are Big Yellow and Zip2 Yellow Pages. To use these directories, you'll need the name of the company and the state in which their office is located.

Many regional phone companies host online yellow pages. BellSouth, which covers the Southeast, has the BellSouth Real Yellow Pages. If you

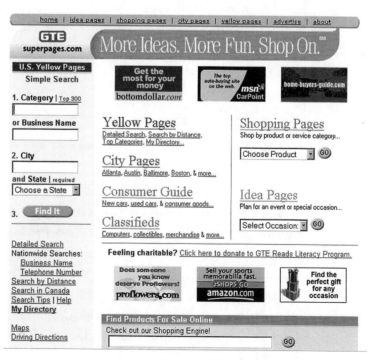

Figure 2. Business Directories

know the name of the regional phone company, look it up online. To do a quick search, use the Go command. Type: go, then the phone company's name, into your browser's address bar. Press **Enter**. Your browser will do a quick search. The phone company's Web site will usually be one of the first ten results.

Some people finders, like Switchboard, have a "nearby" feature. Enter an address, and it will return a list of area businesses, restaurants, parks, entertainment, etc. When on business, vacation, or visiting friends or family, you can use this feature to help plan an outing or side trip or to simply find a place to eat.

Table 3 Business Finders	
Big Yellow	www.bigyellow.com
BigBook Yellow Pages	http://bigbook.com
GTE Superpages	www.superpages.com
InfoSpace	www.infospace.com
Yellowpages.com	www.yellowpages.com
Zip2	www.zip2.com

Privacy

Having your personal information filed on the Internet for anyone to find can be a little unnerving. You can request individual people finders to remove you from their databases. The procedure is different for each people finder. You'll find instructions on how to remove your personal information listed in an FAQ file, the Privacy Policy, or on a separate page accessed by a link. If you can't find what you need, check the contact information found on the home page. Scan the list of contact persons and select the most appropriate one to E-mail. When all else fails, E-mail the webmaster.

Follow instructions to remove all or part of your personal information. Your name, address (with the exception of your E-mail address), and phone number are available to anyone who has access to a large library or local phone book. Since this information is so readily available, some people choose to leave it online while removing all other personal information. You may want to consider changing your E-mail address to a free E-mail address that forwards to the E-mail address assigned by your ISP. This helps protect you from junk E-mailers who might gain access to your address. (For more information on free E-mail accounts, see chapter 18, "E-mail for the Entire Family.")

CHAPTER 29

SENIOR SURFING

Hey, Preach," rang the familiar voice on the other end of the phone. Price was about eighty years old. He was a deacon in my church. More than that, he was a fishing buddy and friend.

"What's up?" I asked.

"I need you to go to West Palm Beach with me in the next few weeks." The pastor side of me kicked in. Price had lost his wife about six months earlier. He'd undergone two different bypass surgeries and also had lung problems. He'd just gotten out of the hospital, so I immediately began to wonder what was wrong. Trying to sound upbeat, I asked, "What are we going for?"

"I want you to help me buy a computer."

"A computer?"

"Yes, a computer. My birthday and Christmas are coming. I thought I'd buy myself a computer as a present and get on the Internet."

A few weeks later, we went to West Palm Beach and purchased a computer and printer. I helped Price get on the Internet, and he participated in the first two Internet for Families seminars I taught at the church.

Within a few weeks, he was E-mailing his nephew in France, as well as family in Atlanta, Tampa, and other parts of the country. A few months later, he walked into my office and announced, "Preach, I'm going to be gone for three weeks. I wanted you to know so you won't worry about me."

"Where are you going?" I asked.

"I'm heading to Georgia. I just found some family I didn't know I had. I'm going to go introduce myself."

"How did you find them?"

"On the Internet, of course," he answered over his shoulder as he headed out the door.

The Internet is getting older. More and more senior adults are logging on. They comprise one of the fastest-growing segments of the Internet. In the United States, senior adults represent almost one in five users of the Internet.

When online, senior adults use the Internet primarily for E-mail and research. News and current events come in third, with investing and finances fourth. Other commonly expressed uses of the Internet by seniors include weather, travel, sports, and online shopping. Many seniors are discovering online communities where they meet and make new friends. Some of these online groups have organized face-to-face gatherings. Members of SeniorNet have booked blocks of rooms on cruises, attended regional luncheons, talked on the telephone, and invited other senior surfers into their offline lives.[1]

Ten Reasons Why Senior Adults Should Be Online

Those who are not seniors and those who don't work with seniors often have the wrong impression about senior adults. They are not technophobic. They aren't afraid of technology. If they were, why would they have a VCR, microwave, answering machine, and television with remote in their home? Most senior adults are not afraid of technology; they're just a little skeptical. They want you to show them why they should embrace the latest technology. If they see the personal benefit, they will embrace it.

With that in mind, if you are a senior adult, let me give you my top ten reasons why you should be on the Internet. I will start at number ten and count down to number one.

10. Fun and Entertainment

If you like to play games, work crossword puzzles, attend movies, listen to the radio, or attend concerts or sporting events, you can find lots to keep you busy on the Internet. Play hearts and chess with players from around the world. Print out the daily crossword puzzle from many major newspapers. Listen to live concerts, sporting events, music, talk shows, news, and press conferences. Check out movie reviews, concert schedules, and ticket information for your favorite sports team.

9. Investments and Money Management

On the Internet, you can research stock and investment information. Check your investments, buy and sell stocks, and balance your checkbook online.

8. Travel

Many senior adults love to travel. If you're one of them, you'll be glad to know you can plan, price, and make almost all travel arrangements online. Discover what sights, sounds, and adventures await you at your destination before ever leaving home. Compare room rates, ticket prices, and car rental rates. Print out turn-by-turn maps and directions. Locate interesting side trips along the way. Surf the Internet and discover a vacation destination you never knew existed.

7. Grandkids

Your grandkids are online. They've probably already talked to you about the Internet, telling you about things they've learned and what they do online. They want to include you in this part of their lives.

6. News and Information

Don't wait for the six-o'clock news. Instead, check out breaking news online. Research topics of interest. Check the weather to see if you'll need a jacket or an umbrella when you go out tonight. Get the latest update on your favorite sports team. Keep abreast of your hometown news, even if you haven't lived there in thirty years.

5. Recreation and Hobbies

Do you have a hobby? Are you looking for a new one? Whatever the hobby, you can usually find dozens of sites on the Internet devoted to it. They provide helpful how-to information, materials, and ideas. You can even network with others who share the same hobby or interest.

4. Grandkids

If you're a grandparent, you probably love receiving pictures of your grandkids. With the right equipment, your children can send pictures of your grandchildren minutes after they are taken. You can also chat online with your grandkids—for free—even if you live hundreds of miles apart. You can even play games together across the Internet.

3. Family and Friends

The Internet makes it possible for you to keep up with family and friends. Find lost friends, even if you haven't seen them in twenty or thirty years. Make new friends.

2. Spiritual Growth

Take advantage of online Bible study tools. Find additional helps for teaching your Sunday school class. Form a prayer chain. Correspond with missionaries. Receive daily devotionals by E-mail. Find help on hard-to-answer questions. Grow in your relationship with the Lord using the Internet.

1. Grandkids

I know I've repeated myself three times, but can you think of a better reason to get on the Internet?

Things to Consider

Before purchasing a computer and signing up for Internet access, there are some considerations to keep in mind. The following five questions will help you make an informed decision about getting on the Internet.

1. Where will you learn to use a computer and the Internet?

According to a 1996 survey conducted by SeniorNet, almost four in ten computer owners taught themselves how to use the computer. Learning at work or from a friend were the next two most common answers.[2] The rest took a class.

Almost every community, large or small, offers computer classes. Some are free; others charge a fee depending on the length and content of the class. Check with your local library, senior adult center, or school board. Most large cities have private tutoring centers, and some retail companies offer computer and Internet classes. SeniorNet has more than fifteen hundred learning centers in the United States offering computer courses for senior adults.

Once you are on the Internet, you can visit many sites that contain beginner guides. These sites help you acquire or polish basic Internet skills. Once you feel comfortable moving around the Internet, you might want to consider taking an online class. Classes are offered on every imaginable subject related to the Internet.

2. What are you going to use the computer for?

In chapter 2 I described three types of computer users. If you haven't read that information, I encourage you to do so. What you plan to do with a computer will determine what kind you should purchase. Always keep in mind that if you really begin to enjoy the computer and the Internet, you'll find yourself doing a lot more than you first thought.

3. What are your limitations?

When purchasing a computer, consider the size of the monitor. To lower costs, many companies bundle smallish, fifteen-inch monitors in computer packages. The small fonts (type) and images on these screens might be hard for you to see comfortably. I recommend you pay the difference to substitute a seventeen-inch for the fifteen-inch monitor. If you think you want to stay with the smaller monitor, be sure to use it in the store before making the purchase.

Listen to the speakers. Can you hear them clearly? If the sound seems muffled or distorted, check into a different pair of speakers or a different system. Do the mouse and keyboard feel comfortable? Makes and models vary. If you can't type comfortably, or if the mouse doesn't fit well in your hand, you are not likely to spend a lot of time at the computer. Test these features out before you buy.

It's easy to check these parts out at a retail store. If you are purchasing a mail-order system, visit a friend who has a similar system and try his.

4. How much traveling do you do?

Do you spend a portion of each year traveling, camping, or splitting time between two residences? If you do, you will not want to go too long without your computer. This is especially true if you spend three to six months away from home. If you travel a lot, you should consider a notebook computer. A lot of senior adults I know are opting for a notebook. Full-size keyboards, large screens, and power rivaling their bigger desktop cousins make notebooks a good choice for people who travel a lot. When back at home, you can plug your notebook into a full-size monitor, mouse, and keyboard.

5. Do you really want a hand-me-down?

Probably not. Especially if it's your first computer. Who will you call if it breaks down? Where will you turn for tech support? Yes, your family member or friend who gave it to you has promised to keep it running. But they have a life too. As much as they may want to help, they can't be there every time you need them. They are usually giving the computer away because they have a new one. That means the one you are receiving is too old, too slow, too unreliable, or has a screen that's too small for them. That is not what you want for your first experience with a computer and the Internet.

If you're an adult child encouraging your parents to go online, you want them to have a good experience. Don't discourage them by offering them an outdated and potentially unreliable computer. If you cannot afford to purchase a new computer for them, consider purchasing the equipment and a one-year subscription to WebTV. It won't cost you as much, and it gives them the opportunity to try surfing the Internet and using E-mail before making a major investment.

CHAPTER 30

GETTING IN TOUCH WITH YOUR ROOTS

A growing number of people are embarking on their own family adventure: they are tracing their roots and ever-growing family trees. Many are turning to the Internet for help. A recent survey reported that as many as one-third of AT&T WorldNet subscribers use the Internet for searching out their roots.[1]

This chapter is merely a genealogical primer designed to get you started. Soon you'll move beyond its limitations. When you do, you'll want to read and talk to others about resources to help you continue your family journey.

What You Need to Get Started

Before you start sketching your family tree, you should read a few guides to getting started. Go to your favorite search engine. Do a keyword search using the word *genealogy*. It will return a long list of sites. Scan the list for beginners' guides. Click on a few of the more promising links and read their suggestions (see figure 1). You'll also find a few suggested sites in the "Using the Internet" section of this chapter.

After reading a few guides and perusing what's available on each site, bookmark the best of them. Later, when you begin tracing your roots, you'll

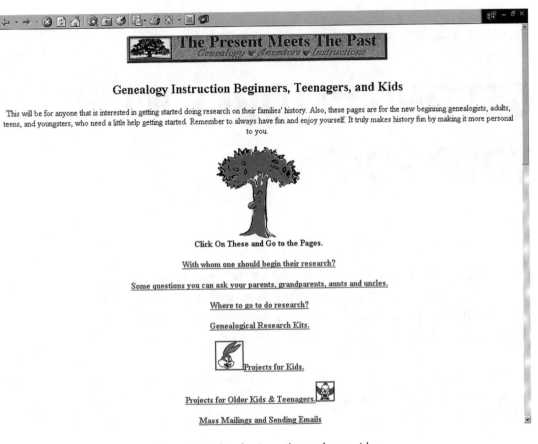

Figure 1. Online beginners' genealogy guide

want to come back to these sites to network with others, find additional how-to help, or do additional research.

When you first get started, you won't need anything more than a pen and notebook. Later you'll want to add some blank genealogy forms and folders. The forms will assist you in collecting all the vital information you need on each member of your family. Some Web sites offer blank forms that you can print out on your own computer. The folders will help you organize and store photos, photocopies of documents, and other records that support your research.

It won't be long before you'll want to invest in genealogy software. There are many good programs available. Choose one that is easy to use, provides a variety of printouts, has guides for unearthing hard-to-find information, and has Web site support. Five of the most popular programs are Family Tree Maker, Family Tree Creator Deluxe, Generations Grande Suite, Personal Ancestral File, and Reunion.

Some of these programs bundle additional CD databases with the software. These databases include Social Security death indexes, military records, marriage licenses, death records, Civil War rolls, and extensive surname directories. Some, like Family Tree Maker, include family trees created by others using that software.

You can also purchase needed CD databases from different sources. For a fee, some Web sites provide online database searching. Before you sign up for one of these online services, however, make sure it offers the type of information you need.

Where to Start

Before logging on to the Internet, begin with the person you know best—yourself. Sit down with a pen and pad of paper and write down what you know about your family. Record the following information for each person: full name (maiden, if married), date and place of birth, date and place of marriage and to whom, military service, date and place of death, and any interesting stories.

Next, either call, write, or E-mail your parents, grandparents, aunts, uncles, and any other living relatives. Tell them what you're doing and ask them to fill in the blanks. If they have any pictures, or birth, marriage, or death certificates, ask them to send you copies.

As you receive information, document and save everything. Record when you received it and from whom. Start with two folders—one for your father's and one for your mother's side of the family. As you add generations, add folders. There isn't one set way of saving the information. Find the method that works best for you and use it. Even when you begin using a program to store your family tree, you'll still need a way of organizing documents.

Once you've traced your family back to your grandparents, begin searching the 1920 and earlier U.S. Census databases. For those born between 1910 and 1919, the 1920 census will give information about their parents, brothers, and sisters. For those born between 1900 and 1909, the information will be in the 1910 census. The same goes for earlier birthdays and census data, back to the 1850 census. Census information prior to 1850 lists only the head of household.

At one time, many states conducted censuses during the middle of the decade. If you know the state in which your ancestors resided, you can search these databases.

As you conduct your search, don't forget family records, such as family Bibles, photos, old letters, wills, land records, legal documents, baptismal records, and printed genealogies. Besides census data on CD, there are printed volumes of birth and marriage records from the 1600s and 1700s. Other groups, such as the Daughters of the American Revolution, may be able to help you trace your roots back to the Revolutionary War and beyond.

Using the Internet

Now that you've gone as far as you can with your immediate family, it's time to turn to the Internet. After collecting information on your parents, grandparents, and great-grandparents, you might want to begin searching online. There are many helpful sites.

Ancestry.com (see figure 2) is the highest-rated family history Web site. It hosts more than 550 million names in over 2000

Where to Start

Beginner's Guide to Family History
    http://biz.ipa.net/arkresearch/guide.html
Ancestry.com
    www.ancestry.com
Cyndi's List
    www.cyndislist.com
Genealogy.com
    www.genealogy.com

databases. Some databases, such as the Social Security Death Index, are free. Others are for members only. Membership costs about $60 a year. Using their templates, you can create a family tree Web site hosted on their site.

Genealogy.com is an award-winning Web site. With their FamilyExplorer, you can learn about family trees and create your own basic family tree. This gives you a taste of what it's like to use family tree software. The site has many how-to articles, step-by-step guides to finding specific family information, and links to public databases and other Web sites.

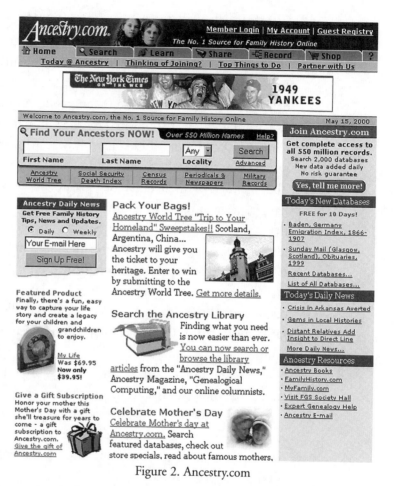

Figure 2. Ancestry.com

Cyndi's List is a directory of more than forty-one thousand links to other genealogy Web sites. Cyndi's site contains lots of research and genealogy Web page construction help.

Heritage Quest is an online genealogy store. It offers software, magazines, books, and hundreds of databases on CDs. In addition, the site contains a beginner's guide, blank forms, and research tools.

The Center for Disease Control—that's right, the CDC—offers helpful information for finding vital-records information. There are links to each state, as well as instructions on how to request specific records.

Family Tree Maker has an extensive Web site. The site supports its software but also has a lot of tools for the average genealogist. Of special interest is the Online Family Finder Index and the Internet Family Finder Index. Enter your ancestor's surname into the search engine, and it will return a list of places for you to continue tracing your family tree.

FamilySearch is sponsored by the Church of Jesus Christ of Latter-day Saints (LDS). Until 1999, the only way to search the Mormon's database was by traveling to Salt Lake City, Utah, or to one of their branch centers. Today, much of their database is searchable online. The Latter-day Saints have a special interest in family history. Family ties are so important to them that they believe they extend beyond the grave. Mormon families try to identify ancestors to make sure they are "in the church." Church "ordinances," such as baptism, are performed on behalf of dead family members.

Some may object to using the LDS database. Though it is compiled for reasons other than those we, as Christians, believe valid, that doesn't necessarily mean you must avoid their information. Only you can decide if it is right for you.

Message boards are electronic versions of the bulletin board. Many larger sites host message boards where you can post the name and other information about an ancestor you're seeking. Others who are tracing their family tree often check such message boards hoping to find leads on their own family. You might find someone who can offer a clue that will help you fill in missing information.

Use a regular search engine. Search for a full name or family name in a search engine such as AltaVista or LookSmart. Perhaps someone else traced their own family back to the same ancestor. If so, they may have posted the information in hopes of finding out more from someone like you.

When using the Internet, always verify sources. Even the person hosting a family Web page has verified the information, but you should do the same. One piece of incorrect information can lead you on a time-consuming, fruitless search.

Going Further

You can't do it all on the Internet. The Internet is limited by the number of online databases. Many records haven't been converted to electronic files. At best, they are on microfiche. Others may still be contained in old, dust-covered books. You will probably need to put on your walking shoes, load film in your camera, grab your notebook, plan a few side trips on your next vacation, and take a few walks around some old cemeteries.

While you're out and about, you'll want to visit the county courthouse to search vital records. It's best to call ahead and find out how to search public documents. Documents on microfilm or microfiche can be printed for less than fifty cents a page.

To further your skills, consider taking an online class. Many genealogy sites, colleges, and virtual universities offer classes. Some are free; others have a fee. Buy a book. Join a local genealogy club; there are more than two thousand of them in the United States. The Genealogist Address Book contains a list of these clubs, along with contact information. Last, but not least, check the Web sites you've bookmarked for additional research tips.

CHAPTER 31

STAYING IN TOUCH

The convenience and instant nature of the Internet provide a great way to keep up with family and friends. From the college student tucked away in a dorm five hundred miles from home, to Grandma and Grandpa traveling cross-country by motor home, to the seaman first-class onboard a ship in the Mediterranean Sea, to your sister four states away—the Internet is a great way to stay in touch with your family.

Hold an impromptu, online family reunion. Plan your annual Thanksgiving get-together, using your keyboard to "chat" with other members of your family. Send Aunt Sally's peanut butter pie recipe to your sister in Oregon. Set your computer to alert you to when friends are online. Send a note asking your best friend to log off the Internet so you can call him or her on the telephone. Send an instant message that your dad will receive immediately the next time he logs on. Log on and find a picture waiting for you of your little sister's first baby, complete with all the "vital statistics."

In this chapter we'll explore three ways you can stay in touch and stay current with what's happening in your family. Instant Messaging programs enable you to send short notes back and forth to family and friends while online. Chat allows you to carry on a keyboard conversation with one or more of those online. Internet Telephony allows you to "chat" using audio and video.

Instant Messaging

Instant messaging is a faster form of E-mail. It allows you to swap messages, exchange files, or "chat" in real time across the Internet. With instant messaging, you're not limited to one-on-one communication. In any conversation, you can include a small group of your family members and friends who are networked together with the same program. One of the best things about instant messaging is that it's free.

Instant messages often resemble the notes you used to pass in study hall—short, to the point, and often written in a personalized shorthand. Many instant messages contain emoticons and acronyms to help communicate a lot in a few words. They are short because most programs limit the number of characters in a message. Long messages must be broken into two or more instant messages or sent by E-mail.

Unlike E-mail, for instant messaging to work, both you and the person you're sending a message to must have the same program. At this writing there are no universal standards for instant messaging. Until there are, AOL Instant Messenger won't work with ICQ. You can run more than one instant messaging program on your system, but it's best to decide among your family members and/or friends which one you will use. All of you can then sign up and download the software. (I personally recommend ICQ.)

Setting Up an Instant Messaging Program

Once you've decided on an instant messaging program, go to the site and download it. If you need help downloading or installing the file, see chapters 25 and 26. During the installation process, it will prompt you to register (see figure 1). You must supply your name

---

Where to Find Instant Messaging Programs

Here are the four most popular instant messaging programs. Once you've settled on the one you will use, go to the listed site to download it.

AOL Instant Messenger
 www.aol.com
ICQ
 http://icq.com
MSN Messenger
 http://messenger.msn.com
Yahoo! Messenger
 http://pager.yahoo.com

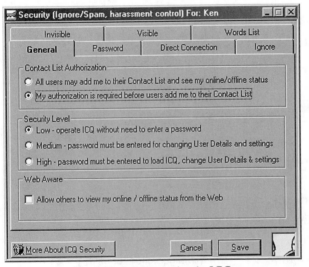

Figure 1. ICQ registration

Figure 2. Privacy setting in ICQ

and E-mail address, but don't offer any more information than you have to. When asked to give a name, select a nickname (instead of your real name) to go by on the Internet.

To maintain privacy, there are two important settings you need to make during installation (see figure 2). First, specify that you must authorize anyone who wants to add you to their list. This way you can control who knows you are online. Those wishing to add you to their list must first get permission from you.

Second, some instant messaging programs allow others not on your buddy list to see you are online. Select the option that blocks this feature. After all, you are using this program to connect with family and friends, not with every stranger lurking on the Internet.

Like E-mail, there are ways to spam instant messaging programs. To block unwanted messages, go to the security and privacy box. Set it to block spam and unwanted or multi-recipient messages. To further protect yourself, set it to accept messages only from those on your contact list. This will not prevent someone from requesting to be added to your list. It will only block instant messages, E-mail, and chat requests from those not on your buddy list. If you have questions about security and privacy, go to the instant messaging program's Web site. Most of the popular programs have a good online help system.

Adding Family and Friends

Once registered, it's time to add people to your "buddy list." This is done by looking them up in the instant messaging database. You can search for them by ID number, name, nickname, or E-mail address. If all else fails, send them an E-mail asking for their ID number and giving them yours.

Once you find those for whom you're looking, add them to your list (see figure 3). If they've selected the authorization feature, you'll have to ask permission to add them. When the instant message box opens, send them a note asking for authorization. Be sure to tell them who you are, especially if you use a nickname. You'll be notified when they give permission for you to add them. If you've selected the authorization feature, you'll have to authorize them when they add you to their list. Repeat this with all your family and friends.

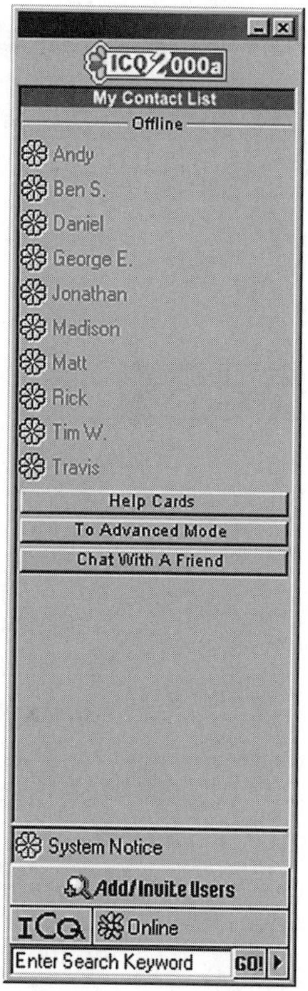

Figure 3. Buddy list

Sending an Instant Message

Now you're set. As people add you to their list and you add them to yours, you'll be notified when they are online. To send them a message:

1. Click on their name.
2. Select **Message** from the pop-up menu.
3. Type your note and click **Send** (see figure 4).

They will receive your message instantly. You will probably have a reply in the amount of time it takes them to jot down their thoughts and hit

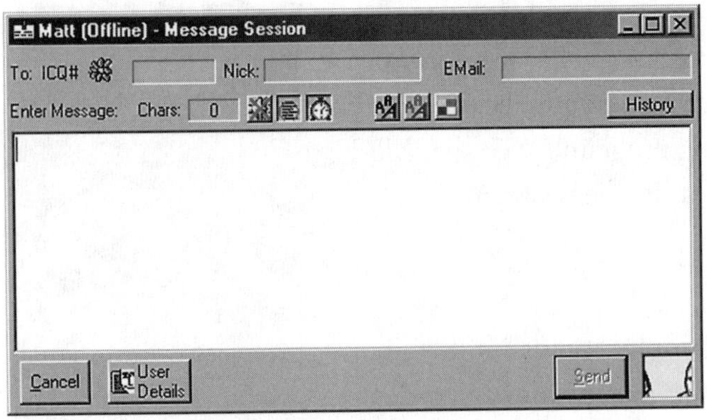

Figure 4. Sending an instant message

Reply. Back and forth the conversation will fly. Don't be surprised if you grow a bit nostalgic, thinking you're back in the cafeteria during study hall.

Chat

Another popular feature of instant messaging programs is "chat." Chat enables you to invite others into a private chat room where you can talk with them. Once you've initiated a chat with one person, you can invite others on your buddy list to join the discussion. See "Hold an Online Family Reunion" in chapter 35 for instructions on how to use this feature with a group of people.

Initiating a Chat Session

To start "talking" to your friends, they must be online. When they are online, ICQ (or other messaging program) will notify you. Once they are online, follow these five steps:

1. Click on their name in the buddy list.
2. Choose **Chat** from the pop-up menu.
3. Send them an invitation to chat.
4. If they accept, the chat screen opens. This screen is divided in half (see figure 5). The top section is your part of the conversation. The bottom half is theirs.
5. Type a sentence or two of greeting and press **Enter**. Your message will immediately appear on their screen. When they reply, you'll receive it instantly.

Unfortunately, with most programs you have to wait for the other person to press the Enter key before you see their message. One program, ICQ, displays your message as you type. This is helpful because you don't have to wait for the other person to compose their thoughts, type, and then press **Enter**. You can read it as they type. You can also type as they type. This is the closest thing to a "real conversation" you'll get using a keyboard.

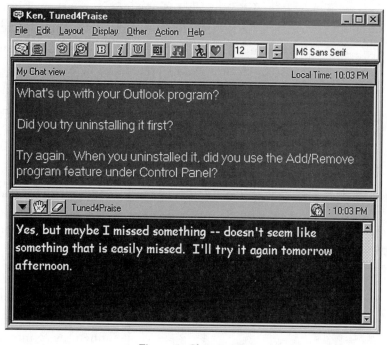

Figure 5. Chat session

Two Other Methods of Chat

There are two other forms of chat I need to mention. The first is Internet Relay Chat, or IRC. IRC requires a special program. Once installed, you connect to an IRC server and select from a list of chat channels. These channels are categorized by subject. Find one you're interested in and join the discussion. Often there will be five, ten, fifteen, or more people chatting back and forth.

Chat rooms are another place people go to chat online. Almost all large Web sites and Online Service Providers (like AOL) host chat rooms. A chat room is like an online coffeehouse. It's a place to go, sit, "listen to a conversation," and join in if you want. Most chat rooms are devoted to a specific topic or age group. Some Web sites host celebrities who will chat with those who log in to the chat room.

IRC and chat rooms pose a number of potential problems for families. The first is the content of the discussion. There are few rules about the language being used. Second, you don't know those in the chat room or on IRC. Someone can pretend to be anyone they choose to be. A forty-five-year-old pedophile can pretend to be a fifteen-year-old. A thirteen-year-old girl can pretend she's twenty-five. Third, someone who is experienced in chat rooms can get enough information from your child to identify them without them realizing they've even given out the information. Fourth, flame wars, spam, and hate E-mail can erupt from those angered by what someone has to say. Fifth, chat can become a distraction, substituting for healthy relationships. Sixth, people have been known to become emotionally involved with someone they've met online, involved to the point of abandoning their own family and friends.

Having said all that, a number of Christian and family-friendly sites host chat rooms. These rooms are monitored and rules are enforced. If someone gets out of line, they are warned. If they continue to ignore the rules or harass others in the room, they are "kicked out" and not permitted back in the room. Chat rooms offer a way to meet people online, exchange ideas, and even grow as a Christian. But chat must be approached carefully.

Rules for Chat

Chat and instant messaging are very popular with teens. It's the new telephone, so you will need to set some guidelines. Here are a few suggestions:

1. Turn off instant messaging programs when using the Internet for homework.
2. The same rules of etiquette apply with chat as would apply with any other form of conversation.
3. Set limits on the time of day and the amount of time that can be spent chatting online.
4. Institute a no-hiding policy. Remind your teens that, as their parents, you have the right to read their messages.
5. Set limits on chat rooms. If you allow your teens to visit chat rooms, visit with them first. Make sure it's a monitored chat room with rules that are enforced. Make a list of acceptable chat rooms, then make sure those are the only ones visited.
6. Set and enforce consequences if rules are broken.

Internet Telephony

Internet telephony takes "chat" one step further. With it, you can actually talk to someone over the Internet. If you have the right equipment, you can even see the person with whom you are talking.

You will need a special program and some hardware to use Internet telephony. If your computer came with a modem, speakers, and a microphone, you have all the hardware you need. If you want to see the person you're talking with, both of you will need the same software and a Web cam.

Don't expect the audio to be the quality of your telephone or the video to be the quality of your television. Internet telephony is still in its infancy. Like everything else on the Internet, it will improve as the technology improves.

As technology advances, it offers more ways to stay in touch with family and friends. Granted, electronic connections can't take the place of a bear hug, but when you're separated by hundreds of miles, technology can help you stay connected to those you love. In addition, technology can help you make plans for those moments when you *can* share a real bear hug.

FAMILY ACTIVITIES AND ADVENTURES

CHAPTER 32

PLANNING A VACATION

Are you tired of traveling to the same old, well-worn vacation spots? No more! Use the Internet to find fresh, new, and exciting family vacations. The challenge for every family is planning a trip that everyone will enjoy.

It used to be that you collected vacation ideas from friends and family, culled a few interesting spots out of magazines or newspapers, called or wrote for information from tourist bureaus, flipped through out-of-date guidebooks at the library, or consulted a travel agent. Now you can find up-to-date information on the Internet, including places to go, sights to see, and activities available. Here are four steps to help you plan a vacation the whole family will enjoy.

1. Dream It

Spend time as a family talking and thinking about where you want to go and what you want to do. Post a "Vacation Wish List" on the refrigerator. As family members think of activities they'd enjoy or places they'd like to go, they can write them down.

As you make your list, encourage creativity and original thinking. At this point no idea is too wild, too way out, or too expensive to consider. You never know when an idea, that at first seems impossible, might become possible with a little planning and budgeting.

Somewhere along the line, everyone in your family may run out of fresh ideas. This is the time to turn to one of the Internet's many family travel collections. The online version of *Family Fun* magazine has a travel index featuring all the travel articles from the magazine. You can browse the index, or search for specific subjects or geographic locations (www.familyfun.com).

America's Best Online is a listing of America's best beaches, parks, hiking trails, ski resorts, fishing, amusement parks, merry-go-rounds, water parks, zoos, roller coasters, and more (see figure 1). Of particular interest to families is their listing of America's Best Family Vacation Spots and links (www.americasbestonline.com).

Figure 1. America's Best Online

If you like outdoor activities, browse the Great Outdoor Recreation Pages (www.gorp.com). Find detailed information and links to hundreds of outdoor activities and destinations. Search the site or browse their "Travel A to Z" feature.

Several other sites worth visiting include: Family.com Travel (www.family.go.com), Travel.com (www.travel.com), and About.com (www.about.com/travel). Both have large collections of family-tested vacation articles. Family.com has a section for families traveling with special-needs children. About.com is a search directory, compiled by "real people." The Travel with Kids section contains a host of links, vacation guides, and travel tips. A number of other major search engines, including AltaVista and Yahoo, have travel directories.

As you make your list, start a file folder of interesting places to go and things to do gleaned from magazines, newspapers, and the Internet. Be sure to bookmark any sites you might need to return to.

At first you might narrow things down to one state or region. Eventually, as you talk and dream, one or two destinations will begin to emerge. Once you've decided where you're going or what you're doing, it's time to start planning.

2. Plan It

How will we get there? Where will we stay? What will the weather be like? Where will we eat? What will we do? What reservations will we need? How much will it cost? These are the kinds of questions you'll want to answer during the planning stage. The Internet is the ideal place to evaluate your vacation options.

Create a Family Vacation Guide

With all the resources available, you will be able to create your own family vacation guide. Depending on where you're going, you might find a personalized miniguide available on Fodors Web site (www.fodors.com).

Fodors has been printing travel guides for decades. Now they've made some of that information available online. Even if you don't find a miniguide for your destination, the time spent looking at their guides will give you an idea of the information you need to gather.

As you collected ideas, you probably noted a few Web sites to return to for additional information. Start with the sites you've already identified, but don't stop there. Do a search for information on all the major cities and towns near your destination. Web sites such as Sidewalk (www.sidewalk.com) and City Guide (www.cityguide.com) offer up-to-date information on major cities. Many chambers of commerce and tourism departments offer online information on both popular and little-known attractions. Online editions of local newspapers contain calendars of activities and local travel features. When conducting your search, be sure to scan the results from two or three search engines, or use a metasearch engine.

If you are traveling by car to and from your vacation destination, print a map from MapQuest, Expedia, or Rand McNally. At MapQuest (www.mapquest.com) (see figure 2), enter your home city and destination. If you need door-to-door directions, start with your address and the physical address of where you are going. MapQuest will provide an overview map and turn-by-turn directions.

As you look at the map, note any cities or towns along the way. List some of them. Ask for volunteers (you can involve the entire family in the planning

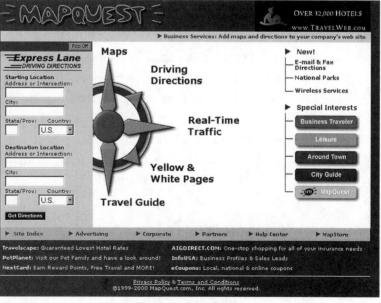

Figure 2. MapQuest

stage) to do an Internet search on those cities and towns. Have them look for anything interesting. You might find a jewel that you never knew existed just a mile or two off the interstate.

Don't forget to check the weather. The Weather Channel (www.weather.com) and the National Weather Service (www.nws.noaa.gov) offer short-term and long-term forecasts for every region of the country. If you're traveling to a small town, enter the name of the closest major city.

Create a Budget

For parents, a key question is "How much is this going to cost?" As you plan, you'll be able to gather much of this information. Many sites post rates. For those that don't, a quick phone call will help you get the information. It's a good idea to confirm all quoted rates. To get an approximate cost on airline tickets, car rentals, and accommodations, do a quick search at a one-stop travel site, like Travelocity. At this point, you're not looking for the best rates; you're trying to write a budget.

File What You Find

As you plan your trip, don't forget to print out the important information. Purchase a three-ring binder and organize the information in it. Because weather and the unexpected might change family plans, I organize information into four sections: maps, accommodations (food and lodging), activities, and reservations. I organize the maps and accommodations by the day I'll need them. The activities section is sorted by "plan to do" and "maybe." This is what works for me. Another option is to organize your notebook by the day of the week.

3. Book It

Once you know when and where you're going, it's time to make your reservations. Travel services, such as Travelocity (see figure 3), American Express, Priceline, and Expedia Travel, are all-in-one Web sites. You can make airline and cruise reservations, book motel rooms, reserve a car rental, and even purchase advance tickets to many attractions. Such one-stop Web sites are quick and provide comparison fares. If your travel dates and times are flexible, you can check the best fare section of many of these Web sites, or try Priceline. One caution: Always read disclaimers and restrictions before purchasing tickets.

If you have a favorite airline or motel, you can go directly to their Web site. Most airlines, major hotel chains, and car rentals offer online reservations.

Before purchasing tickets or making reservations, always compare prices. Compare prices and schedules between all-in-one sites and company sites. At times, I've gotten a better rate or schedule on an individual airline site than I have on an all-in-one site. At other times, the rates have been the same, or better, at the all-in-one site. Remember, to get the best fare and the schedule you want, purchase airline tickets well in advance of your trip.

Make reservations for any activity where space is limited. During their peak season, such activities fill up quickly. When making online reservations, be sure to print out all confirmation information. This is important if your reservations get lost or your tickets don't arrive in the mail.

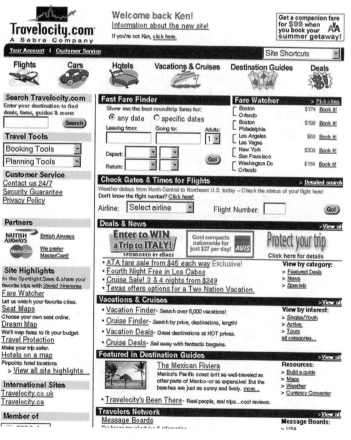

Figure 3. Travelocity

If confirmation information isn't offered online, ask for written confirmation by calling or E-mailing. File all confirmations in your vacation notebook.

4. Take It

You've stopped the newspaper. The post office is holding your mail. The neighbor is watching the dog. The teenager across the street is mowing the lawn. The bags are packed. The alarm is set. Vacation guides, tickets, and other information are on the counter. You're all set. Well, almost. There are a few last-minute items you'll want to take care of before you leave.

1. Print out any additional maps you might need—maps and directions between motels and attractions, and from city to city.
2. Print out any last-minute information on accommodations and attractions.
3. Confirm all flights and reservations.
4. Check the weather forecast.

Don't forget a few things you need to do at home before you leave.

1. Unsubscribe to any newsgroups or E-mail newsletters. You don't want your E-mail clogged with hundreds of messages when you return.
2. E-mail family and friends that you correspond with regularly and let them know you'll be out.
3. If your ISP offers a vacation message feature, set it to reply to all or specific messages, letting people know you are out and when you'll return.
4. When all is done, turn off the computer and unplug it.

One last thing: Now that all the work is done, go have some fun with your family!

CHAPTER 33

EXPRESSING YOUR FAITH

Christians have taken to the Internet like the proverbial duck to water. There are sites for women, men, families, kids, teens, singles, seniors adults, missionaries, Sunday school teachers, businessmen, pastors, musicians, writers, seekers, Christian political activists, Christian book stores, conference centers, online radio, churches, Christian ministries, and more.

Christians are using the Internet to communicate with missionaries, share their faith, grow spiritually, chat with other Christians, build relationships, disciple one another, shop, and listen to music and sermons online. The list could go on. According to an article in *Christianity Online,* there are roughly twenty times more Christian Web pages on the Internet than Buddhist, which runs a distant second.[1] You are not alone in cyberspace. There is a large contingent of believers surfing the net, chatting with others, growing in the Lord, and making an impact for Christ.

Where to Start

For a quick tour of what's out there, start your journey at one of the following megasites. What makes these sites special is the community they strive to build between believers as well as the resources they offer. Each of these sites links to hundreds of others. As you survey these sites, be sure to

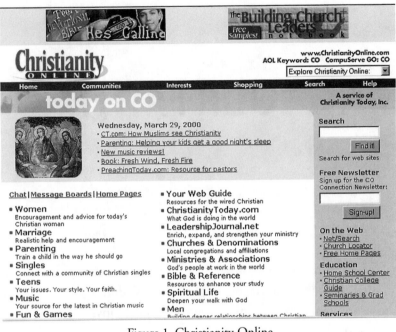

Figure 1. Christianity Online

follow some of the links to partner sites.

Crosswalk, with its daily lineup of chat sessions, forums, various communities, and wide range of content, seeks to address the wide range of needs and interests of Christians. You'll find everything from entertainment to finances, sports to spiritual life, health to home schooling, careers to music. Its filtered search engine allows you to comfortably search all the Web, not just Christian sites. Add your church event to the local Christian events database or search for activities in your area (www.crosswalk.com).

For a number of years now, Gospel Communications Network (Gospel.com) has been the number one Christian Web site on the Internet (based on the number of visits it receives each month). It is the only Christian Web site listed in the Media Metrix 500 list of top Web sites.[2] There is good reason for all the attention it receives. The site has more than 140 of the most familiar Christian ministries as partners. Their CrossSearch search engine lists more than thirteen thousand safe sites of interest to Christians. Gospelcom has now partnered with OnePlace.com, expanding the information and services it offers (www.gospelcom.net).

Christianity Online is a publication of *Christianity Today* (see figure 1). The site offers communities for women, men, singles, families, kids, teens, seniors, and church leaders. Each month it posts selected articles from *Christianity Today*'s long list of magazines. These include *Christianity Today, Campus Life, Christian Parenting Today, Leadership,* and *Marriage.* Christianity Online has two search engines. Net/SEARCH searches for Christian Web sites. Church Locator helps you find a "wired church" (www. christianityonline.com).

Goshen is now a partner site with Crosswalk. What sets Goshen apart are its Bible Study Tools and search engine. A lot of Web sites offer various collections of Bible study helps, but Bible Study Tools offers the most comprehensive, easily searchable set of tools on the net. The Best of the Christian Web called Goshen's search engine the "Yahoo of Christian search engines" (www.goshen.net).

The Best of the Christian Web is just that—a listing of the very best the Christian Web has to offer. Browse their directory by subject, or search it for sites of particular interest to you. It's a great place to begin to familiarize yourself with what's available on the Christian Internet (www.botcw.com).

Spiritual Growth

As you scan the above sites, you'll find links to hundreds of other Christian Web sites. Among those sites are many designed to help you grow personally.

Bible Study

There are many Bible study resources on the Internet. Some sites offer a searchable online Bible. Others offer a lot more. With fourteen Bibles, eight commentaries, five dictionaries, three concordances, and more, Bible Study Tools (sponsored by Goshen) is the most comprehensive Bible study site on the Internet (www.biblestudytools.com).

If you're interested in the history of the English Bible, check out the fine resources at American Bible Society. Click on the Concise History of the English Bible link (www.americanbible.org).

Do you have a desire to delve into the original languages of the Bible? At Ministry of the Word you can learn Greek (the language of the New Testament). If you're a pastor wanting to brush up on your Greek, or someone who'd like to learn how to read the Greek New Testament, this is the place (www.thechristian.org/lrngreek).

Devotionals

There are lots of devotionals online; you just have to know where to look for them. The best place to begin is on one of the sites mentioned above. Use the keyword *devotion* or *devotionals.* Broadman & Holman offers the daily devotional *Experiencing God Today* (see figure 2) (www.broadman-holman.com). Devotional Net includes devotionals by Charles Spurgeon, Walk thru the Bible, and Bible Pathway (www.devotionals.net). Gospel Communication Network links to seventeen different devotionals. These include Daily Wisdom, Christian Quotation for the Day, Today's Thought by John Stott, Keys for Kids, The NIV Quiet Time Bible, Oswald Chambers' *My Utmost for His Highest,* and Our Daily Bread (www.gospelcom.net/welcome/categories/devotionals.shtml).

Some of these devotionals are sent by E-mail; most have to be accessed online. If you find one you'd like to read every day, then make it your home page. (See chapter 13 for help changing your home page.)

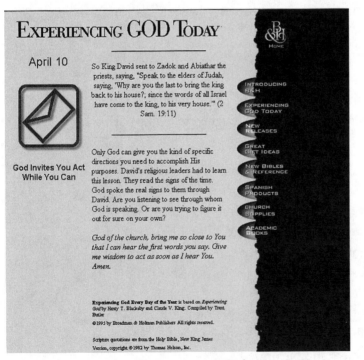

Figure 2. Experiencing God

Ezines

Ezines are online magazines. Some arrive in your E-mail box on a regular basis; others are found online. Almost all of them are free. Most larger sites, and many smaller ones, offer Ezines. Here are five to get you started.

1. Internet for Families Newsletter is a monthly newsletter helping families get the most out of the Internet while avoiding the dangers. Each edition is filled with information, tips, links to family-friendly sites, and family activities (www.internetforfamilies.org/ezine).

2. Internet for Christians is published twice monthly. It's written by Quentin Schultze, the author of *Internet for Christians.* It highlights news stories of interest to Christians, stories affecting society, personal growth and evangelism, resources and entertainment, Internet and technology, E-mail mailing lists, and more. There is also a list of other Ezines on his Web site (www.gospelcom.net/ifc/newsletter.shtml).

3. BreakPoint by Chuck Colson delivers his daily commentary to your E-mail box. To subscribe, go to the following Web page (www.breakpoint.org) and click on **Subscribe**.

4. Leadership Wired by John Maxwell. If you're in any kind of leadership position, this monthly newsletter is a "must read" (www.injoy.com/MonthlyMentoring/LeadershipWired.asp).

5. International Missions Prayer Line is a list of prayer requests sent out every Monday, Wednesday, and Friday by the International Mission Board of the Southern Baptist Convention (www.imb.org/maillist.htm).

E-vangelism

If the apostle Paul were alive today, he'd have a Web site and would be using the Internet for evangelism. In 1 Corinthians 9:19–23, Paul described how he met people where they were in order to bring them to where they needed to be. He summed up his strategy by saying, "I have become all things to all men so that by all possible means I might save some" (v. 22).

Nowadays Christians are using Web pages, E-mail, and chat to reach people for Christ. The methods are as different as the people using them, but they have one thing in common—the building of relationships. Some people are moving into online communities, like Geocities, and doing "door-to-door" evangelism. Geocities' free Web site is laid out in neighborhoods. Having built a Web site, people visit "their neighbor's" Web site. At each site, they find something to compliment and send "their neighbor" an E-mail. In the E-mail, they invite "their neighbor" to visit their own newly created site. Through E-mail, the believer hopes to build a positive relationship that leads to a spiritual dialog.

Figure 3. Five Clicks to Sharing Your Faith

Some Christians are engaging people in thoughtful dialog in chat rooms. Others post Web pages with personal testimonies of what God has done in their lives. Still others are building Web sites that attract the "lost," then engage them through the content of their Web sites and E-mail. Some have added gospel presentations to their Web sites or linked them to sites such as Billy Graham.

If you're interested in building a Web site to reach the lost, begin by reading a few online how-to guides. Start with NetCast E-vangelism (www.netcastevangelism.com) and the Web Evangelism Guide (www.goshen.net/WebEvangelism). Christianity Online is developing the Evangelism Toolbox (www.evangelismtoolbox.com) as a free resource of the best evangelistic resources the Internet offers.

Whether you're planning to share your testimony on- or offline, Five Clicks to Sharing Your Faith Web site will teach you to share it effectively (see figure 3) (www.5clicks.com). This interactive tutorial promises to teach you how to give your testimony and share it in a way that people will come to know Jesus. It is based on Bill Bright's (founder of Campus Crusade for Christ) book, Five *Steps to Sharing Your Faith*.

When you begin to share your faith, there will be times when you're stumped by a question. Don't worry. Admit you're not sure of the answer and promise to find one. Then head over to Christian Answers Net (www.christiananswers.net) or Christian Topics (www.christiantopics.com). Both of these sites offer hundreds of answers to the tough questions both Christians and non-Christians ask about the Christian faith.

Ministry Helps

Are you looking for help in becoming a better servant in your area of ministry? If you teach Sunday school, head over to LifeWay, formerly the Sunday School Board of the Southern Baptist Convention, to find teaching helps (see figure 4) (www.lifeway.com).

Enrich your teaching by taking a cyber pilgrimage at Virtual Holy Land (www.virtualholyland.com). Find sermon resources at Preaching Today (www.preachingtoday.com) and INJOY (www.injoy.com).

Get financial help for yourself or someone else from Mary Hunt at Debt Proof Living (www.debtproofliving.com) or Larry Burkett at Christian Financial Concepts (www.cfcministry.org). Link up with other youth workers at Youthworker Journal (www.youthworker.com). Mine the rich resources at Focus on the Family (www.family.org) and Citizen Link (www.family.org/cforum).

Are you confronted with perplexing ethical and political issues? Surf over to the Ethics and Religious Liberty Commission (www.erlc.com) and the Family Resource Council (www.frc.org).

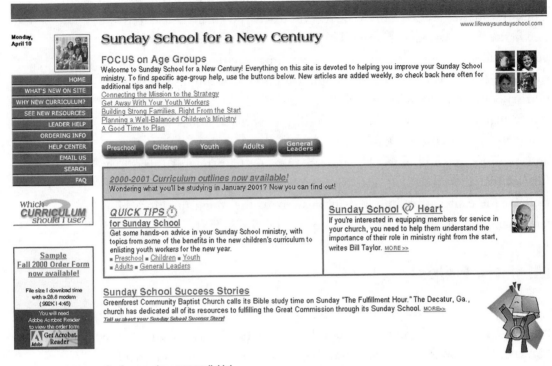

Figure 4. Sunday school helps

Internet Broadcasts

On the Internet, you can listen to live broadcasts of sporting events, concerts, radio programs, music, and other special events. More and more churches and ministries are posting sermons, Bible studies, and devotionals on their Web sites. Others, like The Puzzle Club (on The Lutheran Hour site), have read-along stories for children. At Focus on the Family, you can listen to Dr. Dobson's daily broadcast, *Adventures in Odyssey,* and *Family News in Focus.* Chuck Colson, Chuck Swindoll, Adrian Rogers, *Back to the Bible, Jack Van Impe Presents,* Ravi Zacharias, Steve Brown, *700 Club,* John Hagee, *Renewing Your Mind* (R. C. Sproul), *Country Crossroads,* Beverly

LaHaye, *Precepts with Kay Arthur,* and hundreds more are available online. A growing number of Christian radio stations now broadcast online. These include Moody Broadcast from Chicago and WayFM. There are even Internet radio stations that broadcast only on the Web.

To find Internet broadcasts, start by going to the ministry Web site. If you don't know the address, type: go (followed by the speaker or ministry name) in the Address bar of your browser. The site you're looking for should be listed in the first five to ten hits. If it isn't, try searching for it using one of the Christian search engines listed below. If audio is available, you will find a link on their Web site.

Figure 5. Involved Christian Radio

Another way to find Internet broadcasts is to browse the listings at one of the following Web sites: Involved Christian Radio Network or ICRN (www.icrn.com) (see figure 5); Lightsource.com (www.broadcast.com/lightsource); AudioCentral.com (www.audiocentral.com); TodaysChristianMusic.com (www.todayschristianmusic.com). These are not the only sites on the Internet where you can find links to online music. Larger Christian sites (such as Crosswalk, Gospelcom, One Place, and Christianity Online) offer links to the more popular sites.

Finding Churches, Denominations, and Ministries

No one knows for sure how many churches, ministries, and personal Christian Web sites are on the Internet. Like everything else related to the Internet, the number is growing daily. When searching for a Christian ministry, start with a Christian search engine. The search engines at Crosswalk, Christianity Online, and Goshen, mentioned earlier, are good places to begin.

To locate a ministry, type in the name of the ministry and click **Search**. If you don't find it right away, make sure you have the correct name or try a different search engine. If you still can't find it, try searching for a key member of the ministry. For example: search for James Dobson when looking for Focus on the Family or Chuck Colson when looking for BreakPoint. Follow the same procedure when searching for a Christian denomination.

When searching for a church, start with a church-finder search engine. On most church-finder sites, you can search for churches by name, city, state, and denomination. Many sites offer a directory so you can browse through a list of churches divided by state and/or denomination. Unfortunately, there isn't one comprehensive church-finder search engine. You might have to search through a number of them to find a specific church.

Church Locator, sponsored by Christianity Online, lists more than nine thousand wired churches in the United States and overseas (www. christianity.net/churchlocator/). Goshen's search engine includes a directory of churches divided into forty-nine denominational categories (www.goshen.net). If you don't find the church you're looking for on these two church finders, try Churches Dot Net, Net Ministries, NetChurch, and Christian USA. The Web address for each of these is listed in appendix 2.

To locate a church that's not online, use an online business directory like InfoSpace, GTE Superpages, Big Yellow, and BigBook Yellow Pages. Search by name, category, city, and state. When you search by category, city, and state, the search engine returns a list of all the churches in that city. Some, like BigBook Yellow Pages, supply maps and driving directions to listed churches. If the church is online, many will link to the church's Web site.

I hope I have whetted your appetite for what's available for Christians online. As you'll soon discover, there is more, much more, to be found. If you want to keep up with what's online, regularly visit the sites listed earlier in this chapter under "Where to Begin." Subscribe to one or two Ezines and check the Internet for Families Web site. In addition, you might want to consider subscribing to *Christian Computing, Christianity Online,* or *Scroll.* All three magazines work to keep readers abreast of what's happening in Christianity on the Internet.

CHAPTER 34

PUTTING YOUR FAMILY ONLINE

Before long, someone in your family is going to want to build a Web site. There are many reasons why you would want to put your family online. Building a Web site is an exciting way to stay in touch with your family; on it you can post vacation pictures, your Christmas newsletter, information about an upcoming family reunion, and so on. Hosting a Web site offers a way for you to express your faith. A Web site is another way to stay in touch with those in a Sunday school class or other organization. Creating and hosting a Web site is a skill that will probably help your children in the future. A Web site allows you to connect with others who share a common hobby or interest. What you put on your Web site is limited only by your time and creativity.

This chapter will introduce you to the basics of Web site building. As your interest grows, you'll want to learn more and use more powerful Web authoring software. For now, we will use the software you already have to build a personal Web page.

The Basics

Web sites are built using HyperText Markup Language, HTML. This language tells your browser how to display the text and graphics of a Web page. A few years ago, you had to write Web pages using HTML. For example, if you wanted a line of text to appear in italics, you had to surround it by the HTML tags, <I> and </I>. If you wanted it to be bold, you used <b> and </b>. Today's Web-authoring software inserts these codes automatically. As you build a Web page, you don't even see the tags.

HTML has its limitations. It isn't as flexible or powerful as today's word processors or publishing programs. You can't, for example, use a unique font that you have on your machine. If those viewing your Web page don't have that font, they won't see your page the way you do. People view Web pages using different types of computers, running different software. Therefore, Web pages must be built with a standard that everyone can view.

Building a Personal Web Page

You may already have Web-authoring software on your computer. Internet Explorer comes with FrontPage Express; Netscape includes Netscape Composer with its browser. If it's not already installed on your computer, you'll need to download and install it from their Web site.

In the example that follows, I'll use FrontPage Express. If you're using Netscape Composer, you'll be able to follow along. Both programs have page wizards to help you get started creating Web pages. We will use the Personal Home Page wizard in FrontPage Express to create your home page.

Plan Your Page

The first step in building any site is to know what you want to do and how you want to do it. On a pad of paper, sketch how you want the text and pictures to appear on the page. Collect any photos or clip-art images you'll need. If you plan to use photos, they need to be scanned into your computer and saved in JPG format. If you don't own or have access to a scanner, you can have photos scanned at a photo shop. Many photo shops will take a roll of film and digitize your images, putting them on a CD.

Clip-art images need to be in GIF format or JPG format. You can find free GIF and JPG clip-art images on the Internet. Both Microsoft and Netscape have collections of clip art on their Web sites.

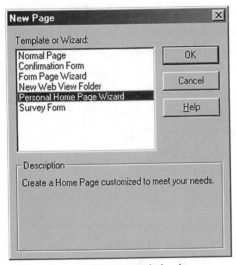

Figure 1. New Page dialog box

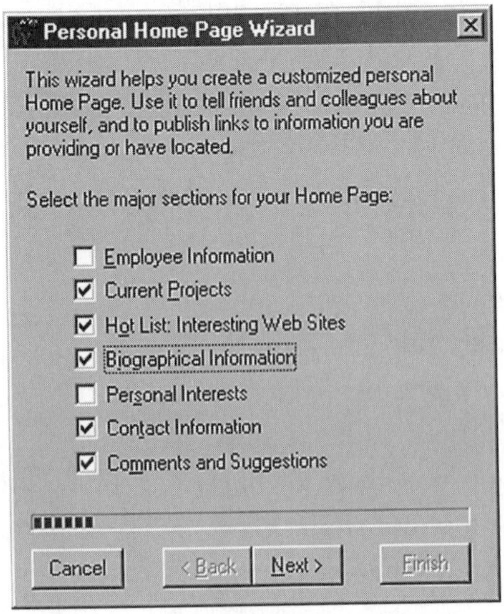

Figure 2. Personal Web Page Wizard

Building Your Personal Home Page

To open FrontPage Express, click **Start** on the taskbar, then choose **Programs, Accessories, Internet Tools, FrontPage Express**. (Netscape Composer is in the Netscape Communicator folder on the Start menu.) There are three toolbars in FrontPage Express: Format toolbar, Standard toolbar, and Forms toolbar. If you use any word processor or Microsoft Office Programs, you'll recognize most of the buttons. If you're unsure of a button, rest the mouse pointer over it for a few seconds and the label will appear.

FrontPage Express includes a number of page wizards and templates. To view them, click **Ctrl-n** or choose **File, New** from the Menu bar. You will use the Personal Home Page Wizard to create your home page. Follow these steps:

1. If the New Page dialog box isn't open, click **Ctrl-n** to open it (see figure 1).
2. Choose **Personal Home Page Wizard** and click **OK**.
3. Select the categories of information you want on your home page. In this example I've selected Current Projects, Hot List, Biographical Information, Contact Information, and Comments and Suggestions (see figure 2). Click **Next** when finished.

4. Your home page needs an address (URL) and a title. Since this is your home page, the URL should be either home.htm or index.htm. Since most browsers look for index.htm first, change it to this. Each page you create needs a unique address. Change the page title to anything you want. If you're creating a personal Web page, add your name. In this example, I named the page Ken's Home Page (see figure 3). Click **Next** when finished.

5. Depending on the items checked in step three, you'll be prompted to add information to and/or choose format options for each section. Click **Next** when finished with each section.

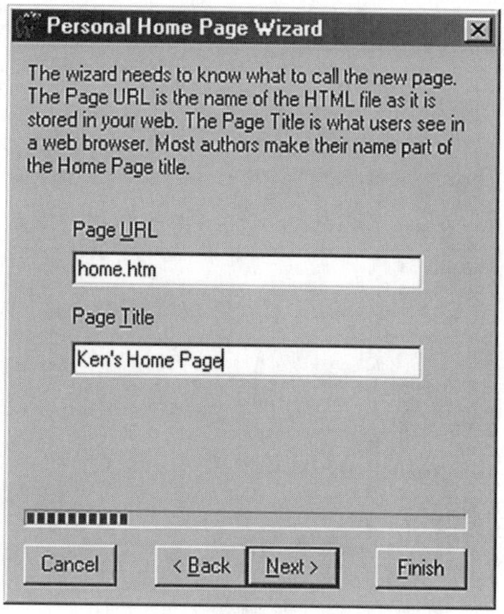

Figure 3: Naming your home page

6. If you chose to add a Comments and Suggestions section to your home page, select how you want the information stored. The Comments and Suggestions section gives visitors the opportunity to tell you what they think of your site. For ease of use, choose **Use link, Send E-mail to this address**. Be sure to include an E-mail address. All comments will then be sent to you as an E-mail message (see figure 4). When finished, click **Next**. Note: To protect your privacy, use a free E-mail address on your Web site.

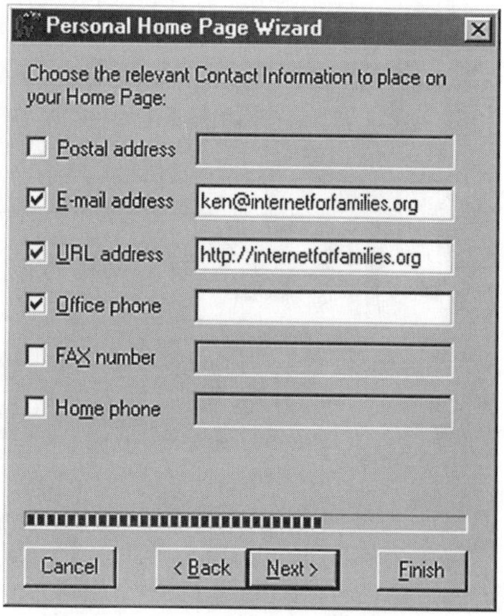

7. Arrange the elements in the order you want them to appear on your page. Highlight a section and use the Up/Down buttons to rearrange them. When satisfied, click **Next**.

8. Now that you've supplied all the information the wizard needs, click **Finish**. FrontPage Express compiles your information and displays your home page (see figure 5).

Figure 4. Comments and Suggestions

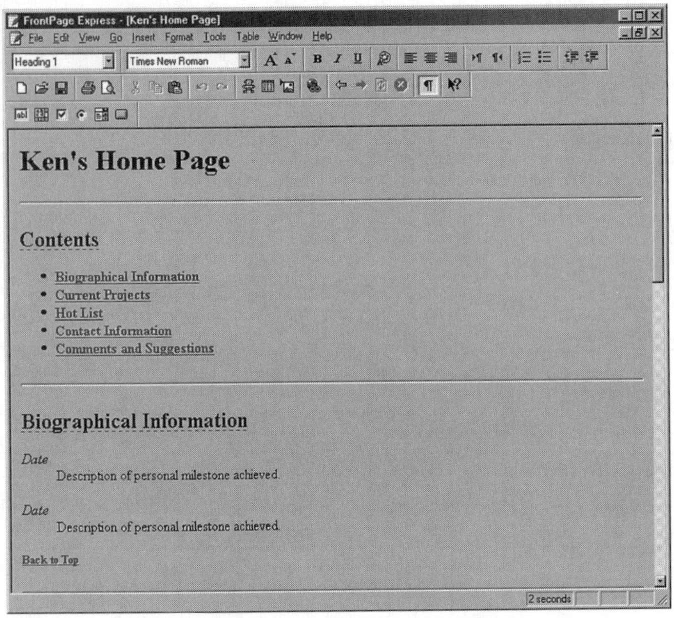

Figure 5. Rough draft of Ken's home page

Figure 6. Link box

Add Text

Now that you have the basic structure of your home page, it's time to add text. Each section of your page has placeholder text. Replace this text with your information. If you create additional pages, you can add links from the Current Projects list to those new pages. For now, leave them as a bulleted list. To add a project to the list, position the cursor at the end of the last bulleted item. Press **Enter** and a new bulleted item is created.

Add Links

In the Hot List section, we're going to add three Web sites to the list.

1. Delete the words "Sample Site 1."
2. Type in the name of a favorite Web site.
3. Highlight the name you just typed and choose **Insert, Hyperlink** from the Menu bar or **Ctrl-k** (see figure 6). In the Link dialog box, type in the address of the Web site. Click **OK**. Notice that the name is changed to hypertext. With the text still highlighted, click **Bold** from the toolbar to set it off from the rest of the text.

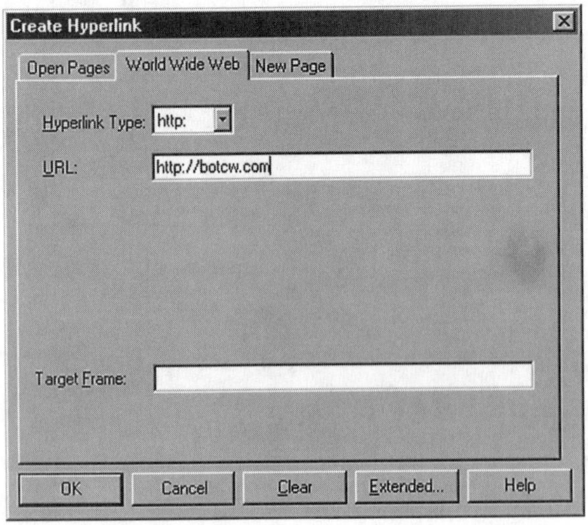

4. Replace the placeholder text with a description of the Web site.

5. Repeat this for additional Web sites.

Add Graphics

Now let's add a picture to your Web site.

1. Position the cursor on the page where you want the graphic to appear.

2. Click the Insert Image icon located on the toolbar.

3. Find the image you want to add on your hard drive. Remember, Web graphics must be in either GIF or JPG format. Click **OK**.

4. You will probably not like how the image first appears on the page. Right-click on the image to adjust it. Choose **Image Properties** from the pop-up menu. Click on **Appearance**. Use the controls to experiment with the size and placement of the graphic (see figure 7).

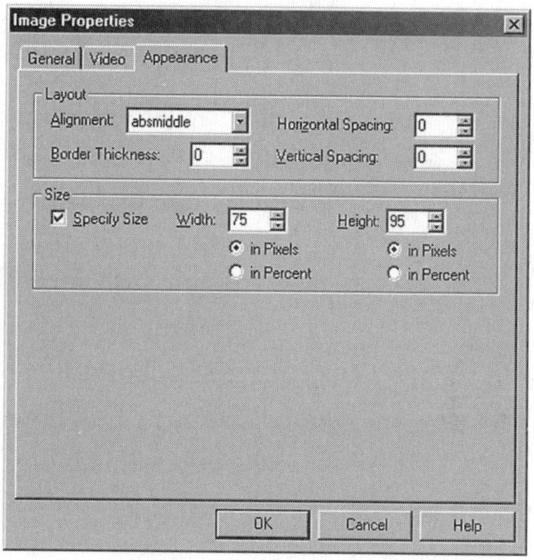

Figure 7. Image Properties

Change Background Color

The last thing we're going to do is change the background color. Select **Format, Background** from the Menu bar. Choose a new color combination from the Page Properties dialog box (see figure 8). Don't be afraid to experiment. If you don't

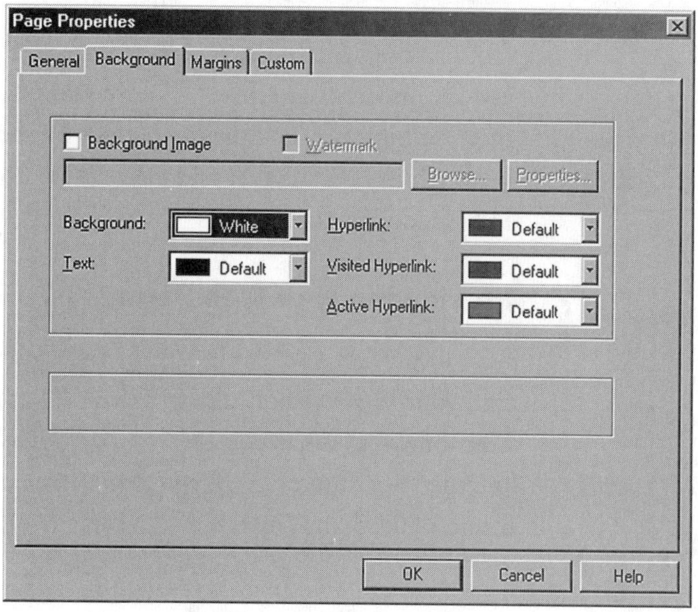

Figure 8. Page Properties

like a combination, change it. Just be sure the color scheme you settle on is easy to read. Before leaving the Page Properties box, notice that you can use a graphic image as a background. There are many sites that offer free background textures and patterns. Here are three sites that contain free backgrounds and clip art for your web site.

- Atlantic Fish Free Christian   http://chr4.tripod.com
  Clip art
- Free-Backgrounds.com   www.free-backgrounds.com
- Microsoft Developer's   http://msdn.microsoft.com/default.asp
  Network (click on
  downloads)

You can find more using a search engine and the keywords "free backgrounds." Remember, with free clip art on the Web, you always run into the problem of finding something offensive in the collection. So, be careful.

Saving Your Page

It's time to save your work. Before you can post it to the Internet, save it as a file on your hard drive. Choose **File, Save As** from the Menu bar, or click the Save button. Click the As File button. Select a location on your hard drive in which to save the file, and click **Save**. Your home page will be saved as an HTML document.

Previewing Your Web Page

To preview your Web page in your browser, open Windows Explorer and find your Web page on the hard drive. Double-click on it. It will open in your Web browser. What you see is what others will see after you post it to the Internet (see figure 9). If you don't like something, reopen it in FrontPage Express and change it.

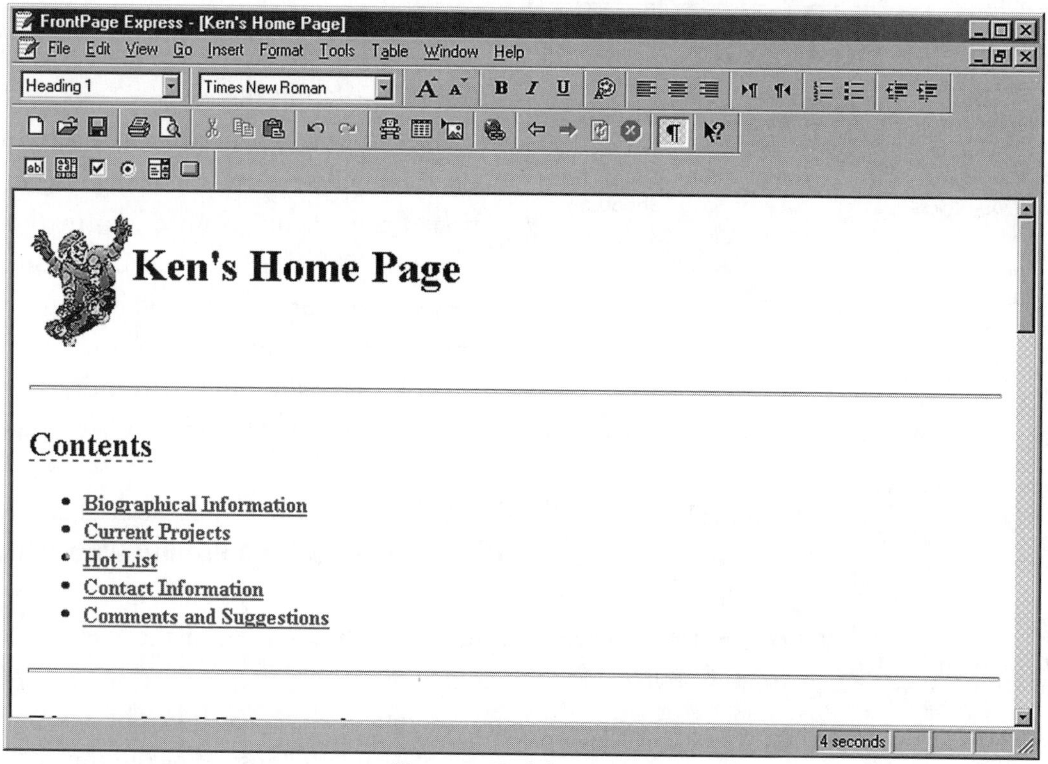

Figure 9. Ken's home page

Posting Your Web Page

Right now, the only way someone can view your new Web page is to come to your house and view it on your computer. It's time we move that page from your computer to the Internet. This is called *uploading*. Both FrontPage Express and Composer include publishing wizards to help you upload your page.

Before you attempt uploading your page, you must have a place to post it. Many ISPs offer a limited amount of space for subscribers to post personal Web pages. If it's not included in your basic subscription, it might be available for a few dollars more a month. You can also subscribe to a free Web hosting service on the Internet (see sidebar). Many of these sites also offer online tools for creating Web pages. In exchange for free Web space, most of these free Web hosting services place pop-up or banner ads on your

Free Web Site Hosting

Angelfire	www.angelfire.com
GeoCities	www.geocities.com
Homestead	www.homestead.com
HowdyNeighbor.com	www.howdyneighbor.com
MyFamily	www.myfamily.com
Tripod	www.tripod.com
TruePath	www.truepath.com
Xoom	www.xoom.com

site. You have no control over these ads. For a small fee, some companies allow you to opt out of these ads.

Once you have a place to host your site, you will need the following information from them: connection method; server or FTP address; name of the directory where your Web site will be stored on their server; and your Web address (URL), user name, and password.

Now that you have that information, it's time to post your Web page.

1. To run the Web Publishing Wizard, choose **Start** from the taskbar, then **Programs, Accessories, Internet Tools, Web Publishing Wizard** (see figure 10). If it's not installed, you will need to install it.

2. Click **Next** to start the wizard. Enter the location of the Web site on your hard drive or the individual file.

3. Click **Next** and enter a name for your Web server. It can be any name you choose. For example: My Web Server. The next time you upload files, select this name from the list.

4. Click **Next**, and select the connection method, if you know it. If you don't, choose **Automatically Select Connection Method**.

5. Click **Next** again and enter the address (URL) to access your Web site. In the Local Directory box, type the full path to where your Web page is located on your hard drive. The path will look

Figure 10. Web Publishing Wizard

similar to this: c:\mydocuments\home.html.e to the folder where your Web site is located on your hard drive.

6. Click **Next** one last time. Click **Finish** and the dial-up connection will open and log on to the Internet.

7. Enter your user name and password in the Network Password dialog box.

8. Click **Finish**. Your Web site will now load.

Helping Others Find You

Now that you've posted your Web site, it's time to let others know it's there. Start by sending all your friends an E-mail. Make sure you type in the Web address correctly. Don't stop there. Include your Web site on business cards, stationery, and Christmas cards. Add your address to your E-mail signature file.

To keep your friends and family coming back to your Web site, add a few more pages. Add some special material to your Web site during the holidays and invite your friends to view it. Make a list of your favorite Web sites, post a few family pictures, or scan and post your preschooler's artistic masterpieces. Be creative. When you've added some special material, send everyone a note inviting them to stop by again.

Where to Go from Here

Do you want to do more? Great. Now that you've learned the basics, experiment. Both FrontPage Express and Netscape Composer are able to do a lot more. Read a few online beginner's guides on building sites. Look for ideas. Sketch out and build additional pages. Build a family Web site, with each member in charge of different sections. Build a site for your Sunday school class. Eventually, you might want to invest in a more powerful Web authoring program, such as Dreamweaver, FrontPage, Page Maker, or WebEasy. Above all else, have fun.

CHAPTER 35

FUN FAMILY ACTIVITIES

Part of the lure and enjoyment the Internet offers is all the "stuff" you can do both on- and offline. Here are twenty-five activities to get you started. As you do some of these, you will discover other things you can do with the help of the Internet.

Family Newsletter (Ezine)

A family newsletter is a great way to keep in touch with family. The easiest newsletter to produce is one limited to text. Such newsletters are easily sent by E-mail. If you want to use photos and children's drawings, you'll have to post your newsletter to a Web site or use a publishing program that converts your newsletter to a format that others can view.

The procedure for producing a newsletter is very simple.

1. Decide who will produce the newsletter. More than one person can participate. Individuals can write and submit articles. Others can edit the articles. Then a more technologically inclined family member can put it together.
2. Determine how often you're going to produce the letter and set deadlines for submitting material.

3. Decide the format of your newsletter. How you plan to send the newsletter will determine your format. Will you send it as an E-mail message or attachment? Will you post it to a Web site? Perhaps you'll do both. Will you need to send it to some people by fax or snail mail?

4. If you're going to post it to a Web site, create a site on a free Web hosting service such as TruePath.com, Homestead.com, or MyFamily.com.

5. Settle on a name and the type of information that will go into your newsletter. Be sure to include a calendar of events for birthdays and anniversaries. If someone's hobby is genealogy research, ask them to write a family tree column. Consider adding a special section to record those humorous incidents that occur in every family. Use the newsletter to help plan, publicize, and highlight special moments like weddings and graduations. The ideas are endless.

6. Have family members send in announcements, family events, anecdotes, and poems. If you plan to post the newsletter to a Web site, have them send photos and children's drawings. Get as many people as possible to send items by E-mail. This saves you time because the items won't have to be scanned. (Note: When family members send items for the newsletter, have them sent in the same word processor format. This will save you time retyping. If they can't send it to you in the specified format, have them send it as a standard E-mail message. Then cut and paste it into the program you're using.)

7. Set up a free E-mail address for the newsletter. This will keep newsletter E-mail separate from personal mail. Even if the editor changes, the E-mail address won't.

8. Send a reminder a few days before the deadline. Include the E-mail address to which items are to be sent.

9. Assemble the newsletter. If you're posting it to a Web site, you'll need to use FrontPage Express, Netscape Composer, or the free Web hosting site's software. For help using this software, see chapter 34. (Note: If you're using WordPerfect or Microsoft Word, you can type and compose your newsletter in your word processor and convert it directly to HTML. Check your word processor's online help for more information.)

10. Before sending out your newsletter, send a copy to yourself. If you're posting it online, upload it and view it. Make sure everything is the way you want it.

11. When everything is to your liking, send out your newsletter. You may need to send it more than one way. Send a message announcing where it's posted online, or send it by E-mail, fax, or, if necessary, the old-fashioned way—by snail mail, to those who don't have Internet access.

12. If you are posting it to the Web, you can keep anyone other than family members from viewing the pages by using a password. If you cannot create a password, then don't place a link to the newsletter on the Web site. Instead, send the link that leads to the family newsletter by E-mail to your family. They must use the link to get to the newsletter.

You can use these newsletter instructions for creating invitations, Christmas cards, flyers, and more.

Hold an Online Family Reunion

This is an easy way to get everyone together without the expense of traveling cross-country. MyFamily.com has free, private chat rooms where you and your family can go to chat. Someone in your family must register for a site. They will list names and E-mail addresses of everyone who will have access to the site. Those people will receive a password so they can log on to the family site. Once registered, set a date and time for your reunion; then, at the appointed time, log on.

Another way to hold an online family reunion is for everyone to sign up for the same chat program, as described in chapter 31. To use ICQ for a family reunion, follow these steps:

1. Make sure everyone has ICQ and has added everyone in the group to their buddy list.

2. Set a date and time for the reunion.

3. At the agreed on time, log on to the Internet. The first two people online will initiate the chat session (see chapter 31).

4. As other family members log on, click on their names and choose **Chat**. When they accept the chat invitation, they will be added to the chat session.

5. Members can log on and off during the chat session. As long as two people are in the chat session, it will continue.

The advantage of using ICQ is twofold. ICQ notifies you whenever a family member logs on while you're online. You can choose to send a quick note or pause for a longer conversation. Second, your chat room is always open. You don't have to register again to use it. If five or six of you are online one evening, you can enter the chat room for an impromptu get-together.

Don't forget those who aren't on the Internet yet. You can still include them. Arrange for them to go to a friend's house who is online, or if they live near an online family member, have them join the conversation from there. You might even schedule your online family reunion when a family member with a notebook computer is visiting someone who isn't online.

Be sure to allow plenty of time for your reunion. Online reunions can stretch into hours. One last note: While you're online, start planning your next face-to-face reunion. If you're looking for help or ideas for your next reunion, check out Family-Reunion.com.

Create an Online Photo Album

Perhaps you don't want to build a Web site, but you do want to share your vacation pictures with your family. Maybe you just had a baby and you want all your friends and family to see how beautiful she is. Then post your pictures in a free, virtual album.

You will need a digital camera, the ability to scan pictures into your computer and save them in JPG format, or a photo CD of pictures you've taken. Photos don't have to be in JPG format, but it's the best format for the

Web. Next, you'll need to select a site and upload your pictures to your virtual album.

Zing.com, ClubPhoto, and PhotoLoft are three online photo communities. All of these sites work about the same way: (1) Create an album by registering with the site. (2) Download and install the software for using the site. (3) Add your pictures to your album. (4) Invite your family and friends to check out your album.

Another option is MyFamily.com. Every free family Web site has a photo album built into it. Uploading photos is simply a process of clicking **Upload** and following the online instructions.

A password protects your photos from all but those whom you want to see them. Once you've posted your pictures, send the URL (Web address) and the password to your family and friends.

> **Online Photo Communities**
>
> | | |
> |---|---|
> | ClubPhoto | www.clubphoto.com |
> | PhotoLoft | www.photoloft.com |
> | MyFamily.com | www.myfamily.com |
> | Zing.com | www.zing.com |

Send an Electronic Greeting Card

Send a card to a friend by E-mail. Sending an electronic greeting card is simple, and most greeting card sites work in a similar manner.

1. Select the site from which you want to send a card.
2. Browse the available cards, selecting the one you want to send. Most sites are divided into categories: Easter, Christmas, Birthday, Mother's Day, Father's Day, Valentine's Day, etc.
3. Add a personal message.
4. Fill out the necessary E-mail information. This usually includes providing the name and E-mail address of the person for whom the card is intended as well as your own name and E-mail address.
5. Click **Send**.

It's that simple! Some sites allow you to preview your card. Your friend will receive an E-mail notifying them that you've sent them an electronic greeting card. When they click on the link in the E-mail, their card will open in a browser window.

Before sending electronic greeting cards, remember a few helpful tips. First, always read the privacy statement on the site. Second, if required to register, give as little information as possible. Most sites will asterisk or otherwise indicate what information is required. Third, always know the site from which you are sending a card. Fourth, make sure you read the whole card, and if there is sound, listen to it. You don't want to be embarrassed by unintentionally sending an offensive card.

To get you started, here are a few of the most popular electronic card sites.

- American Greetings   www.americangreetings.com
- Blue Mountain Arts   www.4bluemountain.com
- Hallmark   www.hallmarkconnections.com
- Postcards from the Web   www.homearts.com/postcards
- Christian Postcards   www.christianpostcards.com

If you still can't find what you're looking for, try CardCentral, a directory of more than 1,200 electronic card sites (www.cardcentral.net).

Send Your Love Some Virtual Flowers

It's the thought that counts, right? Not always, but when your budget doesn't allow for more, or it's just on the spur of the moment, swing over to one of these sites and send someone in your family a virtual bouquet.

- Internet Flowers   www.iflowers.com
- Virtual Flowers   www.virtualflowers.com

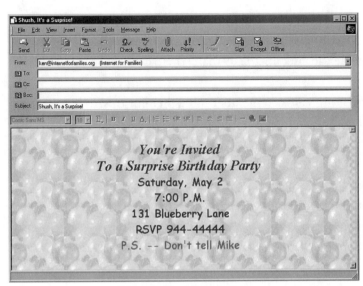

Figure 1. E-mail Invitation

E-mail Invitation

Birthday, anniversary, holiday, class reunion, housewarming, shower—the next time you need to send out invitations, send them by E-mail. With a little creativity, you can send some attention-grabbing invitations (see figure 1). Let's practice.

1. Open your E-mail program and type the following text:

    You're Invited
    To a Surprise Birthday Party
    Saturday, May 2
    7:00 P.M.
    131 Blueberry Lane
    RSVP 944–4444
    P.S. Don't tell Mike!

2. Select the first two lines of text by holding down the left mouse button and dragging it across the two lines. Release the mouse button. The text should remain selected.

3. From the format toolbar, change the font size to 24 points. Choose **bold, italic** and the color **purple**. When finished, click outside the highlighted text to turn off the selection.

4. Select the remaining lines of text. Choose a different font, color, and enlarge it to 18 points. (Be sure to pick a font that most people will have.) Turn off the highlighting by clicking outside the text.

5. Select the last line of text and change the color to red.

6. Select all seven lines of text one more time and choose **Center** justification.
7. Add a background (stationery, in Outlook Express). From the New Message toolbar, choose **Format, Apply Stationery** and select a background image.

Now you're finished. Address your invitation. Add a subject and send it out. If you're sending it to more than one person at a time, use the Bcc: field.

Other uses for this project include birth announcements, garage sales, PTA meetings, sports schedules, Sunday school activities, and youth events.

Plan a Day Trip

In chapter 32 we learned how to use the Internet to plan a vacation. You can also use the Internet to plan shorter outings, such as day trips or weekend getaways. On the Internet, you can find up-to-the-minute information on everything—concerts, community events, theme parks, national park schedules, sports ticket information, and so on. It's also a way to look for those not-too-far-out-of-the-way places to visit. Here are eight steps for planning a family outing:

1. Decide how far from home you want to go. As far as a tank of gas will go? A hundred miles in any direction? Two hours driving?
2. On a map, draw a circle around your city. The size of the circle will depend on how far you are willing to travel from home.
3. List all major cities, towns, state and national parks, and other sites and activities you already know about.
4. Use two or three search engines to search for all the information you can find on the places you listed in number 3. (You don't have to research all the places at once; start with one or two that interest you.) Search city guides offered at travel sites. (MapQuest's local city guides offer a Kids & Family section for more than fifty cities.) Try searching for the phrase "day trips." For example, the Arizona Guide (by the

Arizona Department of Tourism) lists day trips in and around major cities and attractions. If the area in which you live has a regional name, search for it. For example: Southwest Florida.

5. Check online local newspapers, city guides, and city tourism offices for activity calendars.

6. In your browser, create a Bookmarks or Favorites folder called "Day Trips." Bookmark select sites, such as city guides, chambers of commerce, and online local newspapers for future reference.

7. Purchase a file folder and write "Day Trips" on it. File copies of Web pages along with a list of places you'd like to go or things you'd like to do.

8. Before you go, confirm all information online *and* by phone or E-mail. Last-minute changes may not have made it to the Web site.

Take a Virtual Tour of a City or Country

They're called Web cams—small electronic cameras attached to computers—and they're popping up all over the Internet. Many take still shots. Others provide a live video feed. Many Web sites have used them to create virtual tours of cities and countries. Here are three virtual tours—one of an ancient city, one of Israel, and the other of historic, downtown Philadelphia.

* Ancient Rome   www.ancientsites.com/as/
                      rome/academy/tours/index.html
* Tour a Crayon   http://www.crayola.com/factory/index.ctm
    Factory
* Virtual Holy Land   www.virtualholyland.com

Use the following two sites to take a tour of a place that interests your family:

* EarthCam   www.earthcam.com
* WWW Virtual Tours   www.virtualfreesites.com/tours.html

Taking a virtual tour is a great way to get your family excited about taking a vacation to a spot you've never been before.

Visit a Museum Online

Museums are going online. Some museum sites simply post hours of operation, announcements concerning upcoming exhibits, and directions. However, more and more museum sites are adding interactive features—virtual tours of all or a portion of their museum, images of artwork, photos of museum items, activities, and science projects. Naturally, everything in a museum will not be on the Web. Nor does visiting the Web site take the place of visiting the museum. But when you can't make it to the lobby in person, visit a museum online. Here are a few you can try.

- The Smithsonian   www.si.edu
- Oregon Museum of   www.omsi.edu
  Science and Industry
- The Franklin Institute   www.fi.edu/planets/gallery.html
  Science Museum
- Virtual Museums Tours   http://archive.comlab.ox.ac.uk/other/
                                  museums.html

Search tip: To find more museums, use the keyword or words *museum* or *virtual museum.*

Tour the Solar System

There are a number of free science projects at NASA's SpaceKids Web site (see figure 2). One of them enables you to take a virtual tour of the solar system (http://spacekids.hq.nasa.gov/osskids/animate/mac.html). Pick a planet from which to begin your tour. Fly right past Earth on your way to the Sun. After visiting the planets closest to the Sun, zoom out and

Figure 2. NASA's SpaceKid Web site

around to fly by a comet on the way to Jupiter, Saturn, and beyond.

If it's not installed, you'll need to download the Live Picture Viewer. There is a link on the Web page. Be sure to read the Readme file. Please be patient—the photos using Live Picture will take awhile to download.

View Your Neighborhood from Space

Get a new perspective on your neighborhood at Microsoft TerraServer (http://terraserver.microsoft.com). Get a satellite view of your neighborhood or hundreds of famous places.

Around the World in Eighty Days

Here's an exciting project that you can adapt to eight weeks or eight days. Get a copy of Jules Verne's *Around the World in Eighty Days.* Read it yourself before getting your family started on this project. As you read it, plot on a map the countries they flew over and landed in. Select eight to ten of the places mentioned in the book. Have your family use the Internet to research each of those places. Find out all you can about the people, place, and culture. Now read the book as a family, stretching it out over the set period of time. As you read about each of the places you've researched, decorate the dining room appropriately, fix an ethnic meal, or plan some event to highlight what you've learned. If there is a virtual tour on the Internet of that night's designated city or country, sit down as a family after dinner and take the tour together. Be creative. Have fun.

Search tip: To gather information, start with a regular search engine and the CIA World Factbook.

Online Scavenger Hunt

This is a high-tech version of the popular kids' game. This time, instead of actual items, Polaroid photos, or sound recordings, you're going to use the Internet to find things. As in the traditional game, your virtual scavenger hunt can include any item or person you find in real life. For example, you could conduct a scavenger hunt looking for the following:

- a fountain pen
- a picture of Mt. Everest
- a popsicle
- an iron
- a moon lander
- the flag of Madagascar
- a picture of the president of the United States
- Larry Boy
- the music to "Amazing Grace"

You can play this game in teams or singularly. Consider teaming children with adults, or kids against adults. Give each team a time limit on the computer and have at it. Have them print copies of the Web site where they find each item. The one who gets the most results wins. (See www.internetforfamilies.org/fun/scavengerhunt for one possible set of answers.)

Trivial Pursuit

This is an easy game to set up, and it is a fun way to help family members sharpen their searching skills. You'll need a copy of the Trivial Pursuit board game and the Internet. One person goes through the Trivial Pursuit game cards, looking for questions family members aren't likely to know. Select one question from each of the six categories and type them on a piece of paper. On a day decided by the family, post the questions by the computer, along with a schedule of times they can sign up for to use the computer.

For younger family members and those less familiar with the Internet, provide a list of search or homework sites where the information might be found. Give each person a time limit. (Give shorter time limits to handicap those with more Internet savvy.) After each person has finished, the one with the most right answers wins. Make sure each participant records where they found the answer, just in case it differs from the one found in the Trivial Pursuit game.

Build and Fly the Best Paper Airplane

Ken Blackburn holds the world record for a sustained paper airplane flight—27.6 seconds. Print out a pattern for creating your own copy of his world-record-setting airplane or one of the planes at these other sites.

- Ken Blackburn
  www.geocities.com/CapeCanaveral/1817/
- The DC3 of Paper Airplanes
  www.zurqui.com/crinfocus/paper/airplane.html
- Paper Paradise
  www.paperparadise.com/freeindex.cfm

Create Your Own New England Village

Ben and Jerry's, the ice cream moguls, have a fun site that includes puzzles, games, and arts and crafts. There is a page of patterns you can print, cut, and paste together to build your own New England village (http://euphoria.benjerry.com/fun/index.htm).

Dissect a Frog

Hop on over to the University of Virginia and learn how to dissect a frog. There are a number of imitation sites, but this is the original (http://teach.virginia.edu/go/frog).

Find a Craft Project

From preschooler to senior adult, you'll find lots of craft ideas and instructions on the Internet. Here are a few sites to get you started. Search tip: Use the word *crafts, craft project,* or the name of a specific project.

• Hands On! Crafts for Kids	www.crafts4kids.com
• Craftnet Village	www.craftnetvillage.com/ project_library
• Early Childhood Education	www.earlychildhood.com
• Better Homes and Gardens	www.bhg.com/crafts

Follow Your Favorite Sports Team

Get the latest information on your team. Read player profiles. Visit players' personal Web sites. Ask questions of players and coaches. Listen to their games on the Internet, even if you live a thousand miles away from your home team. All four of the major sports are online: football, basketball, baseball, and hockey. So are most major college sports programs. To find your favorite team, start with one of the links below or search for your team by using a search engine. To listen to your team's games online, go to their Web site and find the link to the radio station broadcasting the games locally.

- National Football League   http://nfl.com
- National Basketball Association   http://nba.com
- Major League Baseball   http://majorleaguebaseball.com
- National Hockey League   http://nhl.com
- NCAA   www.ncaa.org

Don't forget to follow your team online, through ESPN and CNN, and by way of your team's hometown newspaper.

Listen to Your Favorite Program

If it's on the radio, it's probably on the Internet. You can find a program by going directly to its Web site or by searching for its broadcast at one of the following sites. When you find the program you want, click on it. If you don't have RealPlayer, you'll need to download it first.

- OnePlace.com   www.oneplace.com
- Broadcast.com   www.broadcast.com
- Involved Christian Radio www.icrn.com
- Lightsource   www.broadcast.com/lightsource
- Today's Christian Music www.todayschristianmusic.com

Make Your Own Paper

Roll up your sleeves, clean off the counter, and prepare to make your own paper. It's a fun and messy project from the Marcal Paper Company (www.marcalpaper.com/how_paper_is_made.html).

Movie and Video Reviews

It's hard to find a good movie or video any more. Often those that promise to provide good family entertainment contain unexpected "surprises" that you'd prefer not to have. Here are four family-friendly movie review sites:

- Christian Spotlight on the Movies — www.christiananswers.net/spotlight
- Preview Online — www.gospelcom.net/preview/
- Screen It — www.screenit.com
- Ted Baehr's Movie Guide — http://movieguide.christcom.net/ccn/movieguide.nsf/main/home

Online Coloring Books

There are pages to color online and pages to print and color offline (see figure 3).

- Christian Answers.Net www.christian-answers.net/kids/clr-indx.html
- Coloring 4 Kids www.coloringpage.org
- Crayola Crayons www.crayola.com

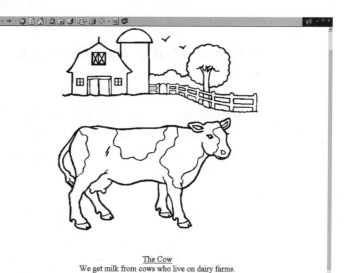

The Cow
We get milk from cows who live on dairy farms.
God made cows to give lots of milk.

Figure 3. Coloring page on Christian Answers.Net

Play Games Online

Do you like to play games? Here are a few sites for kids (young and old). Please be patient. Most of these games are either JavaApplets or Shockwave games. They require some time to load. If you don't have the free Shockwave plug-in, there will be a link that connects you to the download site. There are many other game sites on the Internet. Always use caution when checking out or playing new games.

- Bonus.com   www.bonus.com
- Candystand.com   www.candystand.com
- CCMag Kids 4Jesus   www.gospelcom.net/ccmag/kids
- Guiding Light Games   www.guidinglightvideo.com/games.html
- Microsoft Gaming Zone   http://zone.msn.com
- Shockwave.com   www.shockwave.com

Send Your Name to Mars

NASA invites kids of all ages to send their name to Mars in 2001. Those who do can print out a certificate of participation. To get on board for Mars, just follow the link to NASA's site (http://spacekids.hq.nasa.gov/2001). While you're on this site, check out all the other "cool" activities you can do.

CONCLUSION

Do you remember the diving board back in the introduction? Jumping in over my head was how I learned to dive, and it was how I learned to use the Internet.

Fortunately, when it comes to the Internet, you don't have to jump in over your head. Having read this book and having tried the examples, you now have the tools you need to reap the benefits while avoiding the dangers of the Internet.

What do I like best about the Internet? It's a question I'm often asked; yet I've never been able to answer it. There's so much to like about the Internet.

Knowledge is one of the draws for me. I love to learn. The Internet offers the opportunity to learn new things and connect with others. I'm learning a new hobby—bonsai growing—using the Internet. I've also found medical help for members of my church family. I've taken two online classes. I've searched for and found answers to hundreds of everyday questions.

Relationships are important to me. One of my best friends now lives eight hundred miles away. With instant messaging, we stay in regular contact. Across the Internet, I can encourage a fellow writer. I can receive prayer requests and pray for a pastor friend in another state. My wife, Diane, has built an E-mail web of relationships with friends who are now scattered across the country and overseas. We can even exchange photos across the Web.

My love for adventure is another magnet drawing me to the Internet. There is no way I'll ever climb Mt. Everest, but by way of the Internet I can, and have, stood on the top of the world. I want to be the first pastor or writer in space. I'll probably never get that chance, but I've seen the view out the shuttle window. We wanted to do something special for our kids on a recent vacation. We researched and found where we could swim with dolphins. On a trip to Montana, I went on a white water kayak trip for the first time in my life. We made plans for both trips on the Internet.

Change is another reason I like the Internet. The Internet is far different today from what it was when I first logged on some five years ago— and it promises to be just as different five years from now. (Five years? How about five months from now?) That change brings new skills to learn, new adventures to pursue, and new sites to discover.

There's another aspect of change that appeals to me. It is the potential to influence others for Christ—to point people to Jesus and see them transformed. We are just now beginning to discover the possibilities of what can happen when we engage people in dialogue across the Internet.

Yes, the Internet has its dark side. There are viruses to defend against, places to avoid, and you have a family to protect. But all those dangers also exist in the real world around you, and you've learned where to go and what to do. If you've followed the advice in this book, you've done the same with the Internet.

There are limits to the Internet. The Internet cannot give your spouse a hug. It cannot wrestle your kids into submission on the family room floor. It cannot laugh with you, cry with you, or put a hand on your shoulder. It cannot smile back at you. It cannot replace your sitting in the bleachers at your son's high school basketball game. Nor can it take your daughter horseback riding. You can't smell a flower or feel the cool ocean breeze brush across your face as you watch the sun set. You can't go fishing on the Internet. It cannot replace the company of a friend or a gathering of believers in worship. These things happen in the real world. So be sure you turn the computer off and spend time with your family and friends.

I marvel at what man has achieved with the Internet. I marvel still more at where it will take us. But I marvel most at the picture of my kids' birth tucked away in the pages of a photo album, the sound of my son playing his trumpet, and the laughter of my daughter. I marvel that my wife has put up with me all these years. Above all, I marvel most at what Jesus has done in my life. Yes, the Internet is a marvelous invention, but it doesn't compare to God's marvelous creation.

As a child, whenever I went away for the weekend with my grand-parents, traveled out of town on a school trip, or simply set off into the woods for the day with friends, my mom, in saying good-bye, almost always sent me off with the same farewell: "Be careful and have fun." Those are fit-ting words as we end this journey together through this book. So as you put it down to log back on to the Internet, "Be careful and have fun."

By the way, drop me an E-mail and let me know what *you* like best about the Internet.

Ken
Ken@internetforfamilies.org

TERMS YOU SHOULD KNOW

56K: The standard speed of analog modems today. If you have an older modem, the speed is either 28:8 and 33:6.

ActiveX: Small add-in program, similar to plug-ins, designed to enhance Internet Explorer.

address: Every Web site and Web page has a unique address on the Internet. Entering an address into the browser tells your browser what page of information you want from the Internet. Typically, addresses look like the following: http://www.lifeway.com; http://www.family.org; http://www.nasa.gov. An address can also be called a URL or Universal Resource Locator.

address book: A place to store E-mail addresses.

antivirus software: A program that helps guard against and, if necessary, rid your computer of computer viruses.

attachment: An image, file, or program sent with an E-mail message.

bandwidth: The amount of information that can be transmitted across the Internet at any one time. Bandwidth is affected by the type of connection and the number of people online.

blocking/monitoring software: Programs designed to "block" offensive Web sites and monitor where your family has been online.

Boolean operators: A term such as AND, OR, NOT, usually in capitals, that indicates how terms are related in a search.

browser: The software used to access the Internet. The two most popular are Microsoft Internet Explorer and Netscape Navigator.

cable modem: A newer, faster form of Internet access. Cable modems use the same cable from which you receive your cable television signal.

cache: The place on your hard drive where your browser temporarily stores files and images downloaded from the Internet. Sometimes it is called Temporary Internet Files.

chat: To converse with other computer users by way of a special program, like ICQ or AOL Instant Messenger.

cookie: A piece of information sent to and stored on your computer by a Web site. Cookies can contain information such as log-in or registration information, personal preferences for using their Web site, and online shopping. Cookies cannot read your hard drive or send personal information back to a Web site. They can pass on browsing habits to Web marketers. You can turn off or limit the acceptance of cookies.

directory: A type of search engine compiled by people. Sites can be searched or browsed by categories. Yahoo and About.com are two directory search engines.

domain name: The unique name that identifies a Web site. Names have two or more parts, separated by dots (.). The domain name is always part of the Web address. For example: family.org (Focus on the Family) or eb.com (The Encyclopedia Britannica Online).

download: The act of moving information from a distant computer to the one you are operating.

DSL: Stands for Digital Subscriber Line. This is a much faster form of Internet connection that uses regular phone lines. You'll sometimes see it called ADSL or SDSL.

E-mail: Short for *electronic mail*. Electronic messages sent from one computer to another by way of the Internet. Messages can include pictures, files, and small programs.

E-mail address: An actual address to which E-mail is sent. E-mail addresses have two parts, separated by the @ symbol. The first part is the user's name. The second part is the name of the mail provider.

encryption: Sending information in a coded form to keep it from being read except by the person to whom you send it.

FAQ: Frequently Asked Questions—a special Web page listing answers to commonly asked questions about the site you're visiting.

favorite or bookmark: Like an electronic Rolodex, favorites or bookmarks are set within your browser. When you plan to visit a site often, you can set a favorite or bookmark to remember the Web site's address.

filter: A special tool to automatically sort your incoming mail into various folders or mailboxes. Filters can also be used to block "spam" or other unwanted mail.

flame: Angry or insulting E-mail and chat messages.

FTP: File Transfer Protocol. A set of instructions for moving files from one computer to another across the Internet.

home: *Home* has two different meanings. First, *home* refers to the Web page your browser opens to every time you log on to the Internet. Second, it refers to the "opening page" of any Web site. A Web site's home page is the title and table of contents page rolled into one.

HTML: HyperText Markup Language. The programming language used to create Web pages and other content for the Internet.

http: HyperText Transfer Protocol. These are the first letters you see in the address bar of your browser. It is a "protocol," a set of instructions for how information is transferred across the Internet. Think of it as a "language" your computer uses to "talk" with other computers.

hypertext: Words or text that contain a link to other text or document. When clicked, you are moved to a different page or Web site. Typically, hypertext appears as blue, underlined lettering.

GIF: Graphic Interchange Format. One of two commonly used image formats suitable for the Web.

ISP or Internet Service Provider: Your ISP is the company through which you access the Internet.

Java: A programming language used to add animation and other inter-activity to Web sites.

JPG or JPEG: Joint Photographic Experts Group. The most common format for detailed images and photographs on the Internet.

phrase search: A search for documents containing the exact phrase you specify.

link: A picture, word, button, or graphic image that when clicked moves you to a different Web page or Web site.

load: As a Web page appears on your screen, it is said to be loading.

mailing list: The term has two meanings: (1) A list of individuals who've subscribed to the same online newsletter. (2) An automated E-mail discussion group. A person sends a message to one address, and it is sent to all those on the list.

metasearch engine: A search engine that translates your query into the correct syntax used by different search engines. Metasearch engines include MetaCrawler and ProFusion.

modem: This is the part of your computer that dials up your ISP's phone number and makes the connection to the Internet.

natural language search: A search using normal conversational language. Often framed in the form of a question. Ask Jeeves uses natural language searches.

netiquette: The etiquette of the Internet.

netizen: Someone who uses the Internet.

newbie: Someone new to the Internet.

newsgroup: The name of a discussion group.

Online Service: America Online, Prodigy, and CompuServe are all Online Services. They differ from a standard ISP by providing custom content for their customers. This content consists of Web sites, magazines, entertainment, chat, and more that may or may not be found on the Internet. All Online Services provide Internet access.

password: A word (or combination of letters, numbers, and symbols) that restricts access to data, programs, or accounts.

plug-in: A small program that "plugs in" to your browser, enabling you to run a special piece of software or multimedia.

POP or POP3: Post Office Protocol. It enables you to download your mail from a mail server. The mail server is usually provided by your ISP.

search: Search engines and search sites are the "card catalogs" of the Internet. When you don't know where to go to find what you're looking for, you go to a search site. There you search their catalog of sites by using keyword(s) or phrases.

search engine: A database of Web sites that can be searched. Most search engines collect and categorize information automatically by using software programs. Some search engines are AltaVista, Excite, Crosswalk, LookSmart, and Goshen.

signature: A message, usually including name, E-mail address, and other personal information, attached to the end of your outgoing messages.

SMTP: Simple Mail Transfer Protocol. This is the standard protocol for sending messages. Often your ISP host's address begins with "mailhost."

spam: Anything you don't want. It is most often used to describe unwanted or junk E-mail or mailing list messages.

URL: Universal Resource Locator. The technical name for the unique Web address of each site. See also "address."

userID: Your unique log-on name that identifies you and your computer to your ISP and the Internet.

virus: A small rogue program. Once on your computer, it replicates itself and executes commands that affect the operation of your computer.

webmaster: The person who created or is in charge of the content of a Web site.

Web site/Web page: If the Internet were a library, then each book in the library would be a Web site and each page in that book a Web page. Like the books in a library, some contain hundreds or thousands of pages; others are small, containing just a few pages. Instead of pages made of paper, Web sites and pages are electronic files stored on computers scattered around the world.

www: World Wide Web: The largest section of the Internet. It is the section of the Internet where you'll spend most of your time.

APPENDIX 2

WEB SITES TO VISIT

Here are almost four hundred Web sites to get you started exploring the Internet. They are divided into twenty-four categories. Please keep in mind that not all of these sites are Christian sites. I cannot control all the information you'll find on every site. I've tried to be selective and weigh the good versus any potential danger. I encourage you to surf wisely and as a family.

You can find this list on the Internet at the Internet for Families Web site (internetforfamilies.org). There, it is called Net Compass. Posting this list on the Web site enables me to update it regularly—adding new sites, correcting addresses that have changed, or removing sites that are no longer on the Internet. You can also search Net Compass for relevant sites. To go directly to this page on the Web site, use the following address: http://www.internetforfamilies.org/compass.htm

Children

Ben and Jerry's	http://euphoria.benjerry.com/fun/index.html
Billy Bear 4 Kids	www.billybear4kids.com
Dr. Seuss	www.randomhouse.com/seussville
Family Fun	www.familypcfun.com
Guidepost for Kids	www.gp4k.com
Kids Quest	www.christiananswers.net/kids
KidsCom	www.kidscom.com

KidSurf Online	www.kidsurf.net
Kidz @ Rated-G	http://rated-g.com/channels/kidz.htm
Kidz	www.worldvillage.com/kidz
KinderGARDEN	http://aggie-horticulture.tamu.edu/ Kindergarden/index.html
Larry Boy	www.larry-boy.com
Peanuts & Charlie Brown	www.snoopy.com/comics/peanuts
The Puzzle Club	www.lhm.org
Route 6-16 (Cyber Patrol)	www.microsys.com/616/default.htm

Christian Living

5 Clicks to Sharing Your Faith	www.5clicks.com
Apologia Report	www.gospelcom.net/apologia
Bible Study Tools	www.biblestudytools.com
Christian Answers.Net	www.christiananswers.net
Christian Topics	www.christiantopics.com
Christianity Online	www.christianityonline.com
Devotionals	www.devotionals.net
ICRN – Involved Christian Radio Network	www.icrn.com
Lightsource.com	www.broadcast.com/lightsource
Ministry of the Word	www.thechristian.org
OnePlace.com	www.oneplace.com
TodaysChristianMusic.com	www.todayschristianmusic.com
Virtual Holy Land	www.virtualholyland.com

Christian Organizations and Ministries

Billy Graham	www.billygraham.org
BreakPoint – Chuck Colson	www.breakpoint.org
Campus Crusade for Christ International	www.ccci.org
Christian Broadcasting Network	www.cbn.org
Crosswalk.com	www.crosswalk.com
The Evangelism Toolbox	www.evangelismtoolbox.com
FamilyNet	www.familynet.org
Goshen	www.goshen.net
Gospel Communications Network	www.gospelcom.net
INJOY – John Maxwell	www.injoy.com

Insight for Living – Chuck Swindoll	www.insight.org
Lightsource	www.lightsource.com
Moody Bible Institute	www.moody.edu
NetCast Evangelism	www.netcastevangelism.com
Preaching Today	www.preachingtoday.com
Promise Keepers	www.promisekeepers.org
Renewing Your Mind – R. C. Sproul	www.gospelcom.net/ligonier/index.html
Sports Spectrum	www.gospelcom.net/rbc/ss
TheGoal.com	www.thegoal.com
Trinity Broadcasting Network	www.tbn.org
Walk Thru the Bible	www.walkthru.org
Web Evangelism Guide	www.goshen.net/WebEvangelism

Christian Ethics and Politics

American Family Association	www.afa.net
CitizenLink	www.family.org/cforum
Ethics and Religious Liberty Commission	www.erlc.com
Family Research Council	www.frc.org
Probe Ministries	www.probe.org
Project Vote Smart	www.vote-smart.org
State and Local Government on the Net	www.piperinfo.com/state/states.html

Computers and the Internet

Adobe Acrobat Reader	www.adobe.com
CNET	www.cnet.com
Cyber Patrol	www.microsys.com/cyber
CYBERsitter	www.cybersitter.com
EntryPoint	www.entrypoint.com
McAfee	www.mcafee.com
Microsoft	www.microsoft.com
Net Nanny	www.netnanny.com
Netscape	www.netscape.com
Norton	www.norton.com
PKZIP	www.pkware.com

Quarterdeck	www.quarterdeck.com
QuickTime Player	www.apple.com
RealPlayer	www.real.com
Search Engine Watch	www.searchenginewatch.com
Shockwave	www.shockwave.com
WinZip	www.winzip.com
ZDnet	www.zdnet.com

Free E-mail Web Sites

AmExMail	www.amexmail.com
Bigfoot	www.bigfoot.com
CCNmail (Crosswalk)	www.ccnmail.com
Hotmail	www.hotmail.com
Iname.com	www.iname.com
Juno	www.juno.com
Mail City	http://mailcity.lycos.com
Net@ddress	www.netaddress.com
Yahoo! Mail	www.yahoo.com

Free Web Site Hosting

Angelfire	www.angelfire.com
GeoCities	www.geocities.com
Homestead	www.homestead.com
HowdyNeighbor.com	www.howdyneighbor.com
MyFamily	www.myfamily.com
Tripod	www.tripod.com
TruePath	www.truepath.com
Xoom	www.xoom.com

Online Photo Albums

Club Photo	www.clubphoto.com
MyFamily.com	www.myfamily.com
PhotoLoft	www.photoloft.com
Zing.com	www.zing.com

Electronic Greeting Cards

AARP Celebrates! Send a   www.aarp.org/holiday/
   Birthday Card!   birthday/home.html
American Greetings   www.americangreetings.com
Blue Mountain Arts   www.4bluemountain.com
Cardcentral.net   www.cardcentral.net
Christian Postcards   www.christianpostcards.com
Hallmark   www.hallmarkconnections.com
Postcards from the Web   www.homearts.com/postcards

Electronic Newsletters

ADHD of the Christian Kind   www.christianadhd.com
AnGeL Newsletter   www.christianityonline.com/angel
BreakPoint   www.breakpoint.org
Christian E-mail Mailing Lists   www.gospelcom.net/ifc/mail/view
Christian Homemakers   www.onelist.com/subscribe.cgi/
                                        homefires_hearth
Christianity Online Newsletters   www.christianityonline.com/
                                        community/newsletters
Dummies Daily   www.dummiesdaily.com
International Missions Prayer   www.imb.org
   Line
Internet for Christians   www.gospelcom.net/ifc
Internet for Families   www.internetforfamilies.org
John Stott Ministries   www.gospelcom.net/stott
Leadership Wired   www.injoy.com/MonthlyMentoring/
                                        LeadershipWired.asp
Money Matters   http://money.crosswalk.com
The RoMANtic   www.theromantic.com
TipWorld   www.tipworld.com

Family

ADHD of the Christian Kind   www.christianadhd.com
All About Families   www.allaboutfamilies.org
Center for Family Life Online   www.family-life.org
Family Builder's Ministry   www.familybuilders.net
FamilyLife – Dennis Rainey   www.familylife.com

Family PC Fun	www.familypcfun.com
Family-Reunion.com	www.family-reunion.com
Filtering Facts	www.filteringfacts.org
Focus on the Family	www.family.org
Growing Together	www.gospelcom.net/growingtogether
Internet for Families	www.internetforfamilies.org
KidShield	www.kidshield.com
MyFamily.com	www.myfamily.com
National Center for Fathering	www.fathers.com
Federation for Children with Special Needs	www.fcsn.org
Special Child magazine	www.specialchild.com

Finances

Christian Financial Concepts – Larry Burkett	www.cfcministry.org
Debt Proof Living – Mary Hunt	www.debtproofliving.com
Quicken Financial Network	www.quicken.com
Ronald Blue	www.ronblue.com

Games and Activities

Build and Fly the Best Paper Airplane	www.geocities.com/CapeCanaveral/1817
KinderART	www.kinderart.com
Lego	www.lego.com
Make Your Own Paper	www.marcalpaper.com/how_paper_is_made.html
Paper Paradise	www.paperparadise.com/free/index.cfm
Send Your Name to Mars	http://spacekids.hq.nasa.gov/2001
The DC3 of Paper Airplanes	www.zurqui.com/crinfocus/paper/airplane.html

Online Coloring Books

Christian Answers.Net	www.christiananswers.net/kids/clr-indx.html
Coloring 4 Kids	www.coloringpage.org
Crayola Crayons	www.crayola.com

Online Games

Bonus.com	www.bonus.com
Candystand.com	www.candystand.com
CCMag Kids 4Jesus	www.gospelcom.net/ccmag/kids
Guiding Light Games	www.guidinglightvideo.com/games.html
Microsoft Gaming Zone	http://zone.msn.com
Shockwave.com	www.shockwave.com

Genealogy

Ancestry.com	www.ancestry.com
Beginner's Guide to Family History	http://biz.ipa.net/arkresearch/guide.html
The Center for Disease Control	www.cdc.gov
Cyndi's List	www.cyndislist.com
Family History	www.familyhistory.com
Family Tree Maker	www.familytreemaker.com
FamilySearch	www.familysearch.org
Genealogy.com	www.genealogy.com
Heritage Quest	www.heritagequest.com
Journal of Online Genealogy	www.onlinegenealogy.com
RootsWeb.com	www.rootsweb.com
US Genealogical Project	www.usgenweb.com

Government

Census Bureau	www.census.gov
House of Representatives	www.house.gov
Internal Revenue Service	www.irs.gov
Library of Congress	www.loc.gov
Medicare	www.medicare.gov
National Gallery of Art	www.nga.gov
The Senate	www.senate.gov
Social Security	www.ssa.gov
The White House	www.whitehouse.gov

Hobbies

Crafts

Better Homes and Gardens   www.bhg.com/crafts
Craft Net Village   www.craftnetvillage.com/project_library
Early Childhood Education   www.earlychildhood.com
Hands On! Crafts for Kids   www.crafts4kids.com
Michael's Arts and Crafts   www.michaels.com

Cooking

Crisco Kitchen   www.criscokitchen.com
Lipton Kitchens   www.lipton.com
Sara Lee   www.saraleebakery.com

Follow Your Favorite Sports Team

National Basketball Association   http://nba.com
National Football League   http://nfl.com
Major League Baseball   http://majorleaguebaseball.com
National Hockey League   http://nhl.com
NCAA   www.ncaa.org

Gardening

Better Homes and Gardens   www.bhg.com/gardening
    Gardening Guide
Burpee   www.burpee.com
Garden.com   www.garden.com
National Gardening Association   http://www2.garden.org
Old Farmer's Almanac   www.almanac.com
Organic Gardening   www.organicgardening.com

How-to Guides

Better Homes and Gardens   www.bhg.com/homeimp
    Home Improvement
    Encyclopedia

How2.com	www.how2.com
ImproveNet	www.improvenet.com
Learn2.com	www.learn2.com
The Home Depot	www.homedepot.com

Homework Help

The American Presidency	www.gi.grolier.com/presidents
Ask Dr. Math	www.forum.swarthmore.edu/dr.math
ChemFinder.com	www.chemfinder.com
Chemical Elements.com	www.chemicalelements.com
Dissect a Frog	http://teach.virginia.edu/go/frog
Homework Helper	www.homeworkhelper.com
Homework Help	www.startribune.com/education/homework.shtml
Homework Central	www.homeworkcentral.com
Infoplease Homework Center	www.infoplease.com/homework/index.html
Infoplease Kids' Almanac	http://kids.infoplease.com
KidsClick!	http://sunsite.berkeley.edu/kidsclick
Microsoft TerraServer	http://terraserver.microsoft.com
Ocean Planet	http://seawifs.gsfc.nasa.gov/ocean_planet.html
Researchpaper.com	www.researchpaper.com
Student Navigator	www.nytimes.com/learning/general/navigator/students.html
StudyWeb	www.studyweb.com

Men

Great Dads	www.greatdads.org
Men of Integrity	www.menofintegrity.org
The RoMANtic's Guide	www.theromantic.com
Marriage Builders	www.marriagebuilders.com
Men (Crosswalk.com)	http://men.crosswalk.com
National Center for Fathering	www.fathers.com
New Man Magazine	www.newmanmag.com
Promise Keepers	www.promisekeepers.org

Movie and Video Reviews

Christian Spotlight on Entertainment	www.christiananswers.net/spotlight/home.html
Crosswalk Entertainment Channel	http://movies.crosswalk.com
Familystyle.com	www.familystyle.com
Plugged-In	www.family.org/pplace/pi
Screen It	www.screenit.com

News

ABC News	www.abcnews.com
CNN	www.cnn.com
ESPN Sports	www.espn.com
Los Angeles Times	www.latimes.com
MSNBC	www.msnbc.com
New York Times	www.nytimes.com
PathFinder (Time & Life Magazine)	www.pathfinder.com
U.S. News	www.usnews.com
USA Today	www.usatoday.com
The Wall Street Journal	www.wsj.com
The Washington Post	www.washingtonpost.com

Reference

Britannica Online	www.britannica.com
BioSearch (Biographical Encyclopedia)	www.biography.com
CIA World Factbook	www.cia.gov/cia/publications/factbook/index.html
Dictionary.com	www.dictionary.com
Discovery Channel Online	www.discovery.com
Electric Library	www.elibrary.com
The Elements of Style	www.bartleby.com/14.1
Encyclopedia Britannica	www.eb.com
Encyclopedia.com	www.encyclopedia.com
Healthfinder	www.healthfinder.gov
Information Please Almanac	www.infoplease.com
NASA	www.nasa.gov

National Geographic Online	www.nationalgeographic.com
The National Library of Medicine	www.nlm.nih.gov
Navigator (NY Times)	www.nytimes.com/learning/general/navigator
PC Webopaedia	www.pcwebopaedia.com
Research It	www.itools.com/research-it/research-it.html
Researchpaper.com	www.researchpaper.com
Roget's Internet Thesaurus	www.thesaurus.com
The Virtual Reference Desk	http://thorplus.lib.purdue.edu/vlibrary
The Smithsonian Institute	www.si.edu
The Weather Channel	www.weather.com
The History Channel	www.historychannel.com
WWWebster Dictionary	www.m-w.com

Search Engines

Family-Friendly Search Engines (Filtered)

Ah-ha.com	www.ah-ha.com
AltaVista	www.altavista.com
Crosswalk	www.crosswalk.com
GO Network	www.go.com
LookSmart	www.looksmart.com
Lycos	www.lycos.com
Searchopolis	www.searchopolis.com

Standard Search Engines

About.com	www.about.com
Ask Jeeves	www.aj.com
Excite	www.excite.com
Google	www.google.com
HotBot	www.hotbot.com
Northern Light	www.northernlight.com
Snap.com	www.snap.com
Yahoo	www.yahoo.com

Metasearch Engines

| DogPile | www.dogpile.com |
| Family Friendly Search | www.familyfriendlysearch.com |

MetaCrawler	www.metacrawler.com
ProFusion	www.profusion.com
SavvySearch	www.savvysearch.com

Kids' Search Engines

AOL NetFind Kids Only	www.aol.com/netfind/kids
Ask Jeeves for Kids	www.ajkids.com
Searchopolis	www.searchopolis.com
Yahooligans	www.yahooligans.com
Zeek Search	www.zeeks.com/search/zeeksearch.asp

Christian Search Engines

711.net	www.711.net
All in One Christian Index	www.allinone.org
Christian USA	www.christianusa.net
Church Locator	www.christianity.net/churchlocator
Churches Dot Net	www.churches.net
Cross Search	www.crosssearch.com
Crosswalk	www.crosswalk.com
Goshen	www.goshen.net
Net Ministries	www.netministries.org/churches.htm
NetChurch	www.netchurch.com
NetFINDER	www.christianityonline.com
Searchopolis	www.searchopolis.com
The Best of the Christian Web	www.botcw.com

People Finders

Bigfoot	www.bigfoot.com
InfoSpace	www.infospace.com
Switchboard	www.switchboard.com
The Ultimates	www.theultimates.com
WhoWhere?	www.whowhere.lycos.com
Yahoo! People Search	http://people.yahoo.com

Special People Finders

411 Military Locator	www.military-network.com/411locate/411locate.htm

About.Com Military Locators	http://usmilitary.about.com/business/ usmilitary/msub13.htm
ClassMates.com	www.classmates.com
Planet Alumni	www.planetalumni.com

Business Finders

Big Yellow	www.bigyellow.com
BigBook Yellow Pages	http://bigbook.com
GTE Superpages	www.superpages.com
InfoSpace	www.infospace.com
Yellowpages.com	www.yellowpages.com
Zip2	www.zip2.com

Newsgroups, Mailing Lists, and Ezine Search Engines

Deja.com	www.deja.com
E-zine List	www.meer.net/~johnl/e-zine-list
eGroups	www.egroups.com
Forum One	www.forumone.com
Internet for Christians	www.gospelcom.net/ifc/mail/view
List of Lists	http://catalog.com/vivian/ interest-group-search.html
Liszt	www.liszt.com
One List	www.onelist.com
Reference.com	www.reference.com

Senior Adult

AARP Webplace	www.aarp.org
Access America for Seniors	www.seniors.gov
Administration on Aging	www.aoa.dhhs.gov/aoa/webres/craig.htm
ElderWeb	www.elderweb.com
Fifty-Plus.net	www.fifty-plus.net
Life Lines	www.aarp.org/mmaturity/nov_dec98/ medical.html
Medicare	www.medicare.gov
Modern Maturity	www.aarp.org/mmaturity/home.html
National Council on the Aging	www.ncoa.org
Nursing Home INFO	www.nursinghomeinfo.com

SeniorNet	www.seniornet.org
Seniors' Connection	http://www1.christianity.net/community/seniors
Senior Sites	www.seniorsites.com
SeniorsSearch	www.seniorssearch.com
The Senior Times	www.theseniortimes.com
Social Security Online	www.ssa.gov
Yahoo! Seniors' Guide	http://seniors.yahoo.com

Southern Baptist

Baptist Press	www.sbc.net/bpCurrent.asp
International Mission Board	www.imb.org
LifeWay (Formerly the Sunday School Board)	www.lifeway.com
North American Mission Board	www.namb.net
SBCsearch	www.founders.org/sbcsearch
Southern Baptist Convention	www.sbc.net

Travel and Maps

AAA	www.aaa.com
America's Best Online	www.americasbestonline.com
American Express	http://travel.americanexpress.com
Excite Travel	http://city.net
Expedia Travel	www.expedia.msn.com
Expedia Maps	www.expediamaps.com
Family Fun magazine	www.familyfun.com
Family.com Travel	www.family.go.com
Fodors	www.fodors.com
Great Outdoor Recreation Pages	www.gorp.com
MapQuest	www.mapquest.com
National Weather Service	www.nws.noaa.gov
New York Times Travel Section	www.nytimes.com
Priceline	www.priceline.com
Rand McNally	www.randmcnally.com
TRAVEL.com	www.travel.com
Travelocity	www.travelocity.com
The Weather Channel	www.weather.com

Virtual Tours

Ancient Rome	www.ancientsites.com/as/rome/ academy/tours/index.html
EarthCam	www.earthcam.com
South Pole	http://bat.phys.unsw.edu.au/~aasto
Tour the Solar System	http://spacekids.hq.nasa.gov/osskids/ animate/mac.html
Virtual Holy Land	www.virtualholyland.com/
Virtual Museums Tours	http://archive.comlab.ox.ac.uk/other/ museums.html
WWW Virtual Tours	www.virtualfreesites.com/tours.html

Women

Annie's Home Page	www.annieshomepage.com
Christian Women Today	www.crusade.org
Christianity Online	www.christianityonline.com
Growing Together	www.gospelcom.net/growingtogether
HomeArts.com	www.homearts.com
Moms Online	www.momsonline.com
Parent Soup	www.parentsoup.com
Parents' Place	www.family.org/pplace
ParentsPlace.com	www.parentsplace.com
Peggy's Place	www.gospelcom.net/peggiesplace/dday.htm
Women (Crosswalk.com)	http://women.crosswalk.com

Youth

Boundless	www.boundless.org
Café YouthTalk	www.walkthru.com/cafe/public_html
Christianteens.net	www.christianteens.net
KidSurf Online	www.kidsurf.net
Live the Life	www.livethelife.org
Teen Seen	www.ratedg.com/channels/teens
WWJD	www.wwjd.com
Youthworker Journal	www.youthworker.com

NOTES

Chapter 1

1. eMarketer, *eUser & Usage Report,* http://www.emarketer.com/estats/s_euu_prev.html (23 November 99).
2. Datamonitor, "The Future of the Internet," as quoted in *CyberAtlas: Demographics,* 1 June 1999, http://cyberatlas.internet.com/big_picture/demographics/print/0,1323,5901_150071,00.html (22 November 1999).
3. "OCLC Web Characterization Project," press release, *Online Computer Library Center,* 8 September 1999, (Statistics are for the year ending June 1999), http:/www.oclc.org/news/oclc/press/19990908a.htm (15 September 1999).

Chapter 5

1. Clay Renick, "Parents Fight Back against Online Predators," *Baptist Press,* 14 January 1998, *The Ethics and Religious Liberty Commission,* http://www.erlc.com/family/articles/parentsfight.htm (1 May 1999).
2. Troy Wolverton, "Nissan Privacy Goof Exposes E-mail Addresses," *CNet News,* 15 April 1999. http://news.cnet.com/news/0-1007-200-341234.html?tag=st.ne.1002 (20 June 1999).

3.   "FTC Report on Consumers Online Privacy," *Federal Trade Commission,* 4 June 1998. http://www.ftc.gov/opa/1998/9806/privacy2.htm (15 June 1999).

Chapter 7

1.   "Parents Lack Skills to Supervise Children Online," Arbitron NewMedia, as reported in *CyberAtlas,* http://cyberatlas.internet. com/big_picture/demographics/article/0,1323,5901_164711,00. html (26 July 99).

Chapter 8

1.   Portions of this section first appeared in an article by the author entitled "Finding a Family-Friendly ISP," *SBC Life,* June/July 1999, 14.

Chapter 14

1.   eMarketer, "The Numbers Behind E-mail," *CyberAtlas,* 2 February 1999, http://cyberatlas.internet.com/big_picture/demographics/article/ 0,1323,5931_151911,00.html (5 November 95).

Chapter 20

1.   "OCLC Web Characterization Project," press release, *Online Computer Library Center,* 8 September 1999, (Statistics are for the year ending June 1999), www.oclc.org/news/oclc/press/19990908a.htm (2 November 99).

Chapter 29

1. Ito Muzuko, Annette Linde, Charlotte Mynatt, Elizabeth Mynatt, and Vicki O'Day, "Final Report: Broadening Access: SeniorNet and the Case for Diverse Network Communities," *SeniorNet, 1999,* http://www.seniornet.org/research/snaccess_980303.html (9 May 2000).

2. Richard P. Adler, "Older Adults and Computers: Report of a National Survey," *SeniorNet,* 1996. http://www.seniornet.org/research/survey2.html (8 October 1999).

Chapter 30

1. Reuters, "Tracing Your Lineage Online," *ZDNet,* 24 August 1998, http://www.zdnet.com/filters/printerfriendly/0,6061,2130801-2,00.html (22 September 1999).

Chapter 33

1. Mark Moring, and Matt Donnelly, "Christians in Cyberspace," *Christianity Online,* September/October 1999, 11.

2. "Media Metrix 500" report for September 1999, http://www.rkinc.com/top500/top500.html (14 November 1999).

INDEX

W

Y

Z

Copyright Permissions

All illustrations and screen shots used in *Going Online @ Home* are used by permission. Special thanks goes to the following companies, organizations, or ministries who gave permission to use their sites or materials in this seminar.

5 Clicks, screen shot used by permission of Campus Crusade for Christ (www.5clicks.com).

AltaVista logo and our Search Engine Content are copyright and trademarks of Compaq Corporation (www.altavista.com).

America's Best Online, screen shot used by permission (www.americasbestonline.com).

Ancestry.com, screen shot used by permission (www.ancestry.com).

Ask Jeeves for Kids, screen shot used by permission (www.ajkids.com).

Cartoonworks, illustrations used by permission of Ron Wheeler (www.cartoonworks.com).

Christianity Online, screen shot used by permission of Christianity Today, Inc. (www.christianityonline.com).

Crosswalk, screen shots used by permission (www.crosswalk.com).

EntryPoint, screen shot used by permission of EntryPoint Inc. (www.entrypoint.com).

Experiencing God, screen shot used by permission of LifeWay Inc. (www.lifeway.com).

Genealogy Instruction, Beginners, Teenagers, Kids, used by permission of Jeffery Johnson.

GTE SuperPages, screen shot used by permission (www.gte.com).

Kid Explorer, screen shot used by permission of Christian Answer Network (www.christiananswers.net).

Homework Central, screen shot used by permission (www.homeworkcentral.com).

Involved Christian Radio Network, ICRN, screen shot used by permission (www.oneplace.com).

ICQ, screen shot used by permission of America Online, Inc. (www.aol.com).

LookSmart, screen shot used by permission (www.looksmart.com).

MapQuest, screen shot used by permission (www.mapquest.com).

MetaCrawler, screen shots used by permission of Go2Net, Inc. (www.metacrawler.com).

Microsoft Corporation, for the use of *Microsoft Internet Explorer, Outlook Express,* and *MSN Microsoft home page.* Screen shots reprinted by permission from Microsoft Corporation (www.microsoft.com).

Netscape Communicator, Netscape Netcenter, and related shots, Netscape Communicator browser frame, software, and website © 2000 Netscape Communications Corporation. Screen shots used with permission (www.netscape.com).

RealPlayer, Copyright © 1995–2000 Real Networks, Inc. All rights reserved. RealNetworks, RealAudio, RealVideo, RealSystem, RealPlayer, RealJukeBox [and all other RealNetworks Trademarks within the copied RealPlayer Screenshot] and other names or logos are trademarks or registered trademarks of RealNetworks, Inc. (www.real.com).

Researchpaper.com, screen shot used by permission (www.researchpaper.com).

Space Kids, screen shot used by permission (http://spacekids.hq.nasa.gov).

Sunday School for a New Century, screen shot used by permission of LifeWay, Inc. (www.lifewaysundayschool.com).

Switchboard, screen shot used by permission (www.switchboard.com).

Travelocity, screen shot used by permission (www.travelocity.com).

WinZip, screen shot reproduced with permission of Nico Mak Computing, Inc. Copyright 1991–1998, Nico Mak Computing Inc. WinZip®) is a registered trademark of Nico Mak Computing, Inc. WinZip is available from www.winzip.com.

Note: All logos are registered trademarks of their respective companies.